BOOKBINDERS OF THE UNITED KINGDOM
(*OUTSIDE LONDON*)
1780-1840

BOOKBINDERS OF THE UNITED KINGDOM

(OUTSIDE LONDON)

1780-1840

BY CHARLES RAMSDEN

B. T. BATSFORD LTD
LONDON

Printed and bound in Great Britain by
Anchor Brendon Ltd, Tiptree, Essex
for the Publishers
B. T. Batsford Ltd
4 Fitzhardinge Street
London W1H 0AH

CONTENTS

v

LIST OF
ILLUSTRATIONS

INTRODUCTION

THE present work makes no pretence to do more than provide a handlist of bookbinders operating outside London between the years 1780 and 1840 within the area which was then known as the United Kingdom. (For convenience I have also included Irish binders between 1780-1800, as well as after 1800).

London, as a centre of bookbinding, has been excluded from this survey because it has been very widely covered by the researches of Mr. Ellic Howe, whose work in progress includes his "List of London Bookbinders, 1648-1815", which in many cases provides information about London bookbinders for at least a further fifteen years.

The exception of London from the present work raises the difficulty of defining where "London" began and ended between 1780 and 1840. For my immediate purpose, I have taken London to the East as confined to the "City", while in other directions I have included under "London" the West End (West of Temple Bar), as far as Hyde Park, with some extensions to the North-West, as far as Marylebone Road, and to the South-West, to Brompton, Knightsbridge, Pimlico and Chelsea.

I repeat that this book should be regarded primarily as a handlist. It does not aim at formulating even a preliminary estimate of the value and progress of binding in the United Kingdom between the years 1780 and 1840. Any such estimate would obviously and necessarily have to take into account the preponderating influence of London bookbinders of the period. No definite conclusions can be reached until collections, covering the United Kingdom as a complete whole, well authenticated both with information and with specimens, are available to a far greater extent than they are to-day. I venture to hope that this work will encourage both institutional and private collectors to assemble the material on which to form a definite estimate of the achievements of a period of bookbinding which has been unduly neglected in the past, but which is now receiving ever increasing attention.

My inspiration in undertaking this work, apart from a natural interest in following up my former study of French Bookbinders between 1789 and 1848, stems primarily from curiosity aroused by Vol. IV of the Schiff Catalogue of 1935, which was the first of its kind to illustrate any considerable corpus of binders working in the United Kingdom during the 18th and 19th centuries. My even keener interest was however aroused by the most illuminating Appendix XI attached by G. D. Hobson to his book published in 1940 on English bindings in the collection of Major J. R. Abbey. In that appendix Hobson listed over thirty places, outside London, Oxford and Cambridge where gilt binding was being carried out between 1770 and 1830. He went on to suggest that this period, before the development of the railways, was probably the heyday of English provincial binding. The same no doubt holds good in at least equal degree of Scotland, Ireland and Wales.

THE IMPORTANCE OF PROVINCIAL BOOKBINDERS

The use of the term "Provincial" carried with it the risk not only of offending local susceptibilities, but also of creating confusion in the mind of the reader. Obviously "Capital" cities, such as Edinburgh and Dublin, produced and maintained binders, equal, or even superior to those centred in London. Other towns, such as York, Newcastle, Cambridge, Oxford, Bristol, Worcester, and doubtless many more, would rightly be unwilling to admit that they were, or are "provincial" towns.

The real problem arises however when one comes to consider the "binders" of the smaller country towns. In the past, it has been fairly commonly assumed that they were not really binders at all, but that they merely styled themselves as such and passed on any orders for binding which they might be lucky enough to secure to professed and established binders in London, or in the nearest county capital, or town of importance.

The first serious doubts on this theory were thrown in Appendix XI of Hobson's book referred to above. Further study of actual specimens of provincial bindings, of directories, and of the prevailing conditions of the 1780-1840 period seems to leave no doubt of the existence of many competent and even first-class local bookbinders.

It seems worthy of note that (1) quite a number of local binders were in a position to style themselves as "Binders to"—e.g., H.M. the Queen (and the Princesses); the Royal Dukes, etc; and (2) many productions of local binders are quite individual, such as those of Holl, of Worcester; Lubbock, of Newcastle; Sowler, of Manchester; Edwards, of Halifax; Seacombe, of Chester, etc; and this also applies to such binders as Lyon, of Southampton; Bailey, of Wotton; Ettles and Young, of Elgin; Dodge, of Stockport; Ridge of Newark, etc.

Most smaller country towns had their leather dealer and cutter, and their local saddler, and there seems no reason to suppose that the local gentry were not well able, as seems to have been the case in quite small places, to provide enough work for a local bookbinder, who would be prepared to execute work on the spot and, if required under the patron's supervision, instead of his having to send it to London with all the loss of time and control which that entailed. It is nowadays difficult to appreciate the factors of the time and distance even as late as 1900. My grandfather, who had a considerable library and lived seven miles out of Guildford, practically never bought a book elsewhere than in Guildford.

We all know of firms who within living memory have sold their bound books as "Bound by Messrs. Bookshop" when it is well known that Messrs. Bookshop never had a bindery. But when one has handled books, reasonably bound with some degree of individuality, and signed for example by Hyde & Crewe, Newcastle-under-Lyme; Gresswell, Taunton; E. E. Beardsall, Stamford; J. Levett, Cambridge; Rodford, Hull; D. Forth, Bridlington; T. Langdale, Ripon; J. Brown, Penrith, etc, is one justified 100 to 150 years later in saying that the signatories are all, or even to any great extent, guilty of gross terminological inexactitude?

For the moment I am dealing only with persons who definitely laid claim to be binders by a label, or other equivalent token, or with those who are definitely listed in directories as binders. I shall deal below with the progressively more doubtful members of the binding trade. For the moment, I would only add that not all recognised binders are listed as such in the directories. Mackenzie, of Dame Street, Dublin, is an example, though he inserted a ticket with his address in many of his bindings. Again, Edwards, of Halifax, never appears in the directories otherwise than as a bookseller: in fact almost all the evidence that one or more members of the family was a bookbinder can be regarded as circumstantial and indirect.

(1) Where no note follows the binder's name, it can be assumed that the evidence, whether drawn from directories or from other sources, gives no indication that he practised any other trade.

(2) Other occasional occupations, such as victualler, grocer, umbrella maker, parish clerk, servants' registry, trunkmaker, postmaster, singing master, newsvendor, landmeasurer, tailor, schoolmaster, librarian, etc., etc., seem to present no insuperable barrier to serious bookbinding activities.

(3) Stationer and/or bookseller appears to be the commonest trade combined with bookbinding. To-day they would throw considerable doubt on the genuineness, or at least the extent of the *bookbinding* activities. Between 1780 and 1840 they were, I feel, normal concomitants of an underworked, rather than as it is to-day an overstrained industry, when, as a well known binder put it to me, the handbinders of the country of any merit can, nowadays, be counted on one's two hands.

(4) "Printer", or "Ruler", or "Machine-ruler" are fairly common combinations with "Bookbinder" and the three trades seem natural concomitants. I feel however some doubts in my own mind whether in such cases the binding was generally of the highest order. It was often no doubt very akin to the trade binding of the period which can generally be recognised, but as to whose executants not a great deal is known.

(5) I use "etc" and "etc, etc" to indicate wider ranges of activity in addition to bookbinding. "Etc" may be taken to mean that the person, or firm so designated, besides carrying on bookselling and/or selling stationery in addition to bookbinding, may also be dealer in patent medicines (a very common addition), agent for an Insurance Co., printseller, or card maker, and so on, but had usually only one such ancillary activity. "Etc, etc" goes much further: a good example is Martin Keene, of 6 College Green, Dublin, whose label reads:—"Sold by Martin Keene, Bookseller, Stationer & Patent Medicine Seller" and in the surround "Engraving and Printing neatly executed. Law & Mercantile Stamps. Account books ruled and bound to any Pattern". And yet I feel very little doubt that Keene had a bindery of his own.

(6) Trade and Edition binders are to the best of my knowledge seldom, if ever, listed as such during the period, at any rate outside London, though from circumstantial evidence it is very probable that in fact they did exist in such places

as Edinburgh, Dublin, Manchester, Glasgow, Newcastle, York, etc. In such cases however they no doubt also executed bespoke binding.

(7) Vellum-binders. These constituted a special and often a separate section of the bookbinding profession, employing a different technique. They were not concerned with the often exquisite productions bound in Vellum and executed for special orders or occasions by such binders as Edwards, Frye, Kalthoeber, Staggemeier & Welcher, Barratt, de Caumont, etc. The work of the vellum-binder was to provide solid and durable bindings for legal records, archives, business accounts, etc. Their work usually has little artistic merit, admirably as it no doubt serves the purposes for which it was intended. Outside London, vellum-binders are seldom specifically mentioned.

BINDERS BY PROFESSION

The description given in the preceding paragraphs of the various classes of people appearing to have some claim to bookbinding activities might well lead one to suppose that the professional binders are far less numerous than those who bound as a sideline, or even only claimed to be binders. It seems possible however to controvert such a veiw on statistical grounds.

(a) Consideration of the handlist of binders which forms the main bulk of this work would appear to show that some 77 per cent. of them (including those under heading 2 above) were primarily fulltime binders who did not regard their bookbinding as a catchpenny sideline. In such case we have to account for a remaining percentage of entries of about 23 per cent.

(b) Those included under heading 3, i.e., binders also selling books and/or stationery, seem to work out at 9 per cent. of the entries, leaving 14 per cent. still to be accounted for.

(c) The printer, ruler, plus bookbinder class appears to account for 7 per cent. Allowing for a few miscellaneous tradesmen, such as those who produced bookbinders' tools, etc., probably about 5 or 6 per cent. are left to fall under heading 5, those whose various activities entitle them to the smallest claim to be listed as bookbinders.

THE DIFFICULTIES OF DEALING WITH DIRECTORIES

This brings us necessarily to a defence, or at least an explanation of the lines which I have followed in collecting and collating information from directories.

I do not claim that I have evolved, or followed any infallible system. Later 18th and early 19th-century compilers of directories follow no clear or well defined system. The compiler was often none too competent: he was apt to meet with considerable sales resistance and to be hard up; his antecedents were sometimes not above reproach; his ideas as to whom to include in, or exclude from his directory were often subject to undue considerations of social or professional rank. His usual method was to go straight ahead on an alphabetical basis. When he did try to classify his directory by trades, his choice was often arbitrary and ill-balanced.

When the Pigot and Robson directories reached the stage of being classified, they were apt to have too many omnibus headings such as "Booksellers, stationers, printers and binders", from which I have had to try and extract the binders. On occasion the problem has not been too difficult of solution. There may be an entry "Binder" after the name of a firm, or there may be a reference by asterisk to "Binder" or "Binder only". Otherwise I have followed the wise French advice "Dans le doute, abstiens-toi" and I am reasonably confident that the number of persons, or firms wrongly admitted to my list of bookbinders is very small, a fair margin of doubt probably applying to not more than one per cent. to two per cent. In any case the large number of references given should enable anyone with enough patience to form either the same opinion as my own or a different one.

GENERAL LAYOUT

As will be seen from the general index of contents on page v, I have treated England and Wales together, while handling Scotland and Ireland respectively as separate units. In each of the three sections into which the main portion of this work is divided, I have given (a) a list of the principal directories consulted and quoted, (b) an alphabetical list of localities and the binders working there, and (c) an alphabetical list of the binders and any details which I have been able to discover about them.

Where directories obviously overlap geographical sections (as is the case with Pigot's Commercial Directory of Scotland, Ireland, and the four Northern Counties of England, dated 1820), I have listed such directories under all three sections. Some publishers of directories, notably Pigot, had the habit, when compiling say for example an Hibernian Directory, of adding thereto directories for some of the more important cities in England and Scotland. Any reader, therefore, who finds a reference in the index of Scottish binders to a directory which does not appear in the Scottish directory list, will probably find it under one of the other two directory lists.

Lists of the main sources consulted and referred to (other than directories) and their abbreviations, as well as of the general abbreviations employed in the body of the book, will be found directly after this introduction.

Special references and their abbreviations, applicable to Scotland and Ireland, will be found preceding the sections in question.

CHARLES RAMSDEN

ACKNOWLEDGEMENTS

It gives me great pleasure to have this opportunity of recording the many debts of gratitude which I owe to numerous institutions and individuals all over the country.

I should like to tender my special thanks to the Librarians of the British Museum, the Victoria and Albert Museum, the Guildhall Library, the Bodleian Library, the Scottish National Library, the Edinburgh City Library, Trinity College Library, Dublin and the Royal Irish Academy.

I am also profoundly grateful to the Librarians of innumerable County and City Libraries all over the four Countries with which I have dealt. They have without exception accepted the tiresome task of extracting from directories, etc., particulars of bookbinders in their regions, a work which is particularly difficult and laborious since early directories are usually compiled on a purely alphabetical basis. I am similarly thankful to many private owners of rare directories, not in public libraries, and to collectors of tradesmen's tickets, for placing their material at my disposal.

Finally I should like to mention just a few of the individuals who over many months have generously contributed entries or further particulars to my work, notably Mr. M. Cohen, Mr. M. Craig, Mr. A. Ehrman, Mr. H. Fletcher, Mr. A. Hobson, Mr. E. Howe, Dr. W. Mitchell, Mr. A. Munby, Mr. H. Nixon, Miss J. Norton and Mr. J. Oldham.

C. R.

ABBREVIATIONS

E D   Earliest (probable) date of binding activity. Not given when such date appears from directories, or other reliable sources, but only where no other evidence is available other than circumstantial, drawn from the style of the binding, or of the binder's ticket, date of the work, or its dedication, etc.

L D   Latest (probable) date of binding activity, etc. (see under E.D.). It should, however, be noted that no special effort has been made to examine directories after 1840.

BEP/WM   Watermark on binder's endpaper(s).

B B   Bookbinder.

B S   Bookseller.

P R   Printer.

S T   Stationer.

Etc: Etc, etc   Indicates diminishing degrees of specialisation in bookbinding. Thus, "etc" may mean "bookseller, stationer, bookbinder", while "etc, etc" may indicate a wider range as "Printer, publisher, bookseller, stationer, bookbinder, music and printseller, machine-ruler, patent medicine vendor".

MISCELLANEOUS REFERENCES

(1) AE/COLL .. .. A. Ehrman Collection.

(2) AE/COLL/LAB .. A. Ehrman Collection, Label.

(3) AE/f .. .. Information from A. Ehrman.

(4) AE/HEAL/LAB .. Labels in Heal Collection communicated by A.E.

(5) BKBG/AMER .. *Bookbinding in America*, Portland, 1941.

(6) BS/HOWE/LBB .. Howe: *London Bookbinders*, 1648-1815, Bib/Soc. 1950.

(7) BUSHNELL .. Joint author DBP/1726/75.

(8) DBP/1726/75 .. Bib/Soc. *Dict. of Booksellers & Printers* 1726/75 (1932).

(9) Norton .. .. Miss Norton's *National & Provincial Directories* (outside London) (1950). Does not cover Scotland or Ireland.

(10) HOB/ABB .. G. D. Hobson, *English Bindings, J. R. Abbey Collection* (1940).

(11) JA/XXXX .. .. English Provincial Bindings in Abbey Collection with Cat. No.

(12) JBO/AE .. .. List of Binders, communicated by J. Oldham to A. Ehrman.

(13) LAB/JONES .. Collection of Bookbinders' tickets, etc lent to H. Nixon by Mr. Jones in July, 1951.

(14) LAB/KNA .. Bookbinders' tickets in R. J. Knaster Collection.

(15) LAB/PEARSON .. Collection of Bookbinders' tickets, lent by Dr. Pearson, per H. Nixon. July, 1951.

(16) MUNBY, or
    MUNBY COLL .. Information received from A. Munby, or represented in his Collection.

(17) OLD/SHREW .. J. Oldham. *Bindings in Shrewsbury College Library* (1943).

(18) P/TICKET   .. Album of Binders' tickets, lent by Ivor Poole, Dec., 1950. Dates are those as given in the album.

(19) SCH/S. de R/IV .. British, etc, Bindings in the Schiff Collection, 1935.

(20) TIMP/42 .. .. Timperley's *Encyclopaedia*, 1842.

(21) WHEELER   .. Francis Wheeler, Sale Catalogue, Giraud Badin, 1932.

(22) MAT/OX/a.c. .. Matriculated, Oxford University, in the year quoted. Mr. I. Philip of the Bodleian Library kindly drew my attention to the fact that the University granted Matriculation to certain tradesmen whose activities were useful to the University.

(23) BT/SALOP   .. Llewellyn C. Lloyd: 'Book-Trade in Shropshire'. Transactions of Shropshire Arch. Soc. Vol. XLVIII.

(24) J L D   .. .. J. Douthwaite Collection.

(25) O C   ..   .. Author's own Collection of bindings.

(26) ABB/CBS .. .. 'British Signed Bindings in Abbey Collection', Cambridge Bibl. Soc., Vol. 1, 1949-51, p. 270/9.

(27) WSM/KC/NEW .. Information communicated by Dr. W. Morrison, King's College, Newcastle-upon-Tyne.

NATIONAL DIRECTORIES

(References in the first column are to Miss Norton's *Guide to National and Provincial Directories*, London, 1950).

Norton
No.

9 13 15 18 }	BRI/DIR/91/98:	Univ. Brit. Dir. 91/98.
24	HOLD/11:	Holden's (London &) County Dir., Vol. II & III.
30	PIG/16/17:	Pigot/Com/Dir/16/17.
31	PIG/18/20:	Commercial Dir. Aston-York 18/20.
33	PIG/SIN/20:	Commercial Dir. Scot. Ire., etc 20.
35	PIG/LPCD/22:	Lon. & Prov. Dir. (Midland) 22.
36 {	PIG/SC/23: PIG/LPCD/23: }	Dir. South Counties, 23.
37	PIG/NCD/24:	New Commercial Dir. 24.
38	PIG/DUB/24:	Dublin & Hibernian Dir. 24.
40	PIG/CDS/25:	New Commercial Dir. Scotland, 25.
43	PIG/LPD/26/27:	London & Prov. Dir. 26/27.
47	PIG/NCD/28:	N. Counties Dir. 28.
53	PIG/NCD/30:	S. & Midland Counties Dir. 30.
57	PIG/LPCD/32:	London & Provincial Dir. 32.
60	PIG/LPCD/34:	London Prov. Com. Dir. 34.
61	PIG/SEVEN/DIR/34:	Seven Northern Counties Dir. 34.
62	PIG/MID/DIR/35:	Midland Counties & Wales Dir. 35/36.
64	PIG/CDS/37:	Commercial Dir. Scotland.
67a	PIG/HC/39:	Home Counties Dir. 39.
72	PIG/MND/42:	Midland Counties Dir. 42.
—	PIG/NAT/DIR/28/29:	Pigot's Nat. Directory, 1828/29 (Guildhall).
101	ROB/NINE/DIR/39:	Robson's Commercial Directory (London) & Nine Counties, Vol. II, 39.
103	ROB/SIX/DIR/39:	Robson's Directory for Norfolk Circuit & Oxfordshire, 39.
104	ROB/HOMCO/DIR/39:	Robson's Commercial, 7 (Home) Counties, 39.
105	ROB/LON/DIR/40:	Dir. London & W. Counties.

Norton
No.

127	BED/DIR/85:	Merchants' Miscellany for City of Bedford, 85.
132	READ/DIR/28:	Reading Dir. 28.
133	,, ,, /37:	,, ,, 37.
151	CHES/DIR/40:	Chester Gen. Dir. 40.
152	MACC/DIR/17:	Hist. of Macclesfield, 17.
153	,, ,, /25:	Macclesfield Hist. & Dir., 25.
155	FALM/DIR/15:	Hist. of Falmouth, 1815.
157	CARL/DIR/11:	Cumberland Guide, etc., 11.
158	CUMWES/DIR/29:	,, &Westmorland Dir., 29.
164	CARL/DIR/37:	Carlisle Dir., 37.
165	,, ,, /40:	,, ,, 40.
166	COUNT/DER/29:	Directory County Derby, 29.
169	DERBY/DIR/23/24:	Guide & Commercial Dir. 23/24.
175 to 190	EX/P/J:	Exeter Pocket Journal, 07-40.
207	EX/DIR/28:	Exeter Dir. 28.
208	,, ,, /31:	,, ,, 31.
—	,, ,, /35:	,, ,, 35.
216	PLY/DIR/14:	Plymouth, etc Directory, 14.
217	,, ,, /22:	Plymouth Dir., 22.
218	,, ,, /23:	Tourist's Companion, etc, 23.
219	,, ,, /30:	Plymouth Dir. 30.
221	,, ,, /36:	,, ,, 36.
226	SID/DIR/36:	Sketch of Sidmouth, 36.
233	WEY/DIR/28:	Weymouth Guide, 28.
234	DUR/DIR/27:	Durham Dir. 27.
248	GLOU/DIR/28:	Gloucestershire Dir. 28.
252	BRIS/DIR/85:	Bristol Dir. 85.
253	,, ,, /87:	,, ,, 87.
254	,, ,, /92:	,, ,, 92.
255	,, ,, /94:	,, ,, 93/94.
257	,, ,, /97:	,, ,, 97.

259	BRIS/DIR/99:	Bristol Dir. 99.
260	,, ,, /01:	,, ,, 01.
261	,, ,, /03:	,, ,, 03.
263	,, ,, /06:	,, ,, 06.
266	,, ,, /09:	,, ,, 09.
269	,, ,, /12:	,, ,, 12.
270	,, ,, /13:	,, ,, 13.
272	,, ,, /15:	,, ,, 15.
275	,, ,, /18:	,, ,, 18.
278	,, ,, /21:	,, ,, 21.
281	,, ,, /24:	,, ,, 24.
284	,, ,, /27:	,, ,, 27.
287	,, ,, /30:	,, ,, 30.
290	,, ,, /33:	,, ,, 33
293	,, ,, /36:	,, ,, 36.
297	,, ,, /40:	,, ,, 40.
315	BRIS/IND/18:	Bristol Index, 18.
320	CHELT/DIR/02:	Cheltenham Dir. 02.
321	CHELT/ANN/37:	Cheltenham Annuaire, 37.
322	,, ,, /38:	,, ,, 38.
323	,, ,, /39:	,, ,, 39.
324	,, ,, /40:	,, ,, 40.
340	CHELT/DIR/39:	Cheltenham Dir. 39.
354	HANTS/DIR/84:	Hampshire Dir. 84.
—	PORTS/DIR/23:	Portsmouth Dir. 23 (J L D).
358	SOUTH/DIR/11:	Southampton Dir. 11.
359	,, ,, /34:	,, ,, 34.
360	,, ,, /36:	,, ,, 36.
375	GUER/G/26 ::	Guide to Guernsey, 26.
377	L.C/JER/34:	Guide to Jersey, 34.
378	JERS/DIR/37:	Royal Almanack, etc, 37.
379	GUER/DIR/40:	Privileged Islands (Directory for Guernsey only), 40.
383	JEFF/IM/40:	Isle of Man, New Guide, 40.
395	VECT/DIR/39:	Isle of Wight Dir. 39.
398	KENT/DIR/03:	Hist. Sketch of Kent, 03.
399	,, /DIR/07:	Kent Directory, ? 1807.

402	KENT/DIR/38:	Topography, etc, of East Kent, 38.
411	MAID/DIR/39:	Topography of Maidstone, 39.
414	ROCH/DIR/38:	Topography of Rochester, etc, 38.
422	LANC/DIR/25:	Hist. etc, County Lancaster, 24/25.
432	BOLT/DIR/29:	Bolton Dir. 29.
441	LIV/DIR/77:	Liverpool Dir. 77.
442	,, ,, /81:	,, ,, 81.
443	,, ,, /87:	,, ,, 87.
444	,, ,, /90:	,, ,, 90 (Wosencroft).
445	,, ,, /90:	,, ,, 90 (Gore).
446	,, ,, /94:	,, ,, 94.
447	,, ,, /96:	,, ,, 96.
448	,, ,, /00:	,, ,, 00.
450	,, ,, /03:	,, ,, 03.
451	,, ,, /04;	,, ,, 04.
452	,, ,, /05:	,, ,, 05.
453	,, ,, /05:	,, ,, 05.
454	,, ,, /07:	,, ,, 07.
455	,, ,, /10:	,, ,, 10.
458	,, ,, /14:	,, ,, 14.
459	,, ,, /16:	,, ,, 16.
460	,, ,, /18:	,, ,, 18.
461	,, ,, /21:	,, ,, 21.
463	,, ,, /25:	,, ,, 25.
466	,, ,, /29:	,, ,, 29.
468	,, ,, /32:	,, ,, 32.
469	,, ,, /34:	Liverpool Dir. 34.
483	,, ,, /40:	Robson Liverpool Dir. 40.
488	MAN/DIR/73:	Manchester Dir. 73.
489	,, ,, /81:	,, ,, 81.
490	,, ,, /88:	,, ,, 88.
491	,, ,, /94:	,, ,, 94.
492	,, ,, /97:	,, ,, 97.
493	,, ,, /00:	,, ,, 00.
495	,, ,, /04:	,, ,, 04.
496	,, ,, /08:	,, ,, 08.
497	,, ,, /11:	,, ,, Dean 11.

498	MAN/DIR/11 P:	Manchester Dir. Pigot 11.
499	,, ,, /13:	,, ,, ,, 13.
500	,, ,, /15:	,, ,, 15.
503	,, ,, /21:	,, ,, 21/22.
504	,, ,, /24:	,, ,, 24/25.
505	,, ,, /28:	,, ,, 28.
509	,, ,, /32:	,, ,, 32.
513	,, ,, /38:	,, ,, 38.
514	,, ,, /40:	,, ,, 40.
531	PREST/DIR/21:	Preston Dir. 21.
545	LEIC/DIR/15:	Leicester Dir. 15.
546	,, ,, /27:	,, ,, 27.
548	LINC/DIR/26:	Lincolnshire Dir. 26.
559	NORF/DIR/36:	Hist. etc, Norfolk, 36.
563	NORW/DIR/83:	Norwich Dir. 83.
565	,, ,, /02:	,, ,, 02.
567	,, ,, /11:	,, ,, 11.
583	BERW/DIR/06:	Berwick-on-Tweed Dir. 06.
584	NEW/DIR/78:	Newcastle Dir. 78.
585	,, ,, /82:	,, ,, 82.
586	,, ,, /87:	,, ,, 87.
587	,, ,, /90:	,, ,, 90.
588	,, ,, /95:	,, ,, 95.
589	,, ,, /01:	,, ,, 01.
590	,, ,, /11:	,, ,, 11.
591	,, ,, /24:	,, ,, 24.
592	,, ,, /33:	,, ,, 33.
593	,, ,, /38:	,, ,, 38.
596	NOTTSH/DIR/32:	Nottinghamshire Dir. 32.
601	NOTT/DIR/14:	Nottingham Dir. 14.
602	,, ,, /15:	,, ,, 15.
603	,, ,, /18:	,, ,, 18.
604	,, ,, /25:	,, ,, 25.
605	,, ,, /34:	,, ,, 34.
606	NOTT/REG/40:	,, Register 40.
612	BAN/DIR/27/39:	Banbury Dir. an. cit.
613	OXF/DIR/35:	Oxford University etc, Dir. 35.

614	SALOP/DIR/28:	Dir. of Shropshire.
617	SHREW/DIR/97:	Shrewsbury Companion, 97.
618	,, ,, /03:	Shrewsbury Dir. 03.
621	SOM/DIR/40:	Somerset Dir. 40.
625	BATH/DIR/00:	Bath Dir. 00.
—	,, ,, /01:	,, ,, 01 (J. L. D.).
626	,, ,, /05:	,, ,, 05.
627	,, ,, /09:	,, ,, 09.
628	,, ,, /12:	,, ,, 12.
629	,, ,, /19:	,, ,, 19.
630	,, ,, /24:	,, ,, 24.
631/2	,, ,, /26/27:	,, ,, 26/27.
633/4	,, ,, /29/33:	,, ,, 29/33.
635	,, ,, /37:	,, ,, 37.
636	,, ,, /41:	,, ,, 41.
644	STAFF/DIR/18:	Staffordshire Dir. 18.
646	NEW/LYME/DIR/22:	Newcastle, etc, Dir. 22/23.
647	STAFF/DIR/34:	Staffs. Hist. etc, 34.
651	NEW/LYME/DIR/36:	Newcastle-under-Lyme Dir. 36.
652	,, ,, ,, /39:	,, ,, ,, ,, 39.
655	WOLV/DIR/27:	Wolverhampton Dir. 27.
656	,, ,, /33:	,, ,, 33.
657	,, ,, /38:	,, ,, 38.
672	BRIG/DIR/22:	Brighton Dir. 22 (Boore).
673	,, ,, /22:	,, ,, 22 (Baxter).
674	,, ,, /24:	,, ,, 24 ,,
675	,, ,, /32:	,, ,, 32.
677	,, ,, /39:	,, ,, 39.
687	CHICH/DIR/04:	Chichester Guide, 04.
693	WARW/DIR/30:	Warwickshire Dir. 30.
706	BIRM/DIR /81:	Birmingham Dir. 81.
708	,, ,, /85:	,, ,, 85.
709	,, ,, /87:	,, ,, 87.
711	,, ,, /91:	,, ,, 91.
713	,, ,, /97:	,, ,, 97.
714	,, ,, /98:	,, ,, 98.
715	,, ,, /00:	,, ,, 00.

716	BIRM/MAGN/DIR/00:	Bissett's Birmingham Dir. 00.	
717	„ /DIR/00:	Chapman's Birmingham Dir. 00.	
718/9	„ „ /01/03:	Birmingham Dir. 01 & 03.	
721	„ „ /08:	„ „ 08.	
722	„ /MAGN/DIR/08:	Bissett's Birmingham Dir. 08.	
723	„ /DIR/08:	Birmingham Dir. (Triennial) 08.	
724	„ „ /12:	„ „ „ 12.	
725	„ „ /15:	„ „ „ 15.	
726	„ „ /18:	„ „ „ 18.	
727	„ „ /21:	„ „ „ 21.	
729	„ „ /25:	„ „ „ 25.	
730	„ „ /29:	„ „ „ 29.	
731	„ „ /33:	„ „ „ 33.	
732	„ „ /35:	„ „ „ 35.	
733	„ „ /39:	„ „ „ 39.	
749	LEAM/DIR/33:	Leamington Spa Dir. Fairfax, 33.	
750	„ „ /33:	„ „ „ Moncrieff, 33.	
752	„ „ /37:	„ „ „ 37.	
762	WOR/DIR/20:	Worcestershire Dir. 20.	
778	„ „ /88:	Worcester Dir. 88.	
779	„ „ /90:	„ „ 90.	
780	„ „ /92:	„ „ 92.	
781	„ „ /94:	„ „ 94.	
782	„ „ /97:	„ „ 97.	
783	„ „ /37:	„ „ 37.	
784	„ „ /40:	„ „ 40.	
786	YORK/DIR/22:	York Dir. 22/23.	
788	„ „ /30:	„ „ 30.	
790	WHI/WRY/37/38:	West Riding Dir. 37/38.	
794	WHI/ENR/40:	E. & N. Riding Dir. 40.	
816	HULL/DIR/91:	Hull Dir. 91.	
818/9	„ „ /03:	„ „ 03.	
820	„ „ /06:	„ „ 06.	
821	„ „ /10:	„ „ 10/11.	
822	„ „ /13:	„ „ 13.	
823	„ „ /17:	„ „ 17.	
824	„ „ /21:	„ „ 21.	

826	HULL/DIR/35:	Hull Dir. 35.
827	,, ,, /38:	,, ,, 38.
828	,, ,, /39:	,, ,, 39.
833	LEEDS/DIR/98:	Hist. of Leeds 98.
834	,, ,, /00:	Leeds Dir. 00.
835	,, ,, /07:	,, ,, 07.
836	,, ,, /09:	,, ,, 09.
837	,, ,, /17:	,, ,, 17.
838	,, ,, /28:	,, ,, 28.
840	,, ,, /34:	,, ,, 34.
841	,, ,, /39:	,, ,, 39.
849	SHEFF/DIR/87:	Sheffield Dir. 87.
850	,, ,, /97:	,, ,, 97.
852	,, ,, /21:	,, ,, 21.
853	,, ,, /25:	,, ,, 25.
854	,, ,, /28:	,, ,, 28.
855	,, ,, /33:	,, ,, 33.
861	YORK/DIR/87:	York Guide 87.
868	ABERY/DIR/16:	Aberystwyth Guide 16.
871	CARD/DIR/29:	Cardiff Guide 29.
875	SWAN/DIR/30:	Swansea Dir. 30.
878	ROSS/DIR/25:	Ross Dir. 25 (?).

ENGLISH & WELSH BINDERS BY LOCALITY

ABERYSTWYTH: Pierce.

ALRESFORD: Moody.

ALDSTON: Pattinson.

ALNWICK: Davidson; Fenkle; Graham.

ANDOVER: King; Maud; Rawlings.

APPLEBY: Atkinson; Sewell.

ASHBORNE: Hoon.

ASHBY-DE-LA-ZOUCHE: McNeill.

ASHFORD: Gamber.

ASHTON-UNDER-LYNE: Cunningham; Davies; Neald.

BABCARY: Ball.

BALLINGDON: Hill.

BANBURY: Bloxham; Golsby; Potts; Rusher.

BANGOR: Brown; Roberts.

BARKING: Penn.

BARNARD CASTLE: Clifton.

BARNSTAPLE: Brightwell; Cornish; May.

BARTON-UPON-HUMBER: Warwick.

BASINGSTOKE: Cottle.

BATH: Barratt's Library; Bennett; Beer; Binns; Clement; Cole; Colling's Library; Douglas (3); Evans (2); Farrant; Ford; Fryer; Gibsons; Gurner; Harris; Hazard; Hill; Hocknull; Holloway; Hoskins; Hughes; Keevil; Kennard; Kennington; Lambert; Maybury; Mills; Morris; Murray; Osmond; Price; Raines; Riviere; Simms; Smith (2); Sugg; Taylor (2); Tongue; Toole; Upham's Library; Wigens; Wilson.

BATTLE: Ticehurst.

BECCLES: Gage.

BEDALE: Taylor.

BEDFORD: Perfect; Smith; Stafford; White.

BELPER: Lowe.

BERWICK-ON-TWEED: Hall (3); Henderson; Lauder; Mean; Melrose; Nesbit; Reid; Richardson; Wilson.

BEVERLEY: Scaum; Severs; Stoddart.

BEXHILL: Fleming.

BICESTER: Smith.

BIGGLESWADE: Spong.

BINGLEY: Harrison.

BIRMINGHAM: Aldritt; Allen; Beilby, etc; Belcher; Bishop; Bloomer; Bolton; Bowen; Brettell; Brierley; Carvell; Chapman; Chinery; Clark; Coley; Cooper; Corns; Dark; Dewson; Dunn; Edwards (2); Fisher; Fullwood; Grafton & Reddell; Guest; Hammond; Harlow; Harris; Hodgkins; Hudson; Hunt; Jenkins; Jones; Joseph; Larkin; Male; Martin (2); Mattinson; Maurice; Mills; Murgatroyd; Osborne; Peart (2); Phillips; Pickard; Piercy; Plampin; Pomeroy; Price & Watson; Radcliffe; Ralph (2); Rothwell; Russell; Selkirk; Sheldon; Smith (2); Stone; Suffield; Summers; Taylor; Thomson & Wrightson; Todd; Want; Ward;

Watt; Watton; Webster; Whitehouse; Williams; Wood (2); Wright; Wrightson; Yarrow.

BISHOP AUCKLAND: Fair.

BISHOP'S STORTFORD: Hack; Mulliner.

BLACKBURN: Douglas; Holme; Mellor; Wood.

BLANDFORD: Shipp.

BODMIN: Liddell.

BOLTON: Crook; Gowland; Heap; Holden; Kell; Ogle.

BOSTON: Brown, Noble.

BRADFORD: Dale; Spencer; Taylor.

BRAINTREE: Joscelyne.

BRAMPTON: Lancaster.

BRECON: Partridge.

BRENTFORD: Beasley; Bowden; Jones; Law.

BRIDGNORTH: Partridge.

BRIDLINGTON: Forth; Furley & Pearson.

BRIGHTON: Backwell; Baxter; Burge; Burn; Christopherson; Combe; Cooke; Folthorp; King; Lepperd; Manderson; Nute; Potter; Prudden; Sawyer; Swaine; Taylor (2); Vincent; Woolard.

BRISTOL: Baker; Barry; Becket; Bolt; Brotherton; Browne; Bulgin; Bulvetwell; Carter; Chandler; Chamberlain; Coles; Counsell; Cowley; Cowleys & Pountney; Cross & Cox; Culverwall; Davey; Davis; Davy & Muskett; Dennis; Derrick; Edwards; Escott; Esmand; Essex; Evans; Fenly; Francis; Frost; Fryer (2); Gange & Francis; Ghislin; Goodall; Hillyard & Morgan; Hodges; Hollester (2); Holleston; Huntley; Jackson (2); Jarrett; Jefferies; Jones; Jones & Bolt; King; Kington; Lancaster; Langdon; Lansdowne; Leslie; Leslie & Page; Long; MacCarthy; Macdowall; Major; Masters (2); Matthews; Mills; Mintorn; Moon; Morgan; Norton; Oldland; Oliver; Oram; Otton; Oxley; Parker; Parslow; Parson; Pearce (3); Perry; Pewters (2), Pickering; Player ; Pountney; Price; Pritchard; Pye; Rees; Reid (2); Richardson (2); Robert; Roberts; Sanford; Saunders; Sellick; Smart; Smith (4); Strong; Tamlyn; Thorbran; Turpin (2); Wansbrough (2);

Webber; Whereat; Woods; Wright; Wright & Bagnall.

BRIXTON: Daws; Martin.

BROMPTON: Chard; Denton.

BRUTON: Green; Stevens.

BUCKINGHAM: Seeley.

BUNGAY: Marsden; Smith.

BURNLEY: Rickard; Sutcliffe; Thornton.

BURSLEM: Dodd; McCreery; Scott.

BURTON: Hayes.

BURTON-ON-TRENT: Bellamy.

BURY-ST.-EDMUNDS: Deck; Dutton; Lankester; Morgan; Robinson; Spencer.

BURY (Lancs.): Kay.

CAERPHILLY: Williams.

CALNE: Baily.

CAMBORNE: Edwards.

CAMBRIDGE: Allen; Bowtell (2); Calver; Dickinson; Fitkin & Hart; Gee; Hankin; Hart; Hutt; Ingram; Lawrence (2); Lawrence & Underwood; Levett; Merrill; Newman; Nichols; Nicholson; Page (3); Readhead; Sapsford; Vowell; Wade; Wallis; Wickman; Wiseman; Wootton.

CANTERBURY: Ashton; Colegate; Dean; Hayward; Hunt; Marten; Mason; Prentice; Roalfe; Robertson; Saffery; Ward.

CARDIFF: Mathias.

CARDIGAN: John.

CARLISLE: Arthur; Beck; Brown; Forster; Harris; James; Jefferson; Moss; Scott (2); Slee; Snowden; Somerville; Thurnam; Whitridge.

CARMARTHEN: Davies; Davis; Evans; Lawrence (2); Morris.

CARNARVON: Evans; Poole & Harding; Potter; Preece; Pritchard (3); Roberts.

CHARD: Toms.

CHATHAM: Burrill; Edmed; Etherington; Hogg; Porter; Reynolds; Stockbridge.

CHELMSFORD: Copland; Guy.

CHELTENHAM: Alder; Bucknall; Campbell; Edwards; Long; Lovesey; Marchant; Paine; Parker; Porter; Webb (2).

CHEPSTOW: Stephens.

CHESTER: Batenham (3); Burton; Butler; Clarke; Edwards; Ellis; Forrester; Harding; Parry; Poole; Poole & Boult; Poole & Harding; Pover; Powell; Seacombe.

CHESTERFIELD: Roberts.

CHICHESTER: Angel; Baxter; Hackman; Hodge; Jacques; Jardine; Lefeaux; Smither; Wayment; Williams & Pullinger.

CHIPPING BARNETT: Cowing.

CHORLEY: Bibby; Parker.

CIRENCESTER: Bailey; Haywood; Overthrow; Smith.

CLAPHAM: Wood.

CLITHEROE: Lomax.

COCKERMOUTH: Bailey; Banks.

COGGLESHALL: Gardner.

COLCHESTER: Bailey; Cook & Brown; Dennis; Fenno; Mattacks (2); Rudkin; Totham.

COLESHILL: Tite.

COVENTRY: Carter; Hickling; Lewin; Stott; Whitehead (2).

CROYDON: Durban.

CULLOMPTON: Rowe.

CURRY RIVEL: Sharrock.

DARLASTON: Slater.

DARLINGTON: Clifford; Coates.

DARTFORD: Davids; Downton; Dunkin; Harman; Hubbard.

DARTMOUTH: Price.

DAVENTRY: Hensman; Line.

DEAL: Austen; Baker; Hayward; Kennard.

DENBIGH: Vaughan.

DEPTFORD: Brown (2); Clemison; Crane; Dilly & Stafford; Wilson.

DERBY: Bemrose; Bolton, Drewry; Fitchett; Harwood; Perfect; Pigott; Pike; Richardson & Handford; Smith; Wilkins.

DEVIZES: Bull; Griffin.

DEVONPORT: Gilbert; Granville; Harris; Lampen; Williams.

DONCASTER: Sheardown.

DORCHESTER: Mepham.

DORKING: Langley.

DOVER: Batcheller; Brydon; Duncan; Fox; Harris; Hendry; Horn; Hynes; Johnson; Mate; May; Rigden; Smith; Williams (2).

DOUGLAS: Caine; Cochrane; Dillon; Stewart; Tickell.

DUDLEY: Walton.

DURHAM: Andrews; Brown; George; Henderson; Hopper (2).

EASINGWOLD: Todd.

EAST DEREHAM: Hastings.

ECCLESHALL: Gallimore.

ELLESMERE: Baugh.

ELY: Clements; Hill; Thorpe.

ENFIELD: Smith.

EPSOM: Dorling.

ETON: Ingleton; Pote.

EVESHAM: Agg; Buttersley; May.

EWHURST: Boots.

EXETER: Baird; Beedle; Besley (2); Bird (2); Brayley; Brewer; Burnett (2); Cross; Cullum; Curton; Davies (2); Ellis; Featherstone; Fouracre; Hart & Cole; Hatch; Hill; Hooker; Howe; Hutchings; Mackenzie; Milton; Phillips; Player; Portbury (2); Read; Rodd; Smith; Spark (2); Spreat; Stabback; Stone; Thomson; Trewman; Warren; Yeo.

FALMOUTH: Dixon; Lake; McDowell; Trathan; Tregoning.

FARINGDON: Knapp.

FARNHAM: Fraser; Nichols.

FAVERSHAM: Ratcliffe; Rook; Thiselton.

FOLKESTONE: Stock.

FRODSHAM: Crowther.

FROME: Pearce.

GAINSBOROUGH: Hemsworth; Knaggs; Sherriff.

GARSTANG: Clarke.

GISBURN: Hayes.

GLASTONBURY: Hewitt.

GLOSSOP: Schofield; Sheppard.

GLOUCESTER: Allen; Brotherton; Gumm; Harding; Jew; Lea; Needham; Stokes; Thomas; Walden; Wingate.

GODALMING: Cook.

GOSPORT: Legg.

GRANTHAM: Brown; Perfect (2); Ridge; Storr.

GREENWICH: Cross; Jeffery; Richardson; Wright.

GRIMSBY: Walker.

GUERNSEY: Brouard; Hamilton; Hancock; Hicks; Manger; Short; Weston.

GUILDFORD: Brightwell; Hooke; Martin; Russell.

GUNTON: Downes.

HACKNEY: Pope.

HALESOWEN: Harris.

HALIFAX: Asquith; Baildon; Binns; Edwards; Frye; Garlick; Hirst; Holroyd; Milner (3); Watson; Whitley.

HAMMERSMITH: Page.

HANLEY: Allbutt; Harleston.

HARLESTON: Elliott.

HARTLEPOOL WEST: Thomas.

HARWICH: Ainslie; Rawlings; Trindle.

HASLINGDEN: Ratcliffe.

HASTINGS: Osborne; Pollard; Ranson.

HAVERFORDWEST: Barnikel; Thomas.

HAWKHURST: Wenban & Ransom.

HAWICK: Kennedy.

HAY: Bissell; Wilson.

HEBDEN BRIDGE: Halstead.

HELSTON : Edwards; Mitchell; Painter; Penalune; Roberts.

HEREFORD: Watkins.

HERTFORD: Austen; Simson (2).

HETTON-LE-HOLE: Shields.

HEXHAM: Barker; Bates; Bell; James.

HEYBRIDGE: Chaplain.

HIGH WYCOMBE: King.

HOLBEACH: Hall; Smith.

HOLMFIRTH: Crosland.

HOLYHEAD: Roberts.

HOLYWELL: Carnes; Hughes.

HONITON: Spurway.

HORNCASTLE: Babington.

HUDDERSFIELD: Shaw; Teale.

HULL: Adams; Allen; Atkinson; Bean (2); Bell; Bosomworth; Bradley; Brown (2); Browne (2); Cairns (2); Cherry; Clifford; Cookman; Craggs; Culwells; Darcy; Darcy & Hildyard; Edge; English; Harland; Harper; Hedge; Hewson; Hicks; Holdsworth; Houghton; Howe (2); Hutchinson; Johnson; Johnston; Jubb; Lacey; Lambert; Leadberry (2); Lethe (2); Lison; Lofthouse;

Marshall; Montgomery; Montgomery & Perfect; Mowatt; Nicholson; Peck; Peck & Smith; Penrose (2); Proctor; Purdon (2); Purdon & Brown ; Rawson & Rodford; Rayner; Rodford; Screaton; Smithson; Sutherland; Topping & Dawson; Turner; Wadsworth; Wainman; Warwick; Wild; Wilkins; Wilkinson; Wilson; Wright; Young.

HUNGERFORD: Nobbs.

HUNTINGDON: Wood.

HYTHE: King; Purdey.

IPSWICH: Brooks; Dowsing; Morley; Parker; Punchard; Scopes; Shave; Stebbing; Stow.

IRONBRIDGE: Smith.

JERSEY (see St. Helier).

KELVEDON: Eley.

KENDAL: Bathgate; Bland; Branthwaite; Hudson & Nicholson.

KESWICK: Airey; Bailey.

KING'S LYNN: Hitchcock; Inkson; Oswell; Richardson.

KIRKBY-STEPHEN: Batty; Davis.

KIRKHAM: Richardson; Sconce; Wandlis.

KNARESBOROUGH: Barnby.

KNUTSFORD: Leech.

LANCASTER: Bathgate; Leeming; Miller; Rothery.

LANE END: Forrister; Moss; Watt.

LEAMINGTON: Dark; Foden; Ostler; Robinson.

LEDBURY: Tranter.

LEEDS: Adgie; Bean; Binns; Booth; Braithwaite; Brown; Cross; Cullingworth (2); Cyclick; Dayson; Dodsworth; Dyson; Fowler; Gaines; Gamble; Goodall; Gregson; Harrison; Heaton; Hird; Hobson (2); Holdsworth (see Robinson); Hopps; Hutley; Inchbold (2); Irving; Jameson; Jefferson; Johnson (2); Knight (2); Knight & Bird; Leach; Machell; Mann; Mawson; Mead; Moody; Nichols (2); Nicholson; Reynard; Robinson; Schofield; Shiers; Shires; Simpson; Slocombe; Smith (2); Somerscale; Spence; Spink; Storey; Utley; Vickers; Warwick; Webster; Wilson; Woods; Wright.

LEEK: Moore.

LEICESTER: Brown; Calladine; Chamberlain; Cockshaw (3); Combe; Cook; Cross; Fowler; Hextall; Jacques; Johnson; Roper; Throsby; Tibbutt; Thompson.

LEWES: Baxter; Butland; Lee; Lomas; Lower; Moon.

LEWISHAM: Barratt.

LINCOLN: Drury; Johnston; Keyworth; Learey; Peck.

LISKEARD: Hill.

LITCHFIELD: Lomax.

LIVERPOOL: Atherton; Bankes; Batey; Beesley; Benn; Berry (2); Bradley; Brakell; Brass; Breckell; Broster (2); Carroll; Carson; Case; Cass; Christie; Close; Cox; Davies (2); Dawson; Dilworth (3); Edwards (3); Evans; Fazakerley; Ferguson; Fletcher; Frye; Gale (2); Grapel; Gregory & Taylor; Harris; Hayman; Haymen; Heymen; Horridge; Howard (2); Howell; Hughes (2); Jones (3); Keating; Kendall; Kent; Kirby; Law; Lawson; Lowry; McCre; McCreery; McDougall; McGaffie; Mackey; Maginnis; Marshall; Mayor; Millet, Mollison; Molloy; Moody; Muncaster; Murray;

Osborne; Oswald; Owens; Parkinson; Parry; Peck; Perry & Metcalf; Reston; Reynolds; Richards; Robinson (4); Rockliff & Ellis; Rothery; Sankey; Santley; Scarrat; Shaw; Shute; Simcock (2); Smart; Smith; Southward; Squire; Stanley (2); Stewart; Stewart & Molloy; Studdart; Surtees; Sutton (3); Taylor; Thompson: Tomlinson (2); Tyrer; Underhill; Wade; Wallace; Walmsley (2); Waterson; Webb; Whittingham; Willan; Willans; Williams (2); Wilson; Winter; Wood (2); Woodward; Wosencroft; Wright (4).

LLANELLY: Williams.

LLANERCHYMED: Jones.

LLANFAIR: Jones.

LLANGOLLEN: Hughes.

LLANIDLOES: Atkinson; Jones.

LLANRWST: Jones.

LLANVYLLING: Jones.

LOTH: Smith.

LOUGHBOROUGH: Lee.

LOWESTOFT: Taylor.

LUDDENDEN: Spencer.

LUDLOW : Griffith; Harris.

LYNN REGIS: Garland; Lane; Pigge; Whittingham.

MACCLESFIELD: Bayley; Cooper; Crowder; Hall; Swinnerton; Wright.

MACHYNLLETH: Roberts.

MADELEY: Edmunds; Walters.

MAIDENHEAD: Burnham; Burton & Batty; Sinclair; Wetton.

MAIDSTONE: Austen; Blake, Brown; Hall; Lindridge; Martin; Ostler; Ottoway; Porter; Price; Smith; Wickham; Williams.

MALVERN : Cross; Hickson; Warman.

MANCHESTER: Abrey; Adams; Ainsworth; Alsop; Ambery; Ashworth; Atkinson; Bancks; Beck; Belshaw; Blakeley; Boardman; Booth; Boyer; Brandreth; Broad; Broughton; Brown; Burket & Riley; Clarke; Cox; Coy; Crooks; Cunningham; Darbyshire; Davenport; Denne; Dewhurst; Dixon; Downs; Ellerby; Elliott; Ellis; Fletcher; Ford; Freckleton; Frye (2); Gadsby; Gardner; Gaskell; Gleave; Goodison; Graham; Griffiths; Hall; Hartley; Hatton (3); Hill; Hodgson; Holgate; Holland; Holt; Jackson; Johnson; Jordan; Kent; Leake (3); Lee; Leight & Woolley; Lomas; London ; Love & Barton; Mackey; Minor; Mowbray; Mullins; Nicholson; Phelan; Pigot; Ponder; Proven; Prudden; Robinson (3); Rose; Scholfield; Silburn; Smith (2); Sowler; Stevens; Stones; Story; Taylor; Thompson (2); Thomson (2); Townson; Tuft; Watson (3); Webb & Simons; Wilde; Winstanley; Withers & Hartley; Wright; Wroe.

MANSFIELD: Collinson.

MARGATE: Denne; Stow.

MARKET WEIGHTON: Crabtree.

MARLBOROUGH: Emberlin; Lucy.

MARYPORT: Harrison (2).

MELKSHAM: Cochrane; Waight.

MERTHYR TYDVIL: Evans.

MOLD: Lewis; Lloyd.

MORPETH: Blair; Brownrigg; Mackay.

MORTLAKE: Rothenburg.

NAILSWORTH: Blackwell: Brown; Partridge.

NARBERTH: Phillips.

NEATH: Bowen.

NEWARK: Lincham; Ridge; Sharp; Wells.

NEWBURY: Coxhead; Hall & Marsh; Powell; Price.

NEWCASTLE-EMLYN: Jones.

NEWCASTLE-ON-TYNE: Angus: Auerbach; Brown; Bruce; Carter; Cay; Clarke; Currie & Bowman; Davidson; Dodds; Duke; Edgar; Finlay; Finlay & Charlton; Forster; Gray; Haddock; Hall (2); Handysides ; Hetherington; Kelly; Lambert; Lee; Loraine; Lowther & Douglas; Lubbock; Marshall; Mather; Miller (2); Millet; Musgrave; Newlands; Nisbet; Oviston; Pearson; Potts; Purvis; Rewcastle; Richardson; Robertson, Sanderson; Seth; Simpson; Snowdon; Spark; Stephenson; Sutherland; Thompson; Whitefield; Wilkinson; Young.

NEWCASTLE-UNDER-LYME: Astbury; Bucknall; Hyde & Cross; Machin; Pye; Smith; Williams.

NEWMARKET: Rogers & Clarke.

NEWPORT (I. of W.): Denton; Dunford; French; Lambert; Midlam; Milligan; Morris; Rowden; Thompson; Warne; Yelf.

NEWPORT (Mon.): Newman.

NEWPORT (Salop): Morris; Silvester.

NEWPORT PAGNELL: Mills.

NEWTON ABBOT: Luscombe.

NORTH SHIELDS: Appleby: Ditchburne; Harrison; Walker.

NORTHAMPTON: Birdsall (3); Burnham; Codgbrook; Johnson; Lacy (2); Rea; Wheeler.

NORTON: Snow.

NORWICH: Annis; Barnes; Beatnise; Bush; Campbell; Campling; Colley; Coote; Cranefield; Cupper & Ives; Cushing; Davey; Dawson; Fletcher; Griffin; Grinter; Jungius; Lemmon; Liffen; Morgan; Muskett; Myhill; Norman; Otty; Parsons; Pinson; Quinton; Richer; Rider; Shalders; Soman & Howes; Stacey; Steward; Stewardson; Taylor; Thrower; Thurgar; Upcroft; Wardlaw; Wilkins; Williams; Yarington.

NOTTINGHAM: Allen; Baker; Barber; Bayne; Beastall (2); Beggs; Bull (3); Dearden; Dunn; Field; Hilton; Hodson; Howitt; Ingram; & Cooke; Jones; Kirk; Leighton; Maples; Morehouse; Robinson; Rothera; Shaw; Simpson; Staveley; Sutton; Taylor; Ward; Watson; Whittingham; Wild; Wright.

NUNEATON: Dews.

OLDHAM: Dodge; Evans.

OSWESTRY: Hocker; Marshall; Price.

OXFORD: Amsterdam; Barnes; Barratt (2); Barrell; Bellamy (2); Bliss; Bradstreet; Burton (2); Couldrey; Curtis; Dewe; Doe (2); Godden; Hayes; Kile (2); Mundy; Padbury; Paine; Parker; Rodwell; Salter & Atkinson; Sanders; Shrimpton; Smith; Talboys; Vincent; Ward; Wheeler; Wood.

PADSTOW: Docton.

PAINSWICK: Wheeler.

PECKHAM: Thompson.

PEMBROKE: Barnakel.

PENRITH: Allison; Brown; Shaw; Weightman.

PENZANCE: Lavin; Rowe; Thomas; Treubath; Vigurs.

PETERBOROUGH: Richardson.

PLYMOUTH: Arliss; Bennett; Bond; Byers; Clark; Congdon; Gibson; Gilbert; Hayes; Lidstone; Luke; Martin; Mudge; Munro; Nettleton; Nosworthy; Pardon; Picken; Platt; Roach; Rowe; Thomas; Vicary; Walker (2); Ward; Williams; Willis.

PONTEFRACT: Fox (?).

PONTYPOOL: Prosser.

PORTMADOC: Jones.

PORTSEA : Betts; Germain; Hookey; Jefferies; Pearson; Roe; Sailman; White; Williams.

PORTSMOUTH : Comerford; Hooper.

PRESCOT: Ducker; Franks.

PRESTON: Bailey; Brakell; Gorsuch; Graham; Higginson; Huddleston; Johnson; Sherrington; Thompson; Whittle.

PRINCE'S RISBOROUGH: Stratton.

PUTNEY: Wallace.

RAMSGATE: Burgess; Hunt; Jarman.

RASTRICK: Turner.

READING: Blackwell; Crapp; Drysdale; Harrison; Ingall; Jenkins; Knee; Lovejoy; Snare; Thomas; Whitman (2); Wyly.

REDRUTH: Reynolds.

RETFORD: Peart; Whiteside.

RICHMOND: Craggs.

RIPON: Clifford; Langdale; Thirlway.

ROCHESTER: Bone; Brooks; Evans; Levett.

ROCHDALE: Butterworth, Lancashire; Leach; Littlewood; Westall; Whitehead; Wood.

ROCHFORD: Beckwith.

ROMSEY: Medley.

ROSS: Farror; Powie.

ROYSTON: Smith; Warren.

RUGBY: Partridge.

RUGELEY: Leonard.

RUTHIN: Philips.

SAFFRON WALDEN: Pursey.

St. ALBANS: Johnson.

St. COLOMB: Bath.

St. HELIER: Bethell; Defries, Falle; La Lievre; Payn; Wood.

St. NEOTS: Le Tansur; Tomson.

SALFORD: Mackey; Mullis; Shepherd; Syers.

SALISBURY: Brodie; Clapperton, Earle; Gilmoir; Goddard; Hawker; Hearn; Pitman; Sounders.

SANDWICH: Giraud; Marbrook.

SCARBOROUGH: Foster; Milson (2).

SETTLE: Brown.

SEVENOAKS: Clout.

SHEFFIELD: Anderton; Beighton; Bentham & Ray; Blurton; Brown (2); Bullivant & Priest; Clare; Cockburn; Crome; Crookes; D'Arcy; Ford; Howlden; Laing; Leader; Mowatt; Orton; Pearce;

Ridge (2) ; Saxton; Slater; Stevenson; Sunderland; Sutherland; Thompson; Townsend; Wade (2); Whitaker (3); Williamson.

SHELTON: Gibbs.

SHEPTON MALLET: Masters.

SHERBURNE: Jeffery; Watts.

SHREWSBURY: Cole; Davies (2); Eddowes; Edwards; Evans; Halburt (or Hulbert); Hodges; Hulme; Minshull; Morris; Partridge, Peel; Pryse; Redfern; Steele.

SIDMOUTH: Harvey; Rippon.

SITTINGBOURNE: Nicholls.

SOUTH MOLTON: Tepper.

SOUTH PETHERTON: Barnett.

SOUTH SHIELDS: Bunn.

SOUTHAMPTON: Callen; Cawte; Clark; Coupland; Davis; Fletcher; Johnston; King; Linden; Lyon; Michell; Paul; Smart; Verney; Wilcox.

SPALDING: Maugham.

STAFFORD: Gallimore.

STAMFORD: Beardsall; Burton; Dickenson; Drury.

STOCKPORT: Dodge; Dymock; Lambert; Smart.

STOCKTON-ON-TEES: Appleton.

STOKESLEY: Pratt.

STONEHOUSE: Gilbert; Millman.

STOURBRIDGE: Brown.

STRATFORD-ON-AVON: Ward.

STROUD: Brisley; Bucknall.

SUDBURY: Riley.

SUNDERLAND: Barnes; Dixon; Heron; McLeish; Moir; Wetherald.

SWANSEA: Bluett; Bowen; Branton; Damp; Evans (2); Griffith; Jones; Walters; Wilkins.

TAMWORTH: Beard; Cotton.

TAUNTON: Bishop; Gresswell; Long; Poole; Trood.

TAVISTOCK: Chave.

TEIGNMOUTH: Litton.

TETBURY: Goodwyn.

TEWKESBURY: Jenner.

THETFORD: Fleet.

THORNBURY: Ellis.

TORRINGTON: Fowler.

TREDEGAR: Peaty.

TRING: Gates.

TROWBRIDGE: Diplock; Sweet.

TRURO: Brokenshir; Carthew; Clyma; Edwards; Heard (2); Maynard; Polybank; Roberts; Thomas.

TUNBRIDGE WELLS: Sprange.

TUNSTALL: Seckerson; Stevens.

ULVERSTON: Kirkman; Soulby.

UPTON-ON-SEVERN: Wagstaff.

UTTOXETER: Dunn; Norris; Tomkinson.

UXBRIDGE: Hetherington; Lake.

WAINFLEET: Hall.

WAKEFIELD: Aked; Cryer; Illingworth & Hicks; Nichols; Shuttleworth.

WALSALL: Martin; Pendrill.

WALTHAM ABBEY: Thompson.

WANDSWORTH: Linfield.

WARMINSTER: Dimsdale; Langford; Vardy.

WARRINGTON: Haddock; Woolstencroft.

WARWICK: Foden; Sharpe.

WATFORD: Niddery.

WATH: Woodhead.

WATTON: Hastings.

WELLINGTON: Corder.

WELLS: Backhouse; Grist; Price; Thompson.

WESTBURY: Michael.

WEYMOUTH: Benson; Commins; Delamotte; Thomas.

WHITBY: Griffiths; Laybourn.

WHITEHAVEN: Cook; Gaythorp; Gibson; Grisdale; McCombe; Newton; Robinson; Stuart; Wilson.

WHITTLESEA: Webster.

WIGAN: Collins; Lyon.

WIGTON: Ismay; Rooke.

WINCANTON: Olding; Rutter.

WINCHESTER: Blagden; Gilmour; Hawker; Jacob; Moody (2); Robbins & Wheeler; Thomas; Warren.

WINDSOR: Brown; Dredge; Farndell; Kelly; Morton.

WITNEY: Woon.

WOLVERHAMPTON: Bridgen; Clowes; Denman; Fownes; Fullwood; Large; Marshall; Parke; Ryley; Simpson; Smart; Wilson.

WOODSTOCK: Griggs.

WOOLER: Brand; McDonald.

WOOLWICH: Black; Blanchard; Boddy; Cock & Jackson; Dale; Ghislin; Muir; Scroggie.

WORCESTER: Baskerfield; Child; Condie; Deighton; Eaton; Edgecombe; Fenwick; Freeman; Grainger; Hayes; Holl; Lewis; Stokes; Stratford; Wagstaff; Wood.

WORKINGTON: Dixon; Kirkconel.

WOTTON: Povey.

WOTTON-UNDER-EDGE: Bailey.

WREXHAM: Goodier; Painter.

WYMONDHAM: Forster.

YARMOUTH (Gt.) Alexander; Cobb: Crisp (2); Diboll; Grave; Maryson; Nall; Paul; Shalders; Smith (2); Taylor.

YARMOUTH: Hazard; Keymer. (? Norfolk or I. of W.).

YEOVIL: Boucker.

YORK: Acton; Alexander; Allom; Atkinson; Avison; Barclay; Barker; Brassington (2); Brennard; Brocklebank; Carroll; Croshaw; Dixon (2); Duncanson (3); Hope; Kendrew; Linney; Marsh; Nicolson; Perfect; Perry; Pickering; Ripley; Smith; Spence & Burdekin; Sumner (3); Swinbank; Teasdale (2); Todd; Walker; Weightman; Yule.

ABREY, *Christopher*   Manchester
(Bookbinder's toolcutter.)
Add: 48 Lombard St.
Refs: MAN/DIR/08.

ACTON, *George*   York
Add: 29 Peter Gate.
Refs: YORKS/DIR/30: PIG/SEVEN/DIR/
34: WHI/WRY/37/8: WHI/ENR/40:
PIG/MND/42.

ADAMS, *James*   Hull
Add: 10 Postern Place: Posterngate:
Refs: HULL/DIR/39.

ADAMS, *William, Jun.*   Manchester
Add: 4 Barton's Bldgs, Deansgate.
Refs: MAN/DIR/38.

ADGIE, *John*   Leeds
Add: 10 Trinity St.
Refs: LEEDS/DIR/39.

AGG, *John*   Evesham
(Postmaster, P R &).
Refs: HOLD/11.

AINSWORTH, *James & Co.*
Manchester

AINSWORTH, *Thomas & Sons* (37)
Manchester
Add: 107 Gt. Ancoats St.
Refs: PIG/SEVEN/DIR/34: PIG/CDS/37:
MAN/DIR/38.

AIREY, *John* Keswick (Cumberland)
Refs: CUMWES/DIR/29.

AKED, *William*   Wakefield
Add: bottom of Westgate.
Refs: PIG/MND/42.

ALDER, *Daniel*   Cheltenham
Add: 89 High St.
Refs: ROB/NINE/DIR/39.

ALEXANDER   Yarmouth (? Great)
E D: 20.
Refs: Soth. Cat. 28.11.50/376. T.
Bewick. Sel. Fables. 1820. Boards.

ALEXANDER, *William*   York
Add: Castlegate.
Refs: PIG/18/20.

ALLBUTT, *Thomas* (35)   Hanley

ALLBUTT, *Thomas & Son* (42)
Hanley
Add: Market Place.
Refs: PIG/MID/DIR/35: PIG/MND/42.

AL(L)DRITT, *William* Birmingham
(& Librarian to the Birmingham
Library 29).
Add: Dean St (12): 16 Bromsgrove
St (15 & 25): Worcester St (18):
6 Moat Row & Cannon St (33):
27 Cannon St (35).

Refs: BIRM/DIR/12: 15: 21: 29: 33: 35: PIG/16/17. 18/20: PIG/LPCD/22: PIG/NCD/28: PIG/NAT/DIR/28/29: WARW/DIR/30: PIG/MID/DIR/35: PIG/CDS/37.

ALLEN   Gloucester
   E D: ? 25.
   Refs: LAB/KNA: "A/BINDER/G" ca.
   25.

ALLEN (ALLAN), *Charles*
                        Cambridge
   Add: Green St.
   Refs: PIG/NCD/30: PIG/HC/39: ROB/
   NINE/DIR/39: ROB/SIX/DIR/39.

ALLEN, *Joseph*   Birmingham
   (Printer &).
   Add: 6 Court, High St (35): 11
   Cannon St & 215 Deritend (37).
   Refs: BIRM/DIR/35: 39: PIG/MID/DIR
   /35; PIG/CDS/37: PIG/MND/42.

ALLEN, *Richard*   Nottingham
   Add: Long Row.
   Refs: NOTT/REG/40.

ALLEN, *W. S.*   Hull
   Add: 24 St. John St.
   Refs: HULL/DIR/21.

ALLISON, *Joseph*   Penrith
                        (Cumberland)
   Add: Market Place.
   Refs: CUMWES/DIR/29.

ALLOM, *John*   York
   Add: 16 New Bridge St.
   Refs: PIG/MND/42.

ALSOP, *William*   Manchester
   Add: 131 Oxford St, Chorlton-
   upon-Medlock.
   Refs: MAN/DIR/38.

AMBERY, *Charles*   Manchester
   Add: 91 Market St.
   Refs: PIG/CDS/37: MAN/DIR/38.

AMSTERDAM, *James*   Oxford
   Add: High St.
   Refs: PIG/LPCD/23.

ANDERTON, *William Walker*
                         Sheffield
   Add: 74 Fargate.
   Refs: PIG/CDS/37.

ANDREWS   Durham
   E D: ca. 30.
   Refs: AE/f: Sotheby: 1. 12. 52.
   Nos. 270 & 279.

ANGEL, *Charles*   Chichester
   (& P R, S T).
   Add: South St.
   Refs: PIG/LPCD/34: PIG/HC/39: ROB/
   HOMCO/DIR/39.

ANGUS, *George* Newcastle-on-Tyne
 E D: ? 22.
Refs: I have an excellent full
morocco binding on various pro-
ceedings of the Newcastle Lit. &
Phil. Society, 1807/22. They
appear to have employed a Mr.
George Angus for their binding
work between 1820/22, and this
binding may therefore well be by
him.

ANNIS, *John* Norwich
(B S &).
Add : London Lane.
Refs: NORW/DIR/11: HOLDEN/11.

APPLEBY, *Thomas* North Shields
Add: Clive St.
Refs: PIG/NCD/28: PIG/NAT/DIR/28/
29.

APPLETON, *John* Stockton-on-Tees
(P R &).
Add: Brunswick St (28): Silver St
(34).
Refs: PIG/NAT/DIR/28/29: PIG/SEVEN/
DIR/34.

ARLISS, *W. W.* Plymouth
(P R &).

ARLISS, *Amelia A*: (36).
Add: Market St (23): Bedford St
(36).
Refs: PLY/DIR/23: 36.

ARMSTRONG, *Adam* Liverpool
Add: 18 Temple Lane, St. Cather-
ine's (96): Dale St (00).
Refs: LIV/DIR/96: 00.

ARMSTRONG, *William* Liverpool
Add: 31 King St (24): 55 Bannister
St & King St Chambers (28).
Refs: LANC/DIR/24: PIG/NCD/28.

ARTHUR, *James* Carlisle
Add: 28 Rickergate.
Refs: PIG/SIN/20: CUMWES/DIR/29:
CAR/DIR/37.

ASHTON, *J.* Canterbury
Add: St. Peter's Place: 13 Burgate
St.
Refs: LAB/JONES (2).

ASHWORTH, *Richard* Manchester
Add: 35 Chapel St, London Rd.
Refs: PIG/CDS/37.

ASQUITH, *George* Halifax
Add: 4 Barum Top.
Refs: YORK/DIR/22: YORKS/DIR/30.

ASTBURY, *John*
Newcastle-under-Lyme
Add: 6 Bow St.
Refs: NEW/LYME/DIR/36.

ATHERTON, *John* Liverpool
Add: Jubilee Buildings, 84 Lord St.
Refs: PIG/CDS/37.
Engraved label in Munby Coll. on
book dated 1831.

ATKINSON, *Henry* Appleby (Westmorland)
  Add: Borough Gate.
  Refs: CUMWES/DIR/29.

ATKINSON, *James* Llanidloes
  Add: Churchyard.
  Refs: PIG/MID/DIR/35.

ATKINSON, *James* Manchester
  Add: 1 Marsden Ct.
  Refs: MAN/DIR/00.

ATKINSON, *John* York
  Add: Opposite Belfrey Church, High Petergate (11): Micklegate (22): 29 Peter Gate (28): Spurriergate (? 35).
  Refs: YORK/DIR/22: PIG/NCD/28: PIG/NAT/DIR/28/29: O.C. Euclid 1535. f.m.g. (ca. 35). Label: "Bd. by/JA/Spurriergate/York." J.A./4955.

ATKINSON, *Joseph* Hull
  Add: Silver St.
  Refs: BRI/DIR/91: HULL/DIR/91.

AUERBACH, *E.* Newcastle-upon-Tyne
  (etc).
  Add: 38 Westgate St.
  Refs: NEW/DIR/38.

AUSTEN, *Ambrose* Maidstone
  Add: Week St.
  Refs: PIG/LPCD/23.

AUSTEN, *Stephen* Hertford
  Refs: In Dec. 1948 H. Fletcher had two bindings in the oriental style made for the Oriental Study Exhibition at the Sorbonne dated 1853. He may have bound before 1840.

AUSTEN, *W.* Deal
  Refs: KENT/DIR/03: HOLD/11.

AVISON, *James* York
  Add: 12 Fetter Lane.
  Refs: PIG/SEVEN/DIR/34.

BABINGTON, *James* Horncastle
  (P R, B B & S T). (Lincs.)
  Refs: HOLD/11.

BACKHOUSE, *Benjamin & Sons*
  Refs: SOM/DIR/40. Wells

BACKWELL, *Matthew Price*
  (P R &). Brighton
  Add: 3 Poplar Place, Meeting House Lane (24): 18 Eastcliffe & Union Place (26): 16 East Cliff (34).
  Refs: BRIG/DIR/24: A.E.COLL/26; PIG/LPCD/32/34.

BAILDON, *John* Halifax
  Add: King Cross Lane.
  Refs: YORK/DIR/22: PIG/LPCD/22: AE/f.

BAILEY, *R. & Co.*
  Wotton-under-Edge (Glos.)

BAILEY, *Richard* (39).
Add: Long St (39).
Refs: ROB/NINE/DIR/39:
O.C. Matilda, 1825: f.m.g., possibly contemporary. Ticket: "Bd. by/R. B. & Co./Wotton."

BAILEY, *T.*   Liverpool
Add: 32 Manchester St, Dale St.
Refs: LIV/DIR/40.

BAILEY, *T. Philip*   Cirencester
Add: Market Place.
Refs: ROB/NINE/DIR/39.

BAILEY, *Thomas*   Cockermouth
                            (Cumberland)
(& dealer in paper hangings).
Add: Main St.
Refs: CUMWES/DIR/29.

BAILEY, *Thomas*   Keswick
(Etc).   (Cumberland)
Refs: CUMWES/DIR/29: PIG/SEVEN/
DIR/34.

BAILEY, *W.*   Preston
Refs: Munby Coll: pink printed label "WB/BB, etc, P", binding ca. 1830.

BAILY   Calne (Wilts)
(Etc).
E D: 80?
Add: Church St.
Refs: P. Ticket, "Baily/Printer/Bookseller & Stationer/Church

Street/Calne/sells articles in the above branches on the lowest/Terms/: Books neatly Bound".

BAIRD, *John*   Exeter
Add: 223 High St.
Refs: EX/DIR/28.

BAKER, *W.*   Deal
E D: ?
Add: Esplanade:
Refs: LAB/JONES.

BAKER, *William*   Bristol
Add: Somerset St, Cathay (18): 3 Narrow Wine Lane (24 & 33): 20 Dove St (30): 2 St. Stephen's Avenue, Clare St (39).
Refs: BRIS/IND/18: BRIS/DIR/24: 27: 30: 33: ROB/NINE/DIR/39.

BAKER, *Wm.*   Nottingham
Add: Middle Pavement.
Refs: NOTT/REG/40.

BALL   Babcary (Somerset)
E D: 12?
Refs: Munby Coll: Label "B, BB, B", Tree calf, 1812.

BANCKS & *Co.*   Manchester
Add: 20 Exchange St.
Refs: PIG/CDS/37: MAN/DIR/38.

BANKES, *John*   Liverpool
Add: 9 Derby St.
Refs: LIV/DIR/10.

PLATE I

PLATE II

BANKS, *Pattinson*   Cockermouth
Add: Main St.   (Cumberland)
Refs: CUMWES/DIR/29.

BARBER, *Alfred*   Nottingham
Add: Park St.
Refs: NOTT/REG/40.

BARCLAY, *Alexander*   York
Add: St. Saviourgate.
Refs: PIG/16/17: 18/20.

BARKER, *George*   York
Add: Pavement.
Refs: YORK/DIR/22: PIG/LPCD/22.

BARKER, *M. & J.*   Hexham
Add: Market Place.
Refs: WSM/KC/NEW: Label on 1786
work "B/BS, ST/ & BB/MP/H"
& on MSS 1817/20 "M & J.B/
B/H."

BARNAKEL, *John*   Pembroke
Refs: PIG/NCD/30.

BARNBY *Stephen*   Knaresborough
(B S, S T &).
Add: High St.
Refs: YORK/DIR/22: PIG/SEVEN/DIR/
34.

BARNES, *Charles*   Norwich
Add: Bedford St.
Ref: NORF/DIR/36.

BARNES, *William*   Oxford
Add: High St.
Refs: PIG/LPCD/23.

BARNES, *W. B.*   Sunderland
E D: Ca. 30.
Refs: AE/COLL/LAB.

BARNETT, *Edwin*   South Petherton
Add: Palmer St.   (Somerset)
Refs: SOM/DIR/40.

BARNIKEL, *J. L.*
        Haverfordwest (Pembroke)
(& fancy paper-worker)
Add: King St.
Refs: O.C. Label: "J.L.B./BB/&
FPW/K.S/H" on W. Nichol's
Planter's Kalender, 1820, ½ calf.

BARRATT'S LIBRARY (*Joseph*)
(B S & Cir. Lib.).   Bath
Add: Bond St.
Refs: LAB/JONES/("Bound   at"):
BATH/DIR/01.

BARRATT, *Thomas*   Oxford
(MAT/OX "bibliopegus" 27.4.98).

BARRATT & *Son* (11)
Refs: BRI/DIR/91 as "Barrott.":
HOLD/11: JA/3392.
O.C. Aristotelis Poetica, f.m.g.,
Hex.   ticket:—"Barratt/Binder/
Oxford".
Tighe. Psyche. 4th ed. 12, f.vell.g.
blue silk end papers. Plain oval

ticket "Barratt." Black Stamped oval beaded frame "T. Barratt, Binder" on Junius 1797, 2 vol. Russia at Marks/ May, 1951.

BARRATT, *William*   Lewisham
Refs: PIG/LPCD/32: 34.

BARRETT, *William*   Oxford
(MAT/OX "bibliopegus" 10.2. 1777)? out of period.

BARRY, *B.*   Bristol
(& S T).
Add: Bristol Bridge.
Refs: BRIS/DIR/94.

BASKERFIELD   Worcester
Refs: Dark blue mor. bdg. ca. 1780, signed at base of spine on Cervantes: 2 vol., 4to. 1756. Christie Sale 1.4.53: Lot 256.

BATCHELLER, *William*   Dover
(Etc, etc).
Add: 1 & 2 Snargate St (King's Arms Library).
Refs: PIG/LPD/26/27: PIG/LPCD/34: PIG/HC/39: LAB/JONES(2): ROB/HOMCO/DIR/39.

BATENHAM, *Edward*   Chester
Add: Northgate St.
Refs: CHES/DIR/40: Munby Coll. Label:—"B, B, C": M.g. ca. 38.

BATENHAM, *James*   Chester
Add: City Walls.
Refs: CHES/DIR/40.

BATES, *David*   Hexham
Add: Meal St.
Refs: DUR/DIR/27: PIG/NAT/DIR/28/29.

BATES, *David*   Hexham
Refs: I now (May, 53) have a ticket "Bd/by/B/H" taken from a dilapidated, but formerly nice Russia binding with key pattern on sides on a 1821 book.

BATEY, *Geo.*   Liverpool
Add: 172 London Rd (34): 60 (40).
Refs: PIG/SEVEN/DIR/34: LIV/DIR/40

BATH, *John Eddy*   St. Colomb
(P R &)   (Cornwall)
Refs: PIG/LPCD/23.

BATHGATE, *James*   Lancaster
Add: Anchor Lane.
Refs: PIG/NCD/28: PIG/NAT/DIR/28/9: PIG/SEVEN/DIR/34.

BATHGATE, *Simon*   Kendal
Add: Caroline St.   (Westmorland)
Refs: CUMWES/DIR/29.

BATTY, *William*   Kirby Stephen
Add: Market Place. (Westmorland)
Refs: CUMWES/DIR/29.

BAUGH, *William*   Ellesmere
   Add: High St.   (Shropshire)
   Refs: SALOP/DIR/28: JBO/AE.

BAXTER   Chichester
   Add: North St.
   Refs: CHICH/DIR/04.

BAXTER *& Co.*   Brighton
   Add: 21 North St.
   Refs: BRIG/DIR/22.

BAXTER, *John & Son*   Lewes
   Add: 37 High St.
   Refs: PIG/HC/39.

BAYLEY, *Edward*   Macclesfield
   (Doubtfully a binder).
   Add: Market Place (17):
   Refs: Sch. S. de R.IV, 47: Hob/
   Abb. App. XI, p. 194. MACC/
   DIR/17:25. Ticket seen at Marks,
   April, 1952.
   (Very poor specimen of binding).

BAYNE, *Charles*   Nottingham

BAYNE, *Charles & Son* (? 34-40 and
   again in 42).
   Add: Shop, Bottle Alley, Bottle
   Lane (32).
   Res: Park Sq, Russell St (34):
   Warser Gate (40).
   Refs: NOTTSH/DIR/32: NOTT/DIR/34:
   NOTT/REG/40: PIG/MCD/42.

BEAN, *Benjamin*   Hull
   Add: 3 Robinson's Row.
   Refs: PIG/NCD/28: PIG/NAT/DIR/28/
   29.

BEAN, *William*   Leeds
   Add: 16 Lowerhead Row.
   Refs: YORK/DIR/22: PIG/LPCD/22.

BEAN & LISON   Hull Port
   Add: 17 Grimsby Lane.
   Refs: LINC/DIR/24

BEARD, *Joseph*   Tamworth
   (P R &).
   Add: Market St. (22): Aldersgate
   (28).
   Refs: PIG/LPCD/22: PIG/NCD/28:
   PIG/NAT/DIR/28/29.

BEARDSALL, *E.*   Stamford
   E D: 36?
   Refs: O.C. Cabinet. Mod. Art./36.
   Stamped calf gilt and mor. side
   panels, with Earl's coronet and
   initials "C.L.". Cut label (printed)
   in 3 parts "E.B./B/S."

BEASLEY, *Ebenezer*   Brentford
   (Etc).
   E D: ? 20.
   Refs: LAB/KNA: "B/Binder/B": ca.
   20: PIG/LPCD/32.

BEASTALL, *Francis*   Nottingham
   Add: Rutland St.
   Refs: PIG/MID/DIR/35.

BEASTALL, *Thomas*   Nottingham
   (& S T).
   Add: Houndsgate.
   Refs: HOLD/11.

BEATNIFFE, *Richard*   Norwich
   (& B S).
   b. 1740, d. 9.7.1818.
   Add: 6 Cockey Lane (02).
   Refs: TIMB/ENC/42, p. 868: NORW/
      DIR/02.

BECK, J.   Leamington
   (P R &).
   Add: Regent St.
   Refs: LEAM/DIR/37.

BECK, *John*   Carlisle
   Add: 48 Scotch St.
   Refs: CARL/DIR/37.

BECK, *William*   Manchester
   Add: 25 Queen St, Hulme.
   Refs: PIG/18/20.

BECKET, *J. Brice*   Bristol
   (B S, S T &).
   Add: Corn St.
   Refs: BRIS/DIR/85: 87: 92: Only
      mentioned as B B in 85.

BECKWITH, *Eli*   Rochford (Essex)
   Refs: PIG/LPCD/32: 34: PIG/HC/39.

BEEDLE, *George*   Exeter
   Add: Horse Lane.
   Refs: EX/P/J/33.

BEER, *George*   Bath
   (Leather Binding Manufacturer).
   Add: 8 Wood St.
   Refs: BATH/DIR/41.

BEESLEY, *Henry*   Liverpool
   Add: 34 Basnett St (37): 3 Union
      Bldgs, Cook St, Castle St (40).
   Refs: PIG/CDS/37; LIV/DIR/40.

BEGGS, *Thomas & Co*   Nottingham
   Add: Upper Parlt. St.
   Refs: PIG/MND/42.

BEIGHTON, *Thomas*   Sheffield
   Add: 189 Gibraltar St.
   Refs: PIG/MND/42.

BEILBY, KNOTT & BEILBY
   (Etc).   Birmingham
   Add: 95 High St.
   Refs: WARW/DIR/30: BIRM/DIR/29:
      33.

BELCHER, *James* (Probably two)
   (Etc).   Birmingham
   Add: Bull Ring (97): 5 High St (33).
   Refs: BIRM/DIR/97: 33.

BELCHER *& Son*   Birmingham
   (Etc).
   Add: 5 High St.
   Refs: BIRM/DIR/12: 15: 18: 25.

BELL, *William*   Hexham
   Add: Fox St.
   Rep: PIG/SEVEN/DIR/34.

BELL, *William*   Hull
(& S T).
Add: Market Place.
Refs: HULL/DIR/91.

BELLAMY, *Edward*   Oxford

BELLAMY, *E. Jun.* (39).
Add: St. Clements (11): St. Ebbs.
(30): New Inn Hall (39).
Refs: HOLD/11: PIG/LPCD/23: PIG/
NCD/30: ROB/SIX/DIR/39. Label seen
at Marks in 1949 on a book dated
1817 with Gothic blindstamped
binding in calf. Munby Coll:
Label "B,BB,O" Russia: ? 07.

BELLAMY, *Ephraim*   Oxford
Add: Littlegate.
Refs: ROB/SIX/DIR/39.

BELLAMY, *R. R.*   Burton-on-Trent
Refs: LAB/KNA/: "Bound by RRB/
B-on-T"; doubtfully in period.

BELSHAW, *Thomas*   Manchester
Add: 2 Old Millgate.
Refs: MAN/DIR/38.

BEMROSE, *W. & Son*   Derby
Refs: LAB/JONES.

BENN, *Thomas*   Liverpool
Add: 2 Thomas St.
Refs: LIV/DIR/90.

BENNETT, *John Dimery*   Bath
(& Servants' Register Office in
1841).
Add: McPherson's Cottage, Philip
St (26): 58 Westgate St (29): 6
New Westgate Bldgs (36): 10
Northumberland Place (37): 8
Orange Grove (41).
Refs: BATH/DIR/26: 29: 36: 37: 41.

BENNETT, *W.*   Plymouth
Add: 13 Russell St.
Refs: PLYM/DIR/30.

BENSON, *Benjamin*   Weymouth
(Etc).
Add: 69 St. Mary St.
Refs: WEY/DIR/28.

BENTHAM & RAY   Sheffield
(Etc).
Add: High St.
Refs: PIG/18/20.

BERRY, *John*   Liverpool
Add: 4 Temple Lane, Temple
Court (00): Sweeting St, Castle
St (03): 17 Temple St (05): 31
Matthew St (07): 9 Cook St (10):
No. 2 (13).
Refs: LIV/DIR/00: 03: 05: 07: 10:
13: 16.

BERRY, *William*   Liverpool
Add: 15 William St (16): 8 Ryley's
Gdn (34).
Refs: LIV/DIR/16: 18: 21: 34.

BESLEY, *Thomas & H.* Exeter
(P R, S T &).

BESLEY, *H.* (1835).
Add: 76 Bell Hill, South St (28 &
31); 76 South St (30 & 35).
Refs: PIG/NCD/30: EX/DIR/28: 31:
35.

BETHELL, *W.* St. Helier (Jersey)
(Etc).
Add: 5 Hope St (34): 15 King St
(39).
Refs: LC/JER/34: ROB/NINE/DIR/39.

BETTS, *Joseph* Portsea
Add: 90 Queen St.
Refs: PIG/NCD/30.

BIBBY, *John* Chorley (Lancs)
Add: Cannon St.
Refs: PIG/NCD/28: PIG/NAT/DIR/28/9:
PIG/SEVEN/DIR/34.

BINNS, *A. E.* Bath
(Etc).
Add: 19 Cheap St.
Refs: BATH/DIR/33.

BINNS, *John* Leeds
(Bookseller): d May, 1796.
Refs: Started as a bookbinder under
his father, Nathaniel Binns, of
Halifax. See Timp/Enc. 42, p. 791.
Worked for S. Crowder of Pater-
noster Row, London, and started
in Leeds about 1766. It is not

certain that he bound after that
date. See also DPB/1726/75, p. 26.

BINNS, *Nathaniel* Halifax
E D: ? 1750: d Jan, 1801 ("at an
advanced age" (?)).
Refs: TIMB/ENCL/42, p. 791: DEP/
1726/75, p. 26.

BIRD, *Thomas* Exeter

BIRD, *J.* (35).
Add: 126 Fore Street Hill.
Refs: PIG/NCD/30: EX/DIR/28: 31:
35(J).

BIRDSALL, *A.* Northampton
Add: Wood St.
Refs: W. Sabine, of Hollis, N.Y.,
reports a cloth binding on a 40
vol set, dated 1808.

BIRDSALL, *James* Northampton
(Son of William).
E D: 26 ?: L D: 40 ?
Refs: JBO/AE.

BIRDSALL, *W.* (decd. 23.6.26)
Northampton

BIRDSALL, *W. & Son* (26):
E D: 92 ?
Refs: B.M.: C. 38. e. 29: C.53.
c.5:e. 57 e.7 12: His label has been
seen by me on a calf binding in
the Etruscan style on an undated
(ca. 1810) English translation of
Marmontel's Belisarius.

BISHOP, *Thomas*   Birmingham
(S T, B S & B B).
Add: Fancy Warehouse, opp.
  Bisset's Museum, New St.
Refs: BIRM/DIR/00.

BISHOP, *John*   Taunton
Add: North St.
Refs: PIG/NCD/30.

BISSELL, *Edmund*   Hay (Brecknock)
Add: Castle St.
Refs: PIG/MID/DIR/35.

BLACK, *J.*   Woolwich
(S T, P R &).
Add: Powis St.
Refs: ROB/HOMCO/DIR/39.

BLACKWELL, E.   Reading
(Etc).
Add: 10 London St.
Refs: READ/DIR/37.

BLACKWELL, *J.* Nailsworth (Glos.)
E D: 22 ?
Refs: Ticket on book dated 1822.
  Hodgson's sale 7.3.52 (No. 364).

BLAGDEN, *Thomas*   Winchester
Refs: Active as a printer between
  1784/96. Is recorded as binding a
  Corporation book in "rough
  calf" in early 1789. (Information
  supplied by G. N. Helliwell,
  Winchester City Librarian, Nov.
  1952).

BLAIR, *P.*   Morpeth
E D: 18 ?
Refs: I noted his name in 1948 on a
  book in Soho market.
  LAB/JONES (2).

BLAKE'S *Printing Office*   Maidstone
(P R &).
E D: 80 ?
Refs: Hob/Abb., App. XI, p. 194:
  AE/HEAL/LAB.

BLAKELEY, *John*   Manchester
Add: Ferneley St, Hulme.
Refs: MAN/DIR/28.

BLANCHARD, *H.*   Woolwich
(S T &)
Add: 24 High St.
Refs: ROB/HOMCO/DIR/39.

BLAND, *George*   Kendal
(Book case maker &).
Add: Highgate (34).
Refs: BRI/DIR/91 : PIG/SEVEN/DIR/34.

BLISS, *David*   Oxford
Refs: MAT/OX: 10.1.99: "station-
  arius et librorum glutinator".
  His wife died ca. 8.6.99, see
  Jackson's "Oxford Journal".

BLOOMER, *T.*   Birmingham
Add: Digbeth.
Refs: BIRM/DIR/18.

BLOXHAM, *William*   Banbury
    Add: High St.
    Refs: ROB/SIX/DIR/39.

BLUETT, *George*   Swansea
    Add: Calvert St (22): High St (30).
    Refs: PIG/LPCD/22: PIG/MCD/30.

BLURTON, *John*   Sheffield
    Add: Newton's Court, King St.
    Refs: WHI/WRY/37.

BOARDMAN, *Samuel* Manchester
    Add: Boond St, Salford (08):
    Hardman's Bldgs, Young St (11
    P): 5 Hardman St, Sal. (13):
    16 St. Ann's St: Res: 25 Young
    St (28).
    Refs: MAN/DIR/08: 11P: 13: 32:
    PIG/NCD/28.

BODDY, *J. M.*   Woolwich
    (B S &)
    Add: 33 Artillery Place.
    Refs: ROB/HOMCO/DIR/39.

BOLT, *James*   Bristol
    (See Jones & Bolt).
    Add: Tailors' Ct, Broad St.
    Refs: BRIS/DIR/33: 36: 40: ROB/NINE/
    DIR/39.

BOLTON, *John*   Birmingham
    Add: 85 Weaman St (35): Steel-
    house Lane (37).
    Refs: PIG/MID/DIR/35: PIG/CDS/37.

BOLTON, *John*   Derby

BOLTON, *William* (42).
    Add: Friar Gate (John (29): William
    (42)).
    Refs: COUNT/DER/29: PIG/MID/DIR/
    35: PIG/MCD/42.

BOND, *Robert*   Plymouth
    (Etc, etc).
    Add: Market St: 14 Whimple St.
    Refs: PLY/DIR/22: PIG/LPCD/23.

BONE, *Charles*   Rochester
    Add: Five Bell Lane, St. Margaret's
    Bank.
    Refs: PIG/LPCD/32: 34: KENT/DIR/38.

BOOTH, *James*   Manchester
    Add: 133 London Rd.
    Refs: MAN/DIR/28.

BOOTH, *Nathaniel, Jun.*   Leeds
    Add: Vicar Lane (22): South
    Market, Hunslet Lane.
    Refs: Label in O.C. "NB/BB/SM,
    HL/L": YORK/DIR/22: PIG/FLCD/
    22 (Jun).

BOOTS, *T. W.* Ewhurst (Surrey)
    Refs: LAB/KNA " TWB/BINDER/E" Ca.
    30.

BOSOMWORTH, *John Goodyear*
    (& Copper-plate Printer)   Hull
    Add: 26 Church Lane (34): No. 31
    (37).

Refs: PIG/SEVEN/DIR/34: PIG/CDS/37: WHI/WRY/37/38: HULL/YORK/DIR/38: HULL/DIR/35: 38: 39: WHI/ENR/40: PIG/MCD/42.

BOWDEN, *Matthew*   Brentford
Add: Old Brentford.
Refs: ROB/HOMCO/DIR/39.

BOWEN, *Henry*   Neath (Glam.)
Add: Wind St (22): Strand (30).
Refs: PIG/LPCD/22: PIG/NCD/30.

BOWEN, *Henry*   Swansea
Add: High St.
Refs: PIG/MID/DIR/35.

BOWEN, *Richard*   Birmingham
Add: 45 Constitution Hill.
Refs: BIRM/DIR/39: PIG/MND/42.

BOWTELL, *John*   Cambridge
b 1753: d 1813.
(Binder to the University, 85: & to King's College 94).
Add: All Saints' Passage (89): St. Catherine's Hostel (01) : Trinity St (11).
Refs: Camb. Ant. Soc. Proc. Vol. XI, pp. 347/84. Label in Bartolozzi style and details of examples of bindings, pp. 362/3. JA/3391: HOLD/11.

BOUCHER, *John*   Yeovil
Add: Borough.
Refs: PIG/LPCD/22.

BOWTELL, *John* (*Jun.*)   Cambridge
b 1777, d 1855.
Add: All Saints' Passage (after 1810: Residence before 1810 in Green St).
Refs: HOLD/11: PIG/LPCD/23: PIG/NCD/30: PIG/HC/39: Camb. Ant. Soc. Proc. Vol. XI, pp. 347/84.

BOWTELL, *William*   Cambridge
(Son of J.B. Junior).
Add: All Saints' Passage.
Refs: Camb. Ant. Soc. Proc. Vol XI, pp. 347/84: ROB/NINE/DIR/39: ROB/SIX/DIR/39.

BOYER, *J. F. & J.*   Manchester
Add: 3 Riding's Ct.
Refs: LANC/DIR/25.

BRADLEY, *Benjamin*   Hull
Add: 9 Bishop Lane (26): 6 Bowl-alley Lane (34).
Refs: LINC/DIR/26: PIG/NCD/28: PIG/NAT/DIR/28/29: PIG/SEVEN/DIR/34: HULL/DIR/35: 38: 39: PIG/CDS/37: WHI/WRY/37: WHI/SNR/40: PIG/MND/42.

BRADLEY, *William*   Liverpool
Add: 20 Pinnington St.
Refs: LIV/DIR/18.

BRADSTREET, *Thomas*   Oxford
Add: St. Aldgate's (23): Littlegate (30).
Refs: PIG/LPCD/23: PIG/NCD/30.

BRAITHWAITE, *Joseph*   Leeds
(Binding Manufacturers (sic)).
Add: Meadow Lane.
Refs: LEEDS/DIR/93: 00.

BRAKELL, *Richard*   Liverpool
(? See Breckell) (& Paper Ruler).
Add: 37 Sweeting St.
Refs: LIV/DIR/34: 40.

BRAKELL, *Thomas*   Preston
(& Paper Machine Ruler).
Add: Pleasant St.
Refs: PREST/DIR/21.

BRAND, *W.*   Wooler
(& S T)   (Northumberland)
E D: ca. 24.
Refs: WSM/KC/NEW: Label "Bd by
/WB/BB & ST/W".

BRANDRETH, *William* Manchester
Add: 9 St. Ann's St (34) (37): 5
Pool Fold (38).
Refs: PIG/SEVEN/DIR/34: PIG/CDS/37:
MAN/DIR/38.

BRANTHWAITE, *Mich. & Rd.*
Kendal (Westmorland)
Add: Fishmarket.
Refs: CUMWES/DIR/29.

BRANTON, *John*   Swansea
Add: Goat St.
Refs: PIG/NCD/30.

BRASS, *Charles James*   Liverpool
Add: 23 Shaw's Brow (32): 45
School Lane (37).
Refs: LIV/DIR/32: 34: PIG/SEVEN/DIA/
34: PIG/CBS/37: 40.
O.C. Calf g. binding on Walton's
Lives, Major 1825, with label.

BRASSINGTON, *Edward*   York

BRASSINGTON, *Richard* (28)
Add: High Ousegate (18): Waterloo
Place, Spurriergate (22): Res:
Bishops Hill (40).
Refs: PIG/18/20: PIG/LPCD/22: PIG/
NCD/28: PIG/NAT/DIR/28/29: YORK
/DIR/30: PIG/SEVEN/DIR/34: WHI/
WRY/37: WHI/ENR/40: PIG/MND/
42. Ticket illustrated in WSM/KC/
NEW.

BRAYLEY, *W.*   Exeter
Add: James St.
Refs: EX/P/J/38-40.

BRECKELL, *Richard*   Liverpool
(? see Brakell).
Add: 1 Erwin Court, Vauxhall Rd.
Refs: LIV/DIR/32.

BRENNAND, *J.*   York
Add: 60 Petersgate.
Refs: YORK/DIR/30.

BRETHERTON, *George* Gloucester
Add: College St.
Refs: ROB/NINE/DIR/39.

BRETTELL, *John*   Birmingham
  Add: Mount St.
  Refs: BIRM/DIR/08.

BREWER, John   Exeter
  Add: James St (33): Bartholomew
  Yd (40): Refs: EX/P/J/33: 34: 36:
  40: EX/DIR/31: 35.

BRIDGEN, *Joseph*   Wolverhampton
  (& Machine Ruler).   Printed the
  1833 & 38/Wolv/DIRS.
  Add: Darlington St.
  Refs: PIG/MID/DIR/35: WOLV/DIR/
  38: PIG/MND/42.

BRIERLEY, *Joshua Leonard*
                        Birmingham

BRIERLEY, Y. L.
  Add: 43 Colmore St (28): Hollo-
  way Head (29): Swan Hotel
  Yard & Worcester St (33): 93½
  High St. (35).
  Refs: PIG/NCD/28: PIG/NAT/28/29:
  WARW/DIR/30: BIRM/DIR/35: 39.
  About 1835 some confusion
  arises.   The BIRM/DIR/35 adds
  "machine ruler" to Joshua
  Leonard's bookbinding, and
  under a different entry gives Y.
  L. Brierley at 4 Smallbrook St as
  "machine ruler, paper gilder and
  vellum binder."   In 1839 only
  Joshua Leonard appears at 5
  Smallbrook St as "hosier, haber-
  dasher, paper gilder and vellum
  binder".

BRIGHTWELL   Barnstaple
  E D: 86 ?
  Refs: JA/2971.

BRIGHTWELL, *John*   Guildford
  Refs: London Binder who worked
  in Guildford in 1796 (see Howe,
  London Bookbinders 1648-1815
  Bib/Soc).

BRISLEY, *John Pierce*   Stroud
  (Etc, etc).   (Gloucestershire)
  Refs: ROB/NINE/DIR/39.

BROAD, *Jesse*   Manchester
  (& S T).
  Add: 3 Barlow Ct, Market St (24):
  No. 1 (34): Rcs: (28): St. John's
  Place.
  Refs: P.C.D. 24: PIG/CDS/25/6: LANC/
  DIR/25: PIG/NCD/28: MAN/DIR/24-
  32: 28 (only as S T & P R):
  PIG/SEVEN/DIR/34.

BROCKLEBANK, *Thomas*   York
  Add: 30 North St.
  Refs: PIG/NCD/28: PIG/NAT/DIR/28/
  29: YORK/DIR/30.

BRODIE & *Co.*   Salisbury
  Add: New Canal.
  Refs: ROB/NINE/DIR/39.

BROKENSHIR, *John*   Truro
  Add: 63 Kenwyn St: (23): 19
  Boscawen St (30).
  Refs: PIG/LPCD/23: PIG/NCD/30.

BROOK, *James*   Ipswich
   E D: 40 ?
   Add: Princess St.
   Refs: Binding seen at Marks, 48:
      LAB/JONES.

BROOKS, *J. R.*   Rochester
   (P R &).
   Add: Troy town.
   Refs: KENT/DIR/38.

BROSTER, *John*   Liverpool
   (& Victualler).
   Add: 21 St. Andrew St (13): 6
   Dansie St. (16): No. 7 (18): (no
   longer victualler): No. 33 (29) :
   32 (32).
   Refs: LIV/DIR/13: 16: 18: 29: 32: 34.

BROSTER, *Thomas*   Liverpool
   Add: 32 John St, Dale St (96): 72
   Paradise St (05).
   Refs: LIV/DIR/96: 05.
   Apparently went into bookselling
   business with Joseph Broster for
   a short time (LIV/DIR/00) and
   again in 1807 (LIV/DIR/07).

BROTHERTON, *Frederick*   Bristol
   Add: 23 Clarence Place, Kingsdown
   (30): 3 Denmark St (39).
   Refs: PIG/NCD/30: BRIS/DIR/30: 33:
   36: 40: ROB/NINE/DIR/39.

BROUARD, *Henry*   Guernsey
   (& P R, Publisher) (St. Peter's Port)
   Add: Bordage St.
   Refs: ROB/NINE/DIR/39: GUER/DIR/
   40.

BROUGHTON, *George* Manchester
   Add: Bow Lane.
   Refs: PIG/CDS/37.

BROWN, *Agnes*   Deptford
   Add: High St.
   Refs: PIG/HC/39.

BROWN, *F.*   Nailsworth (Glos.)
   Refs: LAB/JONES.

BROWN, *Fo(r)ster*   Durham
   Add: Church St (20): Sadler St (28).
   Refs: PIG/SIN/20: DUR/DIR/27: PIG/
   NCD/28: PIG/NAT/DIR/28/29: PIG/
   SEVEN/DIR/34. Ticket illustrated in
   WSM/KC/NEW.

BROWN, *George*   Leeds
   Add: Briggate.
   Refs: BRI/DIR/91.

BROWN, *George*   Sheffield
   Add: 35 Arundell St.
   Refs: PIG/MND/42.

BROWN, *George*   Stourbridge
   Add: High St.
   Refs: WOR/DIR/20.

BROWN, *James*   Penrith
(Cumberland)
Add: Market Place (29).
Refs: O.C. Mark Noble: Mint &
    Corns of Durham: Birmingham,
    1780. Ticket:—"Bd. by/J.B./
    Penrith". ½ calf gilt. Date of
    binding cannot be earlier than
    1809, the date of W.M. on E.P.
    though the style might well
    appear earlier. Ticket illustrated
    in WSM/KC/NEW. CUMWES/DIR/29.

BROWN, *James*   Sheffield
Add: 4 Bailey-field.
Refs: SHEF/DIR/97.

BROWN, *J. B.*   Windsor
(Binder to H.M. (W. IV)).
Add: Castle St.
Refs: Ticket on 2 vols. 35/6. Marks,
    April, 51. "J. B. Brown,/Book-
    binder to/His Majesty/ Castle
    Street, Windsor".

BROWN, *T. Garle*   Leicester
(Claims to be a bookbinder, *inter
    alia*, in 1794, 1815 & 1826).
Add: Market Place.
Refs: LEIC/DIR/94: 15: 26.

BROWN, *John* Bangor (N. Wales)
Add: Castle St.
Refs: PIG/NCD/28.

BROWN, *John*   Settle (Yorks.)
(Etc).
Refs: PIG/NAT/DIR/28/29.

BROWN, *Joseph*   Maidstone
Add: 87 Week St.
Refs: PIG/HC/39.

BROWN, *Richard*   Grantham
(& Bird-stuffer).
Add: Swinegate.
Refs: PIG/MID/DIR/35.

BROWN, *Robert*   Hull
Add: 43 Whitefriar Gate.
Refs: PIG/CDS/37: HULL/DIR/38: PIG/
    MND/42.

BROWN, *Sarah & Son*   Boston
Add: Wormgate.   (Lincs.)
Refs: PIG/MID/DIR/35.

BROWN, *Thomas*   Manchester
Add: 17 Back Queen St.
Refs: PIG/18/20.

BROWN(E), *Thomas*
        Newcastle-on-Tyne
BROWN(E), *Thomas & Son* (01).
Add: Entry above Spread Eagle,
    Groatmarket (78): Groatmarket
    (82): Head of the Side (11): Bigg
    Market (20): Nunsgate (24):
    Royal Arcade (33).
Refs: NEW/DIR/78: 82: 87: 90: 95:
    01 (& Son): 11: 24: PIG/SIN/20:
    DUR/DIR/27: PIG/NCD/28: PIG/NAT/

DIR/28/29: NEW/DIR/33: 38: PIG/
SEVEN/DIR/34: PIG/CDS/37: Nuns-
gate ticket, also calling him a
printer, seen late 1951 at Thorp's
on ½ calf novel dated 1821. Name
spelt with an "E". Ticket illustrated in WSM/KC/NEW.

BROWN, *William*   Carlisle
(& S T).
  Add: Botchergate.
  Refs: PIG/NCD/28: CUMWES/DIR/29:
  PIG/NAT/DIR/28/29.

BROWN, *William*   Deptford
  Add: Butt Lane (23): High St (32).
  Refs: PIG/LPCD/23: 32: 34.

BROWN, *William*   Hull
  Add: Vine Court.
  Refs: BRI/DIR/91: HULL/DIR/91.

BROWN, *W.* Newcastle-upon-Tyne
  Refs: Reported by Dr. W. S.
  Mitchell as a bookbinder sub-
  scribing to Mackenzie's Descrip-
  tive and Hist. Acct. of Newcastle
  1827.

BROWNE, *Arthur, & Son*   Bristol
  Add: Tolzey.
  Refs: BRIS/DIR/85.

BROWNE, *George William*   Hull
(& S T, 03).

BROWNE, *Elizabeth Ellen*
(Etc).
  Add: 18 Lowgate (G.W.) (91): No.
  47: /EE(10).
  Refs: BRI/DIR/91: HULL/DIR/91: 03:
  10.

BROWNRIGG, *Thomas*   Morpeth
  Add: Union St.
  Refs: PIG/SIN/20.

BRUCE, *E. & T.*
(Etc).   Newcastle-upon-Tyne
  Add: Grey St.
  Refs: NEW/DIR/38.

BRYDON, *Robert*   Dover
(B S &).
  Add: King St.
  Refs: DEP/1726/75, p 37. Doubt-
  fully of my period.

BUCKNALL, *Benjamin*
          Stroud (Glos.)
  Add: King St.
  Refs: ROB/NINE/DIR/39.

BUCKNALL, *Benjamin & Edward*
          Cheltenham
(& Copper Plate Printers).
  Add: 85 High St.
  Refs: PIG/LPCD/22.

BUCKNALL, *Walter Bagnall*
          Newcastle-under-Lyme
  Add: 67 Fletcher St.
  Refs: NEW/LYME/DIR/36.

BULGIN, *William*   Bristol
(Etc).
Add: Broad St (85), 28 Corn St (24).
Refs: PIG/NCD/24: BRIS/DIR/85: 87.

BULL, *George* (28)   Nottingham
Add: Byard Lane (28): Newton St
(42).
Refs: PIG/NCD/28: PIG/NAT/DIR/28/
29: PIG/MND/42.

BULL, *John*   Nottingham
(? Father of George & Robert).
Add: Byard Lane (15): Newcastle
St (32).
Refs: NOTT/DIR/14: 15: 18: 25: 34:
PIG/18/20: NOTTSH/DIR/32: PIG/
MID/DIR/35: PIG/MND/42.

BULL, *Henry*   Devizes (Wilts.)
Add: St. John St.
Refs: ROB/NINE/DIR/39.

BULL, *Robert*   Nottingham
Add: Fletcher Gate (28) & (42):
Poynton St (40).
Refs: PIG/NCD/28: PIG/NAT/DIR/28/
29: NOTTSH/DIR/32: NOTT/DIR/34:
PIG/MID/DIR/35: NOTT/REG/40: PIG
/MND/42.

BULLIVANT & PRIEST   Sheffield
(& S T).
Add: 68 Orchard St.
Refs: PIG/MND/42.

BULVETWELL, *C.*   Bristol
Add: 20 Castle Green.
Refs: BRIS/DIR/40.

BULVETWELL/CULVERWALL
                              Bristol
Refs: Probably the same, misspelt
in the Bristol Dirs. of 1836 and
40, as the address is identical.

BUNN, *Benjamin*   South Shields
Add: Glebe (28): 28 Waterloo Vale
(34).
Refs: PIG/NCD/28: PIG/SEVEN/DIR/34.

BURGE, *William*   Brighton
Add: 26 King's Road.
Refs: PIG/LPCD/32: 34.

BURGESS & HUNT   Ramsgate
E D: 16 ?
Refs: O.C. Martial's Epig. 1816,
f.c.g. probably 1825/30.   Label
"Bd. by/B & H/R."

BURKET & RILEY   Manchester
(& marbled paper mfrs.)
Add: 24 St. Mary's Gate.
Refs: PIG/16/17.

BURN, *Edmund*   Brighton
Add: 25 St. John St (24): 23 North
St (32).
Refs: BRI/DIR/24: 39: PIG/LPCD/32:
34.

BURNET(T), *James*   Exeter

BURNET(T), *M.* (23).
  Add: Church Yard (11): South St (16): Holloway St (M.23).
  Refs: HOLD/11/: EPJ/16: 25: PIG/LPCD/23(M).

BURNHAM   Northampton
  ED: ? 1790.
  Refs: Marks reports (June, 1951) tree calf binding about end of 18th century with ticket by the above.

BURRILL, *James*   Chatham
  (Etc).
  Add: High St.
  Refs: ROB/HOMCO/DIR/39.

BURTON, *Daniel*   Chester
  Add: 22 Princess St.
  Refs: PIG/NCD/28: PIG/NAT/DIR/28/9.

BURTON, *Frederick Thomas*
                        Stamford
  Add: St. Mary's St.
  Refs: PIG/LPCD/23: LINC/DIR/26.

BURTON, *John*   Oxford

BURTON, *James* (39).
  Add: St. Ebb's (23): Pembroke St (39).
  Refs: PIG/LPCD/23: PIG/NCD/30: OXF/DIR/35: ROB/SIX/DIR/39.

BURTON & BATTY   Maidenhead
  ED: ? 95.
  Refs: Ticket "B & B, Book Binders, Maidenhead", seen at Marks on a 4to by Adam Smith, dated 1795. Binding roughly contemporary.

BUSH, *George*   Norwich
  Add: Crowe's Ct, St. Benedict St (30): Bridge St, St. Andrew's (39).
  Refs: PIG/NCD/30: PIG/HC/39: ROB/NINE/DIR/39: ROB/SIX/DIR/39.

BUTLAND, *James*   Lewes
  Add: 148 High St.
  Refs: PIG/LPCD/34: PIG/HC/39: ROB/HOMCO/DIR/39.

BUTLER, *Daniel*   Chester
  Add: Linen Hall St.
  Refs: PIG/SEVEN/DIR/34.

BUTTERSLY, *Richard*   Evesham
  Refs: HOLD/11.

BUTTERWORTH, *William*
                        Rochdale
  Add: The Butts.
  Refs: PIG/SEVEN/DIR/34.

BYERS, *William*   Plymouth
  (& B S, etc, by appt. to Duke of Clarence).
  Add: 109 Fore St (Ply. Dock) (23): 32 Fore St (30).
  Refs: PLY/DIR/22: PIG/LPCD/23: PIG/NCD/30.

PLATE III

PLATE IV

CAIN(E), *John*   Douglas (I. of Man)
(& B S).
Add: Lord St (24): (without "e")
Gt. George St (37).
Refs: PIG/NCP/24: PIG/CDS/37: JESS/
IM/40: LAB/KNA/ca. 25.

CAIRNS, *Elizabeth*   (Port of) Hull
Add: 11 Bishops Lane.
Refs: LINC/DIR/26: PIG/NAT/DIR/28
/29.

CAIRNS, *John*   Hull
Add: Stamp Office Chambers (16):
2 Bowlalley Lane (17); Silver St
(18): 11 Bishop Lane (22).
Refs: PIG/16/17: 18/20: DIR/YORK/
22: PIG/NPCD/22: HULL/DIR/17:
21.

CALLADINE, *George*   Leicester
(& S T).
Add: Market Place.
Refs: HOLD/11: LEIC/DIR/18: 26:
PIG/18/20: PIG/NCD/28: PIG/NAT/
DIR/28/29.

CALLEN, *Charles Coombs*
(& Gilder)   Southampton
Add: 21 Union Terrace (30): 2
East St (34).
Refs: PIG/NCD/30: SOUTH/DIR/34:
36.

CALVER, *James*   Cambridge
Add: Jesus Lane.
Refs: PIG/LPCD/23.
Ticket on russia binding of good
workmanship seen at Marks,
July, 1951.   Probable date of
binding 1810-20.

CAMPBELL   Cheltenham
Add: Dodd's Row (about 100 yards
from North St).
Refs: CHELT/DIR/02.

CAMPBELL, *John*   Norwich
Add: Opp. St. Clements.
Refs: PIG/LPCD/22.

CAMPLING, J.   Norwich
Add: Wastlegate St.
Refs: NORF/DIR/36.

CARNES, *William*   Holywell, N.W.
Add: Well St.
Refs: PIG/NCD/28: PIG/NAT/DIR/28/9.

CARRALL, *Michael William*   York
Add: Walmgate.
Refs: PIG/PLCD/22.

CARROLL, *Henry*   Liverpool
Add: 7 Villiers St (21): 46 Hanover
St (29): 75 Lord St (Shop, 34):
15 Heath St East (Res. 34): 81
Lord St (37): 26 (40).
Refs: LIV/DIR/21: 29: 32: 34: 40:
PIG/CDS/37.

CARSON, *George*   Liverpool
(& Trunk Maker).
Add: 25 Cable St (32): No. 41 (43).
Refs: LIV/DIR/32: 34.

CARTER, *Edwin*   Coventry
(Etc).
Add: High St.
Refs: PIG/MND/42.

CARTER, *J.*   Bristol
Add: Narrow Wine Lane.
Refs: BRIS/DIR/27.

CARTER, *Robert*
            Newcastle-on-Tyne
Add: Groat Market (33): Fletcher's
    Entry, Groat Market (34): Court
    9, Westgate St (38).
Refs: NEW/DIR/33: 38: PIG/SEVEN/
    DIR/34: PIG/CDS/37.

CARTHEW, *John*   Truro
Add: 13 Prince St.
Refs: PIG/LPCD/23: PIG/NCD/30.

CARVELL, *J.*   Birmingham
Add: 11 Freeman St.
Refs: BIRM/DIR/29: WARW/DIR/30.

CASE, *John*   Liverpool
(By 1813 included bookselling and
    circulating library).
Add: 26 Matthew St (10); 26 Rich-
    mond Row (13): 38 Byrom
    St (16): No. 37 (21): 75 Gt.

Crosshall (28): 29 Sweeting St
(34).
Refs: LIV/DIR/10: 13: 16: 18: 21:
    34: PIG/18/20: 16/17: PIG/LPCD/
    22: PIG/NCD/28.

CASS, *John*   Liverpool
Add: 71 Park Lane.
Refs: PIG/NCD/28.

CAWTE, *Charles*   Southampton
Add: Castle Bldgs (34): Lansdowne
    Ct (39).
Refs: SOUTH/DIR/34: 36: ROB/
    HOMCO/DIR/39.

CAY, *William*   Newcastle-on-Tyne
Add: High-bridge.
Refs: NEW/DIR/82.

CHAMBERLAIN, *Benjamin Storer*
(& B S).   Leicester
Add: Eastgates.
Refs: LEIC/DIR/15: 27.

CHAMBERLAIN, *William*   Bristol
(& S T).
Add: St. Philip's Place (12): 36
    Castle St (13).
Refs: BRIS/DIR/12: 13.

CHANDLER, *Joseph*   Bristol
(& S T).
Add: 3 Clare St (30): 71 Castle St
    (39).
Refs: PIG/NCD/30: BRIS/DIR/30: ROB/
    NINE/DIR/39.

CHAPLAIN, *Charles Henry*
          Heybridge (Essex)
Refs: PIG/LPCD/32: 34.

CHAPMAN, *Thomas*   Birmingham
(Etc, etc).
Add: 76 Bull St.
Refs: BIRM/DIR/00: 03: 08: 12: 15:
    18.

CHARD, *William* Brompton (Kent)
Add: Wood St.
Refs: KENT/DIR/38.

CHAVE, *James*   Tavistock
(Typographer &).
Refs: HOLD/11.

CHERRY, *Septimus*   Hull
Add: 37 Lowgate (37): 20 Scale
    Lane (42).
Refs: WHI/WRY/37/38: HULL/DIR/
    38/39: WHI/ENR/40: PIG/MND/42.

CHILD, *Richard*   Worcester
Add: 66 High St.
Refs: WORC/DIR/37: 40: PIG/DIR/
    WORC/35.

CHINERY, *James*   Birmingham
(Bookbinders' tool-cutter).
Add: Ann St.
Refs: BIRM/DIR/21.

CHRISTIE, *Alexander*   Liverpool
(S T &).
Add: 49 South Side, Old Dock.
Refs: LIV/DIR/90W.

CHRISTOPHERSON, *Charles*
            Brighton
Add: 64 Cavendish St.
Refs: PIG/LPCD/32: 34.

CLAPPERTON, *Kenneth*   Salisbury
Add: Catherine St.
Refs: PIG/NCD/30.

CLARE, *Thomas*   Sheffield
Add: 7 George St.
Refs: PIG/18/20.

CLARK, *Richard*   Plymouth
Add: Basket St.
Refs: PLY/DIR/22: 23.

CLARK, *William*   Birmingham
Add: 11 Park St. (22 & 33): Rea
    St. (29).
Refs: PIG/LPCD/22: PIG/NCD/28: PIG/
    NAT/DIR/28: 29: WARW/DIR/30:
    BIRM/DIR/25: 29: 33.

CLARK, *W. P.*   Southampton
Add: Hanover Bldgs.
Refs: SOUTH/DIR/34.

CLARKE, *John*
         Newcastle-upon-Tyne
Add: Court 52 Side (27): 99 Side
    (28): Theatre Sq (33): 30 Mosley
    St (37).
Refs: DUR/DIR/27: PIG/NCD/28: PIG/
    NAT/DIR/28/29: NEW/DIR/33: 38:
    PIG/SEVEN/DIR/34: PIG/CDS/37.
    Ticket illustrated in WSM/KC/NEW.

CLARKE, *Thomas* Chester (& S T).
Add: City Walls, Eastgate.
Refs: PIG/SEVEN/DIR/34: CHES/DIR/40.

CLARKE, *Thomas* Garstang (Lancs.) (P R &).
Add: Market Place.
Refs: LANC/DIR/24.

CLARKE & Co. Manchester
Add: 22 Market Place.
Refs: PIG/CDS/37: MAN/DIR/38.

CLEMENTS, *John* Ely (& P R).
Add: Market Place.
Refs: PIG/HC/39.

CLEMENT, *W.* Bath
Add: 1 Wood St, Lower Bristol Road.
Refs: BATH/DIR/29.

CLEM(M)ISON, *John* Deptford

CLEM(M)ISON, *Charlotte* (39).
Add: Broadway (23).
Refs: PIG/LPCD/23: 32: 34: PIG/HC/39 (Charlotte).

CLIFFORD, *Edward* Darlington
Add: Priestgate.
Refs: PIG/NCD/28: PIG/NAT/DIR/28/9.

CLIFFORD, *Edward* Ripon
Add: Blossom Gate.
Refs: PIG/LPCD/22.

CLIFFORD, *Thomas* Hull
Add: 6 Engine St.
Refs: LINC/DIR/26.

CLIFTON, *Thomas* Barnard Castle (Etc). (Durham)
Add: Market Place.
Refs: PIG/NAT/DIR/28/29.

CLOSE, *William* Liverpool
Add: 58 Fleet St.
Refs: PIG/NCD/28.

CLOUT, *Thomas* Sevenoaks
Refs: PIG/LPD/26/27: PIG/LPCD/34.

CLOWES, *James Aaron* Wolverhampton
Add: Townwell fold.
Refs: PIG/MND/42.

CLYMA, *George* Truro
Add: 4 Duke St (30): 4 Lemon St (?).
Refs: PIG/NCD/30. Ticket quoted in WSM/KC/NEW.

COATES, *I.* Darlington
E D : ? 29.
Refs: Ticket illustrated in WSM/KC/NEW.

COBB & Co.   Yarmouth
    Add: 14 Hall Plain.
    Refs: NORF/DIR/36.

COCHRANE, John   Douglas
    Add: Duke St.
    Refs: PIG/CDS/37.

COCHRANE, John   Melksham
    (Etc, etc).   (Wilts)
    Add: Bank St.
    Refs: ROB/NINE/DIR/39.

COCK, W. & Jackson, W. F.
    (Etc).   Woolwich
    Add: Green's End.
    Refs: ROB/HOMCO/DIR/39.

COCKBURN, Thomas   Sheffield
    Add: 35 High St (22): 28 Fruit
      Market (25).
    Refs: YORK/DIR/22: SHEFF/DIR/25.

COCKSHAW, J. C. (15)   Leicester

COCKSHAW, Isaac (27)

COCKSHAW, Albert (27)
    Add: High St (15): Isaac: Gallow-
      tree Gate (27): Albert: High St
    Refs: LEIC/DIR/15: 27.

CODGBROOK, Wiles
    E D: ? 26.   Northampton
    Add: Sheep St.
    Refs: PIG/NCD/30 (See Hensman).

COLBY, Richard   Norwich
    Add: Golden Dog Lane.
    Refs: NORF/DIR/36.

COLE, William   Bath
    Add: Abbey Green.
    Refs: BATH/DIR/00: 01.

COLE, William   Shrewsbury
    E D: 1795 ?
    Refs: JBO/AE.

COLEGATE, Robert   Canterbury
    Add: 6 Parade.
    Refs: KENT/DIR/38.

COLES, George   Bristol
    Add: 31 Gloster St and 59 Broad-
      mead (21): 10 Newfoundland
      St and 59 Broadmead (24): 7
      St. Paul St (36): 8 Picton St (39).
    Refs: PIG/LPCD/22: BRIS/DIR/21: 24:
      27: 30: 33: 36: 40: PIG/NCD/30:
      ROB/NINE/DIR/39.

COLEY, William   Birmingham
    Add: 61 Alison St.
    Refs: PIG/MID/DIR/35.

COLLING'S LIBRARY   Bath
    E D: ? 20.
    Add: Saville Row.
    Refs: LAB/JONES ("bound at").
    Ticket mentioned in WSM/KC/
    NEW.

COLLINGWORTH   Leeds
(see Cullingworth).

COLLINS, *John*   Wigan
Decd: 12.2.11.
Refs: Notes & Queries: Vol. 153
(1927), p 453.

COLLINSON, *R.*   Mansfield
Refs: W. Sabine, of Hollis, N.Z.,
reports a rough binding, ca. 1777.

COMBE, *Robert*   Brighton
Add: 31 Great East St.
Refs: BRIG/DIR/22: PIG/LPCD/23:
BRIG/DIR/24.

COMBE, *Thomas* (15)   Leicester

COMBE, *Thomas & Son* (27).
(Etc).
Add: Hotel St (15): Gallowtree
Gate (27).
Refs: LEIC/DIR/15: 27.

COMERFORD, *M.*   Portsmouth
Add: 114 High St.
Refs: PORTS/DIR/23: "Bound by"
ticket in contemporary book
dated 1817 seen at Grant's Edinburgh

COMMINS, *John*   Weymouth
(Etc).
Add: Stationery Warehouse, 77
St. Mary's St (?16): No. 23 (28).

Refs: WEY/DIR/28: Very poor speci-
men seen at Marks in 48. Munby
Coll: Label "B by C, 77 St. M.S.,
W". Sprinkled calf gilt ca. 1816.

CONDIE, *David*   Worcester
(Working Bookbinder).
Add: Mendicity Office, Blackfriars
(37): Friar's Alley, Broad St (40).
Refs: PIG/MID/DIR/35: WOR/DIR/37:
40. ·
O.C. Dickens, Oliver Twist, Paris
39. ½ m.g. label. Two tickets
seen on bindings ca. 1830 at
Fletchers, JA/4087.

CONGDON, *John* Plymouth (Dock)
(P R &).
Add: Fore St.
Refs: PLY/DIR/14.

COOK, *James*   Whitehaven
(Etc).
Add: Queen St.
Refs: PIG/NAT/DIR/28/9.

COOK, *Thomas*   Godalming
(& Cutler).
Refs: BRI/DIR/98 (v).

COOK *Thomas*   Leicester
Refs: Timp/Enc. 42, p 921. Mur-
dered Mr. Pass in May, 1830.

COOK & BROWN   Colchester
(B S, B B & P R).
Add: High St.
Refs: ROB/HOMCO/39.

COOKE, *Matthew*   Brighton
    (& P R).
    Add: 4 Steyne Lane (32): No. 5 (39).
    Refs: PIG/LPCD/34: PIG/HC/39:
      BRIG/DIR/32: 39.

COOKMAN, *Mrs.*   Hull
    (& S T).
    Add: 23 Chariot St.
    Refs: HULL/DIR/39.

COOPER, *C. & Co. Ltd.*
    E D: 21.   Birmingham
    Add: 107/8 Corporation St.
    Refs: LAB/KNA. "Established 1821/
      Bound by, etc." Date of Label
      uncertain.

COOPER, *John*   Birmingham
    Add: 87 Bull St (22): 4 Court, Bull
      St (25): 4 Coachyard, Bull St (35).
    Refs: PIG/LPCD/22: PIG/NCD/28: PIG/
      NAT/DIR/28/29:   WARW/DIR/30:
      BIRM/DIR/25: 29: 33: 35: 39: PIG/
      MID/DIR/35: PIG/CDS/37: PIG/MND/
      42. Ticket on $\frac{1}{2}$ calf binding on
      lot 32, Sotheby sale 9.3.53.

COOPER, *William*   Macclesfield
    (Etc).
    Add: Park Lane.
    Refs: PIG/NAT/DIR/28/29.

COOTE, *George Mark*   Norwich
    Add: Upper Haymarket (PIG/39):
      Hay Hill, St. Peter's Mancroft
      (ROB/39).
    Refs: PIG/HC/39: ROB/NINE/DIR/39:
      ROB/SIX/DIR/39.

COPLAND, *Alfred*   Chelmsford
    (Etc).
    Add: High St.
    Refs: PIG/LPCD/32.

CORNER   Wellington
    E D: ? 20.
    Refs: LAB/KNA.

CORNISH, *Thomas*   Barnstaple
    Add: Anchor Lane.
    Refs: PIG/NCD/30.

CORNS, *George*   Birmingham
    Add: 9 Ann St.
    Refs: PIG/MND/42.

COTTLE, *Robert*   Basingstoke
    (Etc).
    Add: Winchester St (39).
    Refs: A poor binding seen on a
      Gil Blas at Foyle's, 48.
      ROB/HOMCO/DIR/39.

COTTON, *Richard*   Tamworth
    Add: Church St.
    Refs: PIG/LPCD/22: PIG/NCD/28: PIG/
      STAF/28/29: PIG/NAT/DIR/28/29.

COULDREY Oxford
E D: 10 ?
Refs: JA/2925.

COUNSELL, *Thomas* Bristol
Add: Jamaica St.
Refs: BRI/DIR/91: BRIS/DIR/92.

COUPLAND, *John* Southampton
Add: 70 High St.
Refs: PIG/NCD/30.

COWING, *John James*
(Etc). Chipping Barnet (Essex)
Refs: AE/f: JA/3875: POLD/17: PIG/
LPCD/32.
Browning: Paracelsus, 35, green
m.g. vase design, approx. pub-
lisher's mor. seen at F. Hollings,
48.

COWLEY, *Giles* Bristol
(S T &: in 1809).
Add: Stokes Croft (09): 6 St.
Augustine Place (22).
Refs: BRIS/DIR/09: 12: 15: 18: 21
(George?): 24: 27: BRIS/IND/18:
PIG/LPCD/22.

COWLEYS & POUNTNEY
Bristol
Add: 18 Back & 1 Bridewell Lane.
Refs: PIG/LPCD/22.

COX, *Samuel Thomas* Liverpool
(S T &)
Add: 8 Vauxhall St.
Refs: LIV/DIR/94.

COXHEAD, *William* Newbury
Add: Northbrook St.
Refs: PIG/NCD/30.

COY, *James Crew* Manchester
(& S T)
Add: 2 Greengate.
Refs: PIG/CDS/37: MAN/DIR/38.

CRABTREE, *John* Market Weighton
(Etc). (Yorks.)
Add: Market Place.
Refs: YORK/DIR/22: PIG/NAT/DIR/
28/29.

CRAGGS, *John* Hull

CRAGGS & WELLS (21)
(Etc, etc).
(Started as B S, S T &).
Add: 58 Lowgate (13): 9 Silver St
(17).
Refs: HULL/DIR/13: 17: 21: 38: PIG/
18/20: PIG/CDS/37: PIG/MND/42.

CRAGGS, *Mat* Richmond (Yorks.)
(P R &)
Add: Market Place.
Refs: HOLD/11.

CRANE, *George* Deptford
Add: 56 Flagon Row.
Refs: PIG/HC/39.

CRANEFIELD, *Philip* Norwich
Add: 3 Orford Hill (30): Timber-
field St (39).
Refs: PIG/NCD/30: PIG/HC/39.

CRAPP, *J.* Reading
(? B S &)
Refs: Appears in READ/DIR/37 as B S
but in Snare's 1842 Reading
Directory as a B B.

CRISP, *Robert F. T.* Gt. Yarmouth

CRISP, *Fortunatus* (39)
Add: 1 King St (30); Post Office
Row (39).
Refs: PIG/NCD/30: PIG/HC/39.

CROME, *John* Sheffield
(? Abandoned binding for printing
by 1797).
Add: Campo Lane (87).
Refs: SHEF/DIR/87: 97: 17.

CROOK(E), *Thomas* Manchester
(and ? Bolton)
Add: 80 Greengate, Salford (13):
37 Kennedy St (15): 10 Spring
Gdns (21): 13 Newmarket Bldgs,
Res, 241 Gt Ancoats St (28):
100 Market St (32).
Refs: MAN/DIR/13: 15: 21: 24: 28:
32: 38: PIG/16/17: 18/20: PCD/24:
PIG/CDS/25: PIG/NCD/28: PIG
SEVEN/DIR/34, PIG/CDS/37.
BOLT/DIR/39 gives a Thomas
Crook as at Union St and PIG/
SEVEN/DIR/34 mentions Thomas
Crook at Lever St, Bolton.

CROOK(E)S, *Septimus* Sheffield
(& S T & gilder).
Add: 2 Orange St (21): No. 5 (34).
Refs: YORK/DIR/22: PCD/24: SHEFF/
DIR/21: 25: 28: PIG/NCD/28: PIG/
NAT/DIR/28/29: PIG/SEVEN/DIR/34:
PIG/CDS/37: WHI/WRY/37/38.

CROSHAW, *Cornelius* York
Add: 35 Stonegate.
Refs: PIG/MND/42.

CROSLAND, *Joseph* Holmfirth
(B S, S T &). (Yorks.)
Refs: PIG/MND/42.

CROSS, *George* Exeter
Add: 14 High St (28).
Refs: PIG/NCD/30: E.P.J/28: 30: 33:
36: 40: EX/DIR/28: 31: 35: Hob/
Abb. App. XI, p. 194.

CROSS, *James* Greenwich
Add: 6 Prospect Place, South St.
Refs: PIG/HC/39: ROB/HOMCO/DIR/
39.

CROSS, *John* Exeter
(Binder to Q. Victoria).
Refs: Hob/Abb. App. XI, p. 194.

CROSS, *John* Leeds
(B S, S T &).
Add: 2 Commercial St.
Refs: LEEDS/DIR/34: PIG/SEVEN/DIR/
34: PIG/CDS/37: PIG/MND/42.

CROSS, *R.*   Malvern
(B S, etc).
Add: Post Office.
Refs: LAB/JONES/"Bound by".

CROSS & COX   Bristol
Add: 40 Bridge St.
Refs: ROB/NINE/DIR/39.

CROWDER, *John*   Macclesfield

CROWDER, *John & Son* (25).
Add: Chestergate: 106 (17).
Refs: MACC/DIR/17: 25: PIG/LPCD/
22: JA/4760.

CROWTHER, *G. H.*   Frodsham
(Cheshire)
Refs: Sch.S. de R. IV, 37A: Hob/
Abb. App. XI, p. 194.

CRYER, *John*   Wakefield
(Etc).
Add: Ratten Row.
Refs: PIG/NAT/DIR/28/29.

CULLINGWORTH (or Colling-
worth), *Jeremiah.*   Leeds

CULLINGWORTH *& Son* (42)
Add: 10 Trinity St (34): 42 Boar
Lane (42).
Refs: LEEDS/DIR/34: WHI/WRY/37/8:
PIG/MND/42.

CULLUM, *Robert*   Exeter
(P R, B S &).
Add: Goldsmith St (28 & 35);
Waterbeer St (31).
Refs: EX/DIR/28: 31: 35.

CULVERWELL, *C.*   Bristol
Add: 20 Castle Green.
Refs: BRIS/DIR/36.

CUNNINGHAM, *T.*
E D: 36?   Ashton-under-Lyne
Refs: Ticket seen at Marks (late
1951): "Bd by/T.C/A/u/L" on
chag. mor. binding. Trade binding order.

CUNNINGHAM, *Thomas*
Manchester
Add: 24 St Mary's Gate.
Refs: MAN/DIR/13: 15.

CUPPER & IVES   Norwich
E D: 20?
Add: Bank Place.
Refs: Seen on 3 vol. Bible at Marks
in 1948.

CURRIE & BOWMAN
Newcastle-on-Tyne
Add: 32 Collingwood St.
Refs: PIG/CDS/37: NEW/DIR/38 (etc).

CURSON (or CURTON), *William*
Add: High St.   Exeter
Refs: EX/P/J/07 (Curson): HOLD/11
(Curton).

CURTIS, *Daniel* Oxford
Add: St. Aldates St.
Refs: ROB/SIX/DIR/39.

CUSHING, *John* Norwich
Add: 8 Lady's Lane (02): Wymer
St (11).
Refs: NORW/DIR/02: 11.

CYLICK, *Cerf* Leeds
Add: 35 Wade Lane.
Refs: LEED/DIR/39.

DALE Woolwich
(BS/Howe/LBB, p. 28).
E D: 1798. L D: 10.

DALE, *John* Bradford
Add: 4 Ivegate.
Refs: WHI/WRY/37/38.

DAMP, *John* Swansea
(& S T, Toyman).
Add: Wind St (PIG/30): 63 Calvert
St (S/D/30).
Refs: PIG/NCD/30: SWAN/DIR/30:
PIG/MID/DIR/35.

DARBYSHIRE, *William* Manchester
Add: Paradise Ct, Salf (13): 3 Red
Lion St (25).
Refs: MAN/DIR/13: LANC/DIR/25.

DARCY & HILDYARD Hull
(& S T).
Add: Blackfriargate.
Refs: HULL/DIR/03.

DARCY, *James* Hull
(& Victualler in 1810).
Add: Broadley St (06): 5 Sewer
Lane (10): 5 Sewery St (16): New
Dock Walls (22).
Refs: HULL/DIR/06: 10: 13: 21: PIG/
16/17: YORK/DIR/22: PIG/LPCD/22.

D'ARCY, *James* Sheffield
(& S T: ? same as binder previously
at Hull).
Add: 5 New Dock Side (18):
Hawkesworth Ct, High St (25):
11 West St (28): 35 Rockingham
St (34): No. 169 (42).
Refs: PIG/18/20: SHEFF/DIR/25: 28:
PIG/NCD/28: PIG/NAT/DIR/28/29:
PIG/SEVEN/DIR/34: PIG/CDS/37:
WHI/WRY/37/38: PIG/MND/42.

DARK(E), *William* Birmingham
(& S T).
Add: Colmore St.
Refs: BIRM/MAGN/DIR/08: BIRM/DIR/
08: 112: HOLD/11.

DARK, *John* Leamington
(P R &).
Add: 143 Warwick St (37): No. 21
(42).
Refs: LEAM/DIR/37: PIG/MND/42.

DAVENPORT, *Thomas* Manchester
(& pattern-book maker).
Add: 11 Cockpit Hill (88): Newmarket (04).
Refs: BRI/DIR/91: MAN/DIR/88: 94:
04.

DAVEY, *George*   Bristol
(see Davy & Muskett).
Add: 1 Broad St.
Refs: BRIS/DIR/33: ROB/NINE/DIR/39.

DAVIDS, *Charles*   Dartford
Refs: PIG/LPCD/23: PIG/LPD/26/27.

DAVIDSON, *John*   Alnwick
E D: ?23.
Refs: Ticket illustrated in WSM/KC/
NEW.

DAVIDSON, *John*
         Newcastle-upon-Tyne
Add: Close.
Refs: PIG/CDS/37.

DAVIES, *Henry*   Liverpool
Add: Orrwell Place, Lord St (29 &
34 PIG): Res: Clifford St (29):
Warren St (32): 8 Hawke St (34):
32 Lord St (40).
Refs: LIV/DIR/29: 32: 34: 40: PIG/
SEVEN/DIR/34: PIG/CDS/37.

DAVIES, *James*   Ashton-under-Lyne
Add: 111 Old St.
Refs: PIG/SEVEN/DIR/34.

DAVIES, *James*   Shrewsbury
E D: 96?   L D: 14?
Refs: JBO/AE.

DAVIES, *John*   Carmarthen
Add: Bridge St.
Refs: PIG/LPCD/22: PIG/NCD/30: PIG/
MID/DIR/35.

DAVIES, *John*   Shrewsbury
E D: 96?
Refs: JBO/AE.

DAVIES, *R.*   Shrewsbury
E D: 20?
Add: 7 High St.
Refs: Munby Coll. Label "B by R.
D. 7 High S" calf gilt 1820.

DAVIES, *Richard*   Liverpool
Add: Swift's Court, Castle St (37):
26 Jubilee Buildings, Lord St (40)
Refs: PIG/CDS/37: LIV/DIR/40.

DAVIES, *William*   Exeter

DAVIES, *William, Jun.* (23).
('The entries after 1823 possibly
concern W. D. *Jun.*).
Add: 73 Fore St (23): Allhallows
Ct (30).
Refs: PIG/LPCD/23: E.P.J/25: 27:
30: 33: 36: 40: EX/DIR/28: 31: 35.

DAVIS, *Anthony*   Kirkby Stephen
               (Westmorland)
Add: Market Place.
Refs: CUMWES/DIR/29.

DAVIS, *John*   Carmarthen
Add: Lammas St.
Refs: PIG/MID/DIR/35.

DAVIS, *Joseph*   Southampton

DAVIS, *Josiah* (39).
(& S T).
Add: 11 Bernard St.
Refs: SOUTH/DIR/34: 36: ROB/
HOMCO/DIR/39.

DAVIS, *Samuel*　　　　Bristol
(& S T).
Add: 7 Barton Alley (15): No 12
(17): 1 St. James's Parade,
Churchyard (18).
Refs: BRIS/DIR/15-18: BRIS/IND/18.

DAVY, *John*　　　　Norwich
Add: Pottergate St, St. Andrew's.
Refs: ROB/NINE/DIR/39: ROB/SIX/DIR
/39.

DAVY & MUSKETT　　　Bristol
(B S, B B & S T) (See Davey,
George).
Add: 1 Broad St.
Refs: Munby Coll: light blue en-
graved label "D & M, BS, BB &
ST, No. 1 B.S., Bristol" in bl.
mor. Cathedral Binding on 1827
book.

DAWS, *W.*　　　　Brixton
(P R &).
Add: 18 Commerce Pl.
Refs: ROB/HOMCO/DIR/39.

DAWSON, *John*　　　Norwich
Add: Trafalgar St, New Lakenham.
Refs: PIG/NCD/30.

DAWSON, *Samuel, Jun.*　　Liverpool
Add: 76 Lord St (32): 47 King St
(34).
Refs: LIV/DIR/32.

DAYSON, *Robert*　　　Leeds
(& machine ruler).
Add: 1 Saddle Yard, Briggate.
Refs: PIG/NCD/28: PIG/NAT/DIR/28/
29.

DEAN, *Thomas*　　　Canterbury
Add: 23 St. Margaret St.
Refs: KENT/DIR/38: PIG/HC/39: ROB/
HOMCO/DIR/39: LAB/JONES.

DEARDEN, *Wm.*　　　Nottingham
Add: Carlton St.
Refs: NOTT/REG/40.

DECK, *John & Co.*
　　　　　Bury St. Edmunds
Add: 1 Crown St.
Refs: ROB/NINE/DIR/39: ROB/SIX/DIR/
39.

DEFRIES　　　St. Helier (Jersey)
Add: Grove Place.
Refs: LC/JER/34.

DEIGHTON　　　Cambridge
(Binder to the University in 1785).
Refs: Camb. Ant. Soc. Proc., Vol.
XI, p. 359.

DEIGHTON, *Henry*　　Worcester

DEIGHTON, *Mrs.*
Add: 53 High St.
Refs: LAB/KNA. Ca. 30: Munby
Coll: Label: "Bd. by D., W".
?ca. 40.
PIG/DIR/WORC/35 (H.): WOR/DIR/
40: (H. & Mrs.).

DELAMOTTE   Weymouth
E D: 80?
Refs: Hob/Abb. App. XI, p. 195.

DENMAN, *Philip*   Wolverhampton
(He claims so many activities that he
ranks very dubiously as a real
Bookbinder).
Add: High Green.
Refs: PIG/16/17: STAFF/DIR/18.

DENNE, *James*   Margate
(Etc).
Add: 4 Queen St.
Refs: PIG/HC/39: ROB/HOMCO/DIR/
39.

DENNIS, *George*   Colchester
(Etc).
Add: Culver St (23): 10 Trinity St
(26): High St (39).
Refs: PIG/LPCD/23: PIG/LPD/26/27:
ROB/HOMCO/DIR/39.

DENNIS, *Samuel*   Bristol
(B S &).
Add: 42 Bridge St.
Refs: BRIS/DIR/06.

DENTON   Brompton
Add: Wood St.   (near Chatham)
Refs: PIG/LPD/26/7.

DENTON, *James*   Newport
Add: Holyrood St.   (I. of W.)
Refs: PIG/LPCD/23.

DERRICK, *William*   Bristol
Add: 4 Syms's Alley (21): 6 Lower
Arcade (27).
Refs: PIG/LPCD/22:   PIG/NCD/30:
BRIS/DIR/30.

DEWE, *John*   Oxford
Add: Broad St.
Refs: PIG/LPCD/23.

DEWHURST, *Thomas*   Manchester
Add: 22 Market St.
Refs: PIG/SEVEN/DIR/34: PIG/CDS/37.

DEWS, *William*   Nuneaton
(Etc).
Add: Bedworth.
Refs: PIG/MND/42.

DEWSON, *Thomas*   Birmingham
(& machine ruler).

DEWSON & *Son*
(S T, P R &) (33).
Add: Navigation St (15): Lower
Temple St (18): No. 22 (25): 107
New St (33).
Refs: BIRM/DIR/15: 18: 21: 25: 29:
33: 35: 39: PIG/16/17: 18/20:
PIG/LPCD/22: WARW/DIR/30.

DIBOLL, *J. Wm.*   Great Yarmouth
  Add: Howard St.
  Refs: NORF/DIR/36.

DICKENSON, *George*   Stamford
  Add: St. Mary St.
  Refs: PIG/LPCD/22.

DICKENSON   Cambridge
  Add: St. Edward's Passage.
  Refs: Munby/Coll: e.g. binding,
    ? 1814. Yellow engraved label
    "Bd. by/D/SEP/C." May be
    the same as J. Dickinson (q.v.).

DICKINSON, *J.*   Cambridge
  E D: ? 15 to 22.
  Add: Trumpington St.
  Refs: O.C.: Label on Crabbe:
    Borough, 1813: "J. Dickinson,
    Trumpington St, C."

DILLEY & STAFFORD   Deptford
  Add: Newcross Road.
  Refs: PIG/HC/39.

DILLON, *William*   Douglas
  (& B S).
  Add: North Quay.
  Refs: PIG/CDS/37: JEFF/IM/40.

DILWORTH, *Richard*   Liverpool
  Add: 32 Lionel St.
  Refs: LIV/DIR/32: 34.

DILWORTH, *Robert*   Liverpool
  E D: 00.
  Add: 25 John St, Dale St (00): No.
    32 (03): No. 33 (07): No. 3 (10):
    No. 5 (13): 43 Shaw's Brow (16):
    No. 46 (18): No. 50 (21): No. 28
    (25): No. 32 (29): No. 31 (32):
    No. 65 (40).
  Refs: LIV/DIR/00: 03: 05: 07: 10:
    13: 16: 18: 21: 25: 29: 32: 34:
    PIG/16/17: 18/20: PIG/LPCD/22:
    PIG/SEVEN/DIR/34: PIG/CDS/37.
    O.C. Pictorial label: "RD/BS/
    BINDER/& ST/45 Sh. Br./LIV"
    on full m.g.b. on Vol. 1/11 in
    one: T. Hope: Costume of the
    Ancients, 1812.

DILWORTH, *Robert, Jun.*
  E D: 29.   Liverpool
  Add: 78 Gerard St (29): & 5 St.
    John St. (32): 78 Gerard St (only)
    (34).
  Refs: LIV/DIR/29: 32: 34.

DIMSDALE, *G. L.*   Warminster
  (Etc).   (Wilts.)
  Add: Market Place.
  Refs: ROB/NINE/DIR/39.

DIPLOCK, *John*   Trowbridge
  (P R &)   (Wilts.)
  Add: Union St.
  Refs: ROB/NINE/DIR/39.

DITCHBURN, *Gavin (or Gowan).*
North Shields
Add: Bedford St (20): Camden Lane (34).
Refs: PIG/SIN/20: PIG/NCD/28 (Gowan): PIG/NAT/DIR/28/29: PIG/SEVEN/DIR/34.

DIXON, *Henry John* Sunderland
Add: High St, Bishop Wearmouth.
Refs: PIG/NCD/28: PIG/NAT/DIR/28/29: PIG/SEVEN/DIR/34.

DIXON, *Hezekiah* Manchester
Add: 79 Gt Ancoats St.
Refs: PIG/SEVEN/DIR/34.

DIXON, *James* York

DIXON, *Jane* (42).
Add: 6 Colliergate: No. 5 (40).
Refs: YORK/DIR/22: PIG/LPCD/22: WHI/WRY/37/8: WHI/ENR/40: PIG/MND/42 (Jane).

DIXON, *T. P.* Falmouth
(B S, etc).
E D: ?
Refs: LAB/JONES ("Bound by").

DIXON, *William* Workington
Add: Wilson St (Cumberland)
Refs: CUMWES/DIR/29.

DOCTON, *Thomas* Padstow
(Tailor &) (Cornwall)
Add: Trewickett St.
Refs: PIG/LPCD/23.

DODD, *Lawrence* Burslem
Add: Swan Square.
Refs: PIG/STAF/28/9: PIG/NAT/DIR/28/29.

DODDS, *Robert* Newcastle-on-Tyne

DODDS, *M. S.* (38).
Add: High-bridge (11): 4 Saville Court (34): 1 Quayside (38).
Refs: PIG/SEVEN/DIR/34: PIG/CDS/37: NEW/DIR/11: 38 (Manufacturing Stationer, etc).

DODGE, *John* Oldham
(Etc).
Add: High St.
Refs: PIG/SEVEN/DIR/34.

DODGE, *John & Samuel/Samuel*
(& S T). Stockport
E D: 10?
Add: Church Gate (21): Little Underbank (24, Samuel only, with several etcs): Little Underbank (34).
Refs: MAN/DIR/21: 24: PIG/SEVEN/DIR/34.
O.C. Arabian Nights, 6 vol. 1811. Vell. gilt, inlaid velvet panels (Ticket I & S). Sotheby. 18. XII. 50. No. 122. Hist. Rep. Romaine. 1810. f.m.g. (Samuel).

DODSWORTH, *Henry* Leeds
Add: Boar Lane: Park Lane.
Refs: HOLD/11: LEEDS/DIR/07: 09.

DOE, *Benjamin*   Oxford

DOE, *Charlotte* (39)
   Add: Holywell.
   Refs: PIG/LPCD/23: ROB/SIX/DIR/39.

DORLING, *John*   Epsom
   E D: ?
   Refs: LAB/JONES ("Bound by").

DOUGLAS   Blackburn
   E D: 18?
   Ref: (Note by A. Hobson) Ld.
   Newton's copy of Ottley's Engs.
   of Ld. Stafford's Pictures, 2 vol.
   1818, cont. blue mor. LAB/KNA
   "D/Bookbinder/B" ca. 25.

DOUGLAS, *K.*   Inverness
   (B S, S T &).
   E D: ca. 27?
   Refs: MUNBY/COLL. ca. 1827.

DOUGLAS, *Samuel* (01)   Bath

DOUGLAS, *William* (05)

DOUGLAS, *William, Jun.* (24).
   Add: Green St (91): 11 Margaret's
   Bldgs (01): No. 3 (12): Res.: 9
   Bath St (19): 6 Hetling Ct (26):
   23 Westgate Bldgs (24): Hetling
   Court (33): 1 Hot Bath St (41).
   Refs: BRI/DIR/91: BATH/DIR/01: 12:
   19: 26: 29: 33: 37: 41: PIG/LPCD
   /22: PIG/NCD/30.

DOWNES, *John Dawson*   Gunton
   E D: 14?   (Norfolk)
   Add: Gunton Old Hall.
   Refs: Marks Cat. No. 51 (1934):
   Item 1268: G. Turberville: Booke
   of Falconrie & Noble Art of
   Venerie, 1611: 2 vol. in 1: early
   XIX cent. calf gilt: 2 portraits on
   sides drawn by P. M. La Cave,
   & certified by Downes, & George
   Reading Leathes (the then owner
   of the work) as having been
   printed on the sides by a process
   of which Downes was the inventor.

DOWNS, *John*   Manchester
   Add: 8 Bradshaw St, Hulme.
   Refs: PIG/CDS/37: MAN/DIR/38.

DOWNTON, *Arthur*   Dartford
   (& P R).
   Add: Lowfield St.
   Refs: PIG/LPCD/32: 34: PIG/HC/39.

DOWSING, *Daniel*   Ipswich
   Add: St. Mary at Elms St (30):
   Queen St (39).
   Refs: PIG/NCD/30: PIG/HC/39.

DREDGE, *R.*   Windsor
   E D: 20 ?
   Refs: Hob/Abb. App. XI, p. 195.

DREWRY, *John*   Derby
   (P R &).
   Add: Mercury Newspaper Office,
     Iron Gate.
   Refs: DERBY/DIR/23/24.

DRURY, *John*   Lincoln
   (P R &).
   Refs: BRI/DIR/91.

DRURY   Stamford
   (B S &)
   Refs: Yellow ticket in Munby Coll.

DRYSDALE, *W.*   Reading
   (B S, B B & S T).
   Add: Bridge St (?): 7 High St (28).
   Refs: Hob/Abb. App. XI, p. 194:
     READ/DIR/28.

DUCKER, *Antony Tyrer*   Prescot
   (B S, P R &).   (Lancs.)
   Add: Toll Bar.
   Refs: PIG/NAT/DIR/28/29.

DUKE, *George*   Newcastle-on-Tyne
   Add: Thompson's Entry: Cloth
     Market.
   Refs: NEW/DIR/33: PIG/SEVEN/
     DIR/34.

DUNCAN, *J.*   Dover
   Add: 9 Snargate St (?): Russell St
     (39).
   Refs: LAB/JONES: ROB/HOMCO/
     DIR/39.

DUNCANSON, *Robert* (87)   York

DUNCANSON, *Catherine* (91).
   Add: Davy Gate.
   Refs: YORK/DIR/87: BRI/DIR/91.

DUNCANSON, *George*   York
   Add: High Petergate.
   Refs: PIG/18/20: YORK/DIR/22.

DUNKIN & *Son*   Dartford
   (& P R).
   Add: Lowfield St: High St (39) &
     Gravesend: 10 New Road (39).
   Refs: PIG/LPCD/32: 34: PIG/HC/39.

DUNN, *Charles*   Birmingham
   Add: 33 Digbeth.
   Refs: BIRM/DIR/08: PIG/18/20: PIG/
     LPCD/22.

DUNN, *Charles*   Uttoxeter
   Add: Carter St.
   Refs: PIG/STAF/28/29: PIG/NCD/28:
     PIG/NAT/DIR/28/29.

DUNN, *Jonathan & Son* Nottingham
   Add: South Parade.
   Refs: NOTT/REG/40.

DURBAN, *Frederick John*   Croydon
   (& S T).
   Add: High St.
   Refs: PIG/HC/39.

DUTTON, *Thomas Dodson*
    Bury-St.-Edmunds
Add: 2 Corn Market.
Refs: PIG/NCD/30.

DYMOCK, *William*   Stockport
Add: Market Place (16): Cobourg
 Steps (25): Turner's Buildings
 (34).
Refs: PIG/16/17: LANC/DIR/25: PIG/
 NCD/28: PIG/NAT/DIR/28/29: PIG/
 SEVEN/DIR/34.

DYSON, *John*   Leeds
(& Illustrator (26)).
Add: Square (07): Old Square,
 Korkgate (16): 3 Fish St (26):
 Meadow Lane 30 (34): No 21
 (42).
Refs: HOLD/11: LEEDS/DIR/07: 09:
 17: 26: 34: 39: PIG/LPCD/22:
 YORK/DIR/22: 30: PIG/NCD/28:
 PIG/NAT/DIR/28/29: PIG/SEVEN/
 DIR/34: PIG/CDS/37: WHI/WRY/
 37/38: PIG/MND/42: PIG/18/20:
 16/17.

EACOTT, *W.*   Bristol
(see Escott).

EARLE, *Thomas*   Salisbury
E D: 05?
Refs: Hob/Abb. App. XI, p. 194.

EATON, *Thomas & Son*   Worcester
Add: College St.
Refs: WOR/DIR/40.

EDDOWES, *Joshua*   Shrewsbury

EDDOWES, *W. & J.* (28).
Add: Corn Market (28).
Refs: Hob/Abb. App. XI, p. 194:
 Old/Shrew, p. 127 (binding
 stamped with name & date 1781).
 Signature "Eddowes, Book-
 binder, Salop", seen stamped on
 the inner edge of a handsome but
 badly rubbed quarto at Pratley's,
 Tunbridge Wells, April 1951.
 Date of volume 1821. Style
 heavily gilt morocco of Lewis
 style. LAB/KNA ca. 20. Eddowes,
 J. & W. occur as B S & P R in
 SHREW/DIR/97.

EDGAR, *Robert T.*
(Etc.).   Newcastle-upon-Tyne
Add: 129 Pilgrim St.
Refs: NEW/DIR/24: PIG/NAT/DIR/28/
 29.

EDGE, *John*   Hull
(? see Hedge, John).
Add: Back of Market Place (10):
 Whitehorse Yard (13).
Refs: HULL/DIR/10: 13: PIG/16/17:
 18/20.

EDGCOMBE, *Thomas*   Worcester
Add: College St.
Refs: WOR/DIR/40.

EDMED, *Richard*   Chatham
Add: Ordnance Row.
Refs: PIG/LPD/26/27.

EDMUNDS, *Daniel*   Madeley
   E D: 17?.   L D: 35?   (Shropshire)
   Refs: JBO/AE.

EDWARDS, *Edward*   Truro
   Add: 7 St. Nicholas St.
   Refs: PIG/NCD/30.

EDWARDS, *Edward Richard*
                   Birmingham
   Add: 33½ New St.
   Refs: PIG/MID/DIR/35: PIG/CDS/37.

EDWARDS, *I. H. G.*   Camborne
                    (Cornwall)
   Refs: PIG/LPCD/23.

EDWARDS, *J.*   Helston (Cornwall)
   Refs: PIG/LPCD/23.

EDWARDS, *James*   Liverpool
   Add: 1 Portland Place.
   Refs: LIV/DIR/29.

EDWARDS, *R.*   Cheltenham
   Add: 80 High St.
   Refs: ROB/NINE/DIR/39.

EDWARDS, *Richard*   Bristol
   Add: 21 Union St.
   Refs: PIG/LPCD/22.

EDWARDS, *Thomas*   Chester
   Add: Fletcher's Bldgs.
   Refs: PIG/SEVEN/DIR/34: CHES/DIR/
   40.

EDWARDS & Co. (11)   Halifax

EDWARDS, *Thomas* (18)
   (B S, S T &).
   Add: Old Market Place.
   Refs: HOLD/11: PIG/18/20.

EDWARDS, *Thomas*   Liverpool
   (& Victualler in 1829).
   Add: 41 Christian St (28): 44 Circus
   St (29).
   Refs: PIG/NCD/28: LIV/DIR/29.

EDWARDS, *William & Co.*
                   Birmingham
   Add: Bull St.
   Refs: PIG/MID/DIR/35: PIG/CDS/37.

EDWARDS & WELSBY   Liverpool
   Add: Lower Castle St.
   Refs: LIV/DIR/10.

ELEY, *Jos*   Kelvedon (Essex)
   (P R &).
   Refs: PIG/LPCD/32.

ELLERBY, *William*   Manchester
   Add: 15 Piccadilly (28): No. 31 (32).
   Refs: PIG/CDS/37: MAN/DIR/32: 38.

ELLIOTT, *John Milburn*   Manchester
   Add: 6 Portland St.
   Refs: PIG/CDS/37.

ELLIOTT, *William*
             Harleston (Norfolk)
   Add: Broad St.
   Refs: ROB/NINE/DIR/39: ROB/SIX/
   DIR/39.

ELLIS, *John*   Exeter
   (B S &).
   Add: Mint Lane.
   Refs: EX/JP/38-40.

ELLIS, *John*   Manchester
   Add: 1 Hanging Ditch (18): Bridge
     St, Strangeways (21).
   Refs: PIG/18/20: MAN/DIR/21.

ELLIS, *Richard*   Thornbury (Glos.)
   (Etc).
   Add: High St.
   Refs: ROB/NINE/DIR/39.

ELLIS, *Thomas*   Chester
   (& machine ruler).
   Add: Eastgate Back Row.
   Refs: CHES/DIR/40.

EMBERLIN, *Mrs.*   Marlborough
   E D: 30 (?).
   Refs: A ticket in my O.C. was
     taken from the 4th Ed. of
     Bewick's Nat. Hist. The volume
     had been rebacked, but the book-
     seller described the original half
     binding as dating about 1830/40.

ENGLISH, *A. D.*   Hull
   Add: 15 Silver St (37): 54 White-
     friar Gate (42).
   Refs: PIG/CDS/37: PIG/MND/42.

ESCOTT, *J.*   Bristol

ESCOTT, *W.* (39) (or E*acott*).
   Add: 5 Bedminster Causeway (36):
     Low Maudlin St (39) (Wm).
   Refs: BRIS/DIR/36: 40: ROB/NINE/
     DIR/39.

ESMAND, *Joseph*   Bristol
   (& S T)
   Add: John St.
   Refs: BRIS/94.

ESSEX, *Humphrey W.*   Bristol
   (& S T).
   Add: St. Michael's Hill (06): 22
     Upper Maudlin Lane (18): ditto
     St (21).
   Refs: HOLD/11: BRIS/DIR/06: 12: 15:
     18: 21: 24: 27: 30: 33: 36: 40:
     BRIS/IND/18: PIG/LPCD/22: PIG/
     NCD/30: ROB/NINE/DIR/39.

ETHERINGTON, *A.*   Chatham
   (Etc).
   Add: High St.
   Refs: ROB/HOMCO/DIR/39.

EVANS, *D.*   Oldham
   E D: 30 (?).
   Refs: JA/3688.

EVANS, *Daniel*   Swansea
   E D: 91.
   Refs: BRI/DIR/91.

EVANS, *David*   Carmarthen
   Add: Spurrell's Ct.
   Refs: PIG/NCD/30.

EVANS, *Evan*   Carnarvon
    Add: South Penrallt St.
    Refs: PIG/NCD/28: PIG/NAT/DIR/
    28/29.

EVANS, *John*   Shrewsbury
    E D: 94?   L D: 99?
    Refs: JBO/AE.

EVANS, *John*   Swansea
    Add: St. Mary St (22) & (35):
    Calvert St (30).
    Refs: PIG/LPCD/22: PIG/NCD/30: PIG/
    MID/DIR/35.

EVANS, *Morgan*   Merthyr Tydvil
    Refs: PIG/NCO/30.

EVANS, *Thomas*   Bath
    Add: (1) 2 Brunswick St (2) 41
    Broad St.
    Refs: BATH/DIR/37.

EVANS, *Thomas*   Bristol
    Add: St. James's Churchyard.
    Refs: BRIS/DIR/99: 01: 03.

EVANS, *Thomas*   Rochester
    Add: St. Margaret's Bank.
    Refs: PIG/LPCD/23: PIG/LPD/26/27.

EVANS, *William*   Bath
    (Successor to Mr. Price).
    Add: 3 Wade's Place (29): 11
    Wade's Passage & 4 Grove (33).
    Refs: BATH/DIR/29: 33.

EVANS, *William & Co.* Carmarthen
    Add: Guildhall Sq.
    Refs: PIG/MID/DIR/35.

EVANS, CHEGWIN & HALL
                         Liverpool
    Add: 15 Castle St.
    Refs: PIG/NCD/28: PIG/CDS/37: LIV/
    DIR/40.

FAIR   Bishop Auckland
    (S T &)   (Durham)
    E D: 12?
    Refs: Label in O.C. from J. Aikin's
    Lives of J. Selden & Archbishop
    Usher: London, 12, plain, blind-
    stpd. calf. "Bound by, etc".

FAIRFAX, *J.*   Leamington Spa
    Add: Gloucester St (30): 37 Bath St
    (37).
    Refs: LEAM/DIR/30: 33: 37.

FALLE, *Philip*   St. Helier
    (Etc).   (Jersey)
    Add: Royal Sq.
    Refs: ROB/NINE/DIR/39.

FARMER, *J.*   ? Gibraltar
    E D: 35?
    Refs: B.M.C.68.L.10: Black S.G.
    mor. gilt on Catalogue of Gib-
    raltar Garrison Library.

FARNDELL, *I.*   Windsor?
(Bookbinder to H.R.H. Princess
Charlotte of Wales, who died
1817 at Windsor).
E D: 09?
Refs: BM: RM: 26. a. 5.

FARRANT, *Thomas*   Bath
(& machine ruler in 1837).
Add: 2 St. Michael's Place (22):
No. 1 (37).
Refs: PIG/LPCD/22: BATH/DIR/24:
26: 29: 33: 37: 41: PIG/NCD/30.

FARROR   Ross (Monmouth)
(Doubtfully a bookbinder).
E D: ca. 1825.
Refs: ROSS/DIR/25.

FAULKNER, *Thomas William*
                          Aylesbury
Add: Walton.
Refs: PIG/NCD/30.

FAZAKERLEY, *Thomas* Liverpool
(& shopkeeper in 1832).
Add: 27 Clayton St (28): No. 30
(29): 30 Chesnut St (32): 44
Greenland St (34); 11 Atherton
St (37): 2 Devonshire Place,
Clayton St (24): 21 Atherton
St (40).
Refs: HOB/ABB. App. XI, which
states that he began to study
bookbinding in 1813 and retired
in 1877.

LANC/DIR/24: PIG/NCD/28: LIV/
DIR/29: 32: 34: 40: PIG/CDS/37.
Bookbinder, Vol. 5, p. 57.

FEATHERSTONE, *William C.*
                          Exeter
Add: 73 Fore St.
Refs: PIG/NCD/30.

FENKLE, *Joseph*   Alnwick
Add: Graham St.
Refs: Ticket reported by Dr. W. S.
Mitchell on 1807 book, but
binding probably later.

FENLY, *John*   Bristol
Add: Broad-mead.
Refs: BRI/DIR/91: BRIS/DIR/85: 92:
97: 99: 03: 06: 09: 11.

FENNO, *J.*   Colchester
(B S, B B & S T).
Add: Opp. the George in the High
St.
Refs: Munby/Coll: tree calf,
gilt spine, with red label: oval
red label "Fenno fecit" on Hist.
& Antiquities of Colchester,
Printed and sold by J. Fenno, etc.,
1789. O.C. Common Prayer,
Cambridge, 1785, f.m.g., gilt
spine and sides, signed at base of
spine "Fenno fecit".

FENWICK, *Jesse*   Worcester
Add: Carden St (20): Pump St (40).
Refs: WOR/DIR/20: 40.

FERGUSON, *Robert*   Liverpool
  Add: 140 Dale St.
  Refs: LIV/DIR/90.

FIELD, *Wm.*   Nottingham
  Add: Granby St.
  Refs: NOTT/DIR/34: PIG/MID/DIR/35:
    NOTT/REG/40; PIG/MND/42.

FINLAY, *James*
          Newcastle-upon-Tyne

FINLAY & CHARLTON
  (Etc).
  Add: 9 Mosley St (28): 46 Pilgrim
    St (38).
  Refs: PIG/NAT/DIR/28/29: NEW/DIR/
    38.

FISHER, *Samuel*   Birmingham
  Add: Hurst St (16): 26 Walsall St
    (27) & (35): 59 Inge St (28).
  Refs: PIG/16/17: 18/20: PIG/LPCD/
    22: PIG/NCD/28: PIG/NAT/DIR/28/
    29: WARW/DIR/30: PIG/MID/DIR/
    35: PIG/CDS/37.

FITCHETT, *Thomas*   Derby
  Add: Bridge St.
  Refs: COUNT/DER/29.

FITKIN & HART   Cambridge
  (see Hart).
  Add: Bridge St.
  Refs: ROB/NINE/DIR/39: ROB/SIX/
    DIR/39.

FLACKTON & MARRABLE &
  CLAIRIS
  Refs: LAB/JONES.

FLEET, *James*   Thetford
  Add: Earl's Lane.
  Refs: NORF/DIR/36: PIG/HC/39.

FLEMING, *John* (or FLEMMING)
          Bexhill
  Refs: PIG/LPD/26/27: PIG/LPCD/34:
    PIG/HC/39.

FLETCHER   Southampton
  (Etc, etc).
FLETCHER *& Son* (ca. 20).

FLETCHER, FORBES *& Co.*
  (ca. 40).
  Add: 143 High St (34).
  Refs: P. Labels: LAP/KNA, ca. 20.
    O.C. W. Cowper. Table talk,
    f.m.g. 17: SOUTH/DIR/34: 36:
    ROB/HOMCO/DIR/39.

FLETCHER, *Edgar*   Liverpool
  Add: 2 Langhorne Place (29): 7
    Islington Row (32): 81 White-
    chapel St (34): 39 Whitehall (40).
  Refs: LIV/DIR/29: 32: 34: 40.

FLETCHER, *John*   Liverpool
(& paper ruler).
  Add: 8 Hackin's Hey: Dale St (96):
    No. 21 (00): No. 5 (05): & shop
    at 31 Chapel St: 7 Temple St (10):
    14 George St (13): No. 32 (16):
    No. 15 (18): No. 16 (21): 21
    Temple St (28).
  Refs: LIV/DIR/96: 00: 03: 05: 07:
    10: 13: 16: 18: 21: 25: 29: 32:
    34: YORK/DIR/22: PIG/LPCD/22:
    LANC/DIR/24: PIG/NCD/28: PIG/
    CDS/37: PIG/16/17: 18/20: PIG/
    SEVEN/DIR/34.

FLETCHER, *John*   Manchester
  Add: 173 Chapel St, Salford (04):
    7 Thomson St, Salford (13):
    5 Fish Market (37).
  Refs: MAN/DIR/04: MAN/DIR/08: 13:
    PIG/CDS/37.

FLETCHER, *Josiah*   Norwich
E D: 20?
  Refs: LAB/KNA: ca. 20. Munby
    Coll: Label "B by JF, N"
    grained calf, ca. 20.

FODEN   Warwick
  Refs: Hob/Abb. App. XI, p. 195

FODEN, *Edward*   Leamington
  Add: 37 Regent St (33): No. 50
    (37): 39 Park St (42).
  Refs: LEAM/DIR/33: 37: PIG/MND/
    42.

FOLTHORP   Brighton
  E D: ? 38.
  Add: North St.
  Refs: O.C.: Full citron mor. gt.,
    with ticket, on engravings for R.
    Reinick's "Liedern eines Malers"
    Dusseldorf, 38.

FORD   Bath
  Add: Bond St.
  Refs: Munby reports a label (ca.
    1828) "Bd. at Ford's, late Barratt's
    Library, BS, B".

FORD, *J.*   Manchester
  E D: 00?
  Add: *2 St. Ann Sq (?00): 39
    Market St (?24).
  Refs: Label seen at C. Richardson
    on vol. dated 1809. Nice blind-
    stamped calf, but I should date
    binding not before 1824. *AE/
    Coll/Label suggests about 1800.

FORD, *William & Thomas*
                         Sheffield
  Add: 9 Change Alley.
  Refs: PIG/NCD/28: PIG/NAT/DIR/28:
    29.

FORRESTER, *William*   Chester
  Add: City Walls, Eastgate.
  Refs: PIG/LPCD/22: PIG/NCD/28: PIG/
    NAT/DIR/28/9. Munby Coll.
    "W.F, BB, CW.C" on 1819
    work.

FORRISTER, *Samuel*   Lane End
(& Postmaster in 1818). (Potteries)
Add: Market St.
Refs: PIG/18/20: PIG/LPCD/22.

FORSTER, *George*   Carlisle
Add: Union Court (37): Shakes-
peare Tavern, St. Cuthbert's
Lane (40).
Refs: CARL/DIR/37: 40.

FORSTER, *Joseph*
          Newcastle-upon-Tyne
Add: 61 Pilgrim St.
Refs: PIG/SEVEN/DIR/34.

FORSTER, *Robert*   *Wymondham*
          (Norfolk)
Add: Church St.
Refs: ROB/NINE/DIR/39: ROB/SIX/
DIR/39.

FORTH, *W.*   Bridlington (Yorks)
(Sometimes calls himself "Book-
seller & Stationer", sometimes
"Bookbinder & Stationer", but
there seems no doubt that he
actually bound).
Add: High St (22).
Refs: PIG/LPCD/22: Also LAB/JONES.
I have two specimens in my
O.C.: One is Merigot's Ruins of
Rome, ca. 1798, mottled calf
BEP/WM/1816, and the other
Belzoni's Egypt & Nubia 1820,
in citron morocco. In both cases
they have leather backs and
surrounds to the sides and mottled
paper sides. Both carry tickets
(one white, one green) reading
"Bound by/WF/BB & S/B".

FORTUNE, *J.*   Kingston
(B S, B B & S T).
Add: Market Place.
Refs: SOTH/CAT/15/10/51, No. 164:
Yellow mor. g. on Goldicutt's
Donations from Pompeia, 1825.

FOSTER, *John Andrew* Scarborough
Add: 3 Crawford's Yard, Newborough St.
Refs: PIG/SEVEN/DIR/34: WHI/ENR/
40.

FOURACRE, *T.*   Exeter
Add: Sidwell St.
Refs: EX/DIR/35.

FOWLER, *John*   Leicester
(Etc).
Add: Gallowtree Gate (15): Cank
St (27).
Refs: LEIC/DIR/15: 27.

FOWLER, *Joseph*   Leeds
Add: 5 Harper St, Kirkgate (16):
83 Call Lane (22): No. 32 (26):
Central Market (28): Old Rotation Office Yard, 115 Kirkgate
(30): Rotation Passage, Central
Market (34).

Refs: PIG/16/17: 18/20: (?John):
LEEDS/DIR/17: DIR/YORK/22: PIG/
LPCD/22: PIG/NCD/28: PIG/NAT/
DIR/28/29: YORK/DIR/30: PIG/
SEVEN/DIR/34.

FOWLER, *Thomas*   Torrington
E D: 34?   (Devon)
Refs: Sotheby Cat. 3/VII. 46. Label.

FOWNES, *Henry*   Wolverhampton
(& Machine Ruler).
Add: St. Peter's Sq.
Refs: WOLV/DIR/33: STAF/DIR/34:
PIG/MID/DIR/35.

J. F. (? OX)   Pontefract
(Printer &).
E D: ?
Refs: LAB/JONES.

FOX, *John*   Dover
(& Printer, etc).
Add: Hawkesbury St (32): 119
Snargate St (39): 2 Albion
Place (?).
Refs: PIG/LPCD/32: 34: PIG/HC/39:
ROB/HOMCO/DIR/39: LAB/JONES
(2).

FRANCIS, *E. C.*   Bristol
(See Gange & Francis).
Refs: BM. C 37. b. 51 ("Bound in
Bristol by E. C. Francis, Anno.
1831").

FRANKS. *T. H.*   Prescot (Lancs.)
Add: Market Place.
Refs: PIG/18/20.

FRASER, *Thomas*   Farnham
(Etc).
Refs: PIG/LPCD/23: ROB/HOMCO/
DIR/39.

FRECKLETON, *William* Manchester
(& S T).
Add: 52 Oldham St (08): 15 Green-
gate (15): 38 Toad Lane (16):
Fennel St (21): Hilton's Ct,
Fennel St (37).
Refs: MAN/DIR/08: 15: 21: 38:
PIG/16/17: 18/20: PIG/CDS/37.

FREEMAN, *Edward*   Worcester
Add: 102 High St.
Refs: WOR/DIR/40.

FRENCH, *R. M.* Newport (I. of W.)
E D: 00?
Add: Opposite Town Hall.
Refs: AE/COLL/LAB.

FROST, *C.*   Bristol
(P R, B S, S T &).
E D: 25?
Add: 3 Broad St.
Ref: P. Labels.

FRYE, *Bartholomew.* Halifax
E D: 93? L D: 20?
Add: The Causeway.
Refs: HOB/ABB. 101. O.C.
Metrical Misc'y. 02. f. light blue
m.g. (ticket): Heraldry M.S.,
n.d., green m.g. (ticket). Hanson
(the authority on Edwards of
Halifax) believes Frye to have
been a German, in which case his
original name was no doubt
FREI. PIG/16/17: 18/20.

FRYE, *Bartholomew* Liverpool
Add: 34 Clare St.
Refs: LANC/DIR/24.

FRYE, *B(artholomew)* Manchester
See Frye, B., Halifax, & Frye, G. B.,
Manchester, & Frye, Bar-
tholomew, Liverpool).
Refs: See extract below from Soth.
Cat. 24.7.51. Except for "Manchester" for "Halifax" the ticket
is exactly the same as that on
O.C. Metrical Misc'y. (See B.F.,
Halifax).
"75. FORE-EDGE PAINTING.
The Book of Common Prayer,
etc, contemporary English vellum
gilt, g.e., with a view of Hadfield
Hall, Yorkshire, painted under
the gilt on the fore-edge, by
Bartholomew Frye of Man-
chester, with his ticket; sold as a
binding, not subject to return.
12mo. For J. Reeves, n.d.
Oxford, 1817".

FRYE, *G. B.* Manchester
Add: 2 Park St, Redbank (18):
Riding's Court, St. Mary's Gate
(21).
Refs: PIG/18/20: MAN/DIR/21: 24:
PCD/24: PIG/CDS/25/26.
He may well be a successor of B.
Frye of Halifax and Manchester
(q.v.).

FRYER, *James* Bristol
Add: St. Michael's Hill (01): Queen
St, St. Michael's (06): 8 Steep St
(12).
Refs: BRIS/DIR/99: 01: 06: 09: 11:
12: HOLD/11.

FRYER, *James B.* Bath
Add: Wade's Passage (24): 22 Westgate St (26): 6 Monmouth St (30):
5 St. John's Place (33).
Refs: BATH/DIR/26: 33: PIG/NCD/30.

FRYER, *John* Bristol
Add: 75 Stoke's Croft (30 & 40):
7 Broad St (36).
Refs: PIG/NCD/30: BRIS/DIR/30: 33:
36: 40: ROB/NINE/DIR/39.

FULLWOOD, *James*
Wolverhampton
Add: Cleveland Place.
Refs: PIG/MND/42.

FULLWOOD, *James (& Co.)*
Birmingham

FULLWOOD, *Watt & Fraser* (39)
  Add: 124 Lionel St (25): 29 Ann St
  (33 "& Co.").
  Refs: PIG/NCD/28: PIG/NAT/DIR/28/
  29: WARW/DIR/30: BIRM/DIR/25:
  29: 33: 35: 39: PIG/MID/DIR/35:
  PIG/CDS/37.

FURLY & PEARSON Bridlington
  (Etc, etc).
  Add: High St.
  Refs: PIG/NAT/DIR/28/29.

GADSBY, *John*   Manchester
  Add: 12 Newall Bldgs.
  Refs: MAN/DIR/38.

GAGE, *Edward*   Beccles (Suffolk)
  Add: Blyburgate St.
  Refs: ROB/NINE/DIR/39: ROB/SIX/
  DIR/39.

GAIN(E)S, *Jeremiah*   Leeds
  (& Stationer in 1830: and Ruler in
  1834).
  Add: Lanes Lane (30): 1 Wood St
  (37): Entrance to Wood St from
  Briggate (39).
  Refs: YORK/DIR/30: PIG/CDS/37:
  WHI/WRY/37/8:   LEEDS/DIR/34:
  39: PIG/MND/42.

GALE, *John*   Liverpool
  Add: Wellington St, Everton:
  (shop) 15 North John St (34).
  Refs: LIV/DIR/34.

GALE, *Philip*   Liverpool
  (At times also styles himself as paper
  ruler & stationer).
  Add: 24 Prince's St (05): 5 Temple
  Lane (07): No. 7 (13): 6 John St
  (16): No. 16 (18): 4 Temple
  Court (28): No. 6 (32): 15 N.
  John St: Res: 6 Wellington St,
  Everton (34).
  Refs: LIV/DIR/05: 07: 10: 13: 16:
  18: 21: 32: 34: PIG/16/17: 18/20:
  PIG/LPCD/22: DIR/YORK/22: LANC/
  DIR/24: PIG/NCD/28: PIG/SEVEN/
  DIR/34: AE/COLL.

GALLIMORE, *Ambrose*
          Stafford & Eccleshall
  Add: Market Place (Stafford) and
  High St (Eccleshall).
  Refs: PIG/MND/35.

GAMBER, *John*   Ashford (Kent)
  (S T &).
  Refs: HOLD/11.

GAMBLE, *George*   Leeds
  Add: 5 West Bar.
  Refs: YORK/DIR/30.

GANGE & FRANCIS   Bristol

GANGE, *H. B.* (see also E. C.
  Francis).
  Add: 39 Maryport St (30): Adam
  & Eve Passage, Wine St (33).
  Refs: PIG/NCD/30 (G. & F.): BRIS/
  DIR/30 (H.B.): 33.

GARDNER, *John*   Manchester
   Add: 32 Canal St, Gt. Ancoats St
    (28): 89 Gt. Ancoats St (38).
   Refs: MAN/DIR/28: 38.

GARDNER, *Mathias*   Coggeshall
   (P R, B B & S T).   (Essex)
   Add: Church St.
   Refs: ROB/HOMCO/DIR/39.

GARLAND, *Thomas*   Lynn Regis
   Add: 47 High St.
   Refs: ROB/NINE/DIR/39: ROB/SIX/
    DIR/39.

GARLICK, *Michael*   Halifax
   (b. 1786).
   Refs: Binding on Ackermann's
    Microcosm 1808/10, sold at
    Hodgson's 23.2.45. Lot 510.

GASKELL, *James Hesketh* Manchester
   Add: Welcomb St, Hulme (28):
    3 Red Lion St, St. Ann's Sq (38).
   Refs: MAN/DIR/28: 38.

GATES, *Thomas*   Tring (Herts.)
   (Etc).
   Add: Market St.
   Refs: PIG/LPCD/32.

GAYTHORP, *John*   Whitehaven
   (& Cir. Library)   (Cumberland)
   Add: 80 King St.
   Refs: CUMWES/DIR/29.

GEE, *Henry*   Cambridge
   Add: St. Andrew's Parish.
   Refs: PIG/LPCD/23.

GEORGE, *John*   Durham
   Add: Clay-path.
   Refs: PIG/SIN/20: PARS/WHI/27: PIG/
    NCD/28: PIG/NAT/DIR/28/9: PIG/
    SEVEN/DIR/34.

GERMAIN, *Isaac*   Portsea (Hants.)

GERMAIN, *G.* (39).
   Add: 34 Britain St (23): 5 Butcher
    St (30): No. 16 (39).
   Refs: PIG/LPCD/23: PIG/NCD/30:
    ROB/HOMCO/DIR/39.

GHISLIN, *James*   Bristol
   Add: 36 Back St.
   Refs: BRIS/DIR/06.

GHISLIN, *James*   Woolwich
   Add: Thomas St.
   Refs: PIG/LPCD/23.

GIBBS, *George*   Shelton (Stoke)
   Add: Piccadilly, Brunswick St.
   Refs: STAFF/DIR/34.

GIBSON, *John*   Plymouth
   (& Publisher).
   Add: Frankfort St.
   Refs: HOLD/11.

GIBSON, *Robert*　　　Whitehaven
(& Printer).　　　　(Cumberland)
Add: Cumberland Packet Office,
　26 King St.
Refs: CUMWES/DIR/29.

GIBSONS, *T.*　　　　　Bath
　E D: 00?
　Add: 5 Argyle St.
　Refs: AE/COLL/LAB.

GILBERT, *Philip* Plymouth (14) and
　　　　　Stonehouse (30) (Devon)
　Add: Willow St (14): 6 Union St.
　Refs: PLY/DIR/14: PIG/NCD/30.

GILBERT, *William*　　　Devonport
　Add: 5 Chapel St (30): King St(36).
　Refs: PIG/NCD/30: PLY/DIR/30: 36.

GILMOUR, *Andrew*　　　Salisbury

GILMOUR, *C. & F.* (39).
　Add: High St. (30): Minster St.
　　(39).
　Refs: BRI/DIR/91: PIG/NCD/30: ROB/
　　NINE/DIR/39.　Oval label in black
　　on white "Gilmour/Sarum" seen
　　at Foyle's on f.m.g. work dated
　　1805. Mainly blind-stamped and
　　might be as late as 1815.　Oval
　　label in red "Gilmour/Book-
　　binder/ Copper Plate/ Printer
　　etc" on Blomefield's Norfolk,
　　05, f.c.g. (seen at Marks, Sept., 51).

GILMOUR, *George*　　　Winchester
(P R &)
　Add: Cathedral Yard.
　Refs: PIG/NCD/30: ROB/HOMCO/DIR/
　　39.

GIRAUD, *E. F.*　　　Sandwich
　Add: Market St.
　Refs: ROB/HOMCO/DIR/39.

GLEAVE, *Joseph* (*& Son*) Manchester
(& P R in 1808).
　Add: 63 Alport St (08 "& Printer"):
　　62 Market St (28 "& Son"): 191
　　Deansgate & 61 Market St (28,
　　etc, etc, not specified as B B):
　　244 Deansgate & 82 Market St
　　(32).
　Refs: MAN/DIR/08: 32: 38: PIG/NCD/
　　28: PIG/CDS/37: AE/COLL/LAB.

GODDARD, *Charles*　　　Salisbury
　Add: High St (30).
　Refs. A. Matthews Cat. 32. Aut.
　　1948, Bewick's Aesop's Fables 23
　　(ticket): PIG/NCD/30.

GODDEN, *E.*　　　　　Oxford
　Add: 23 Pembroke St.
　Refs: ROB/SIX/DIR/39.

GOLSBY, *William*　　　Banbury
　Add: Horse Fair (23): North Bar
　　St (39).
　Refs: PIG/LPCD/23: PIG/NCD/30: ROB
　　/SIX/DIR/39.

GOODALL, *John*   Leeds
(Agent to W. Warwick, Gold-
   beater, London (26)).
Add: 11 St. Peter's St (26): 11
   Wade Lane (37).
Refs: LEEDS/DIR/26: WHI/WRY/37/8.

GOODALL, *Joseph & Co.*   Bristol
Add: Tower Lane.
Refs: BRIS/DIR/92.

GOODIER, *William*   Wrexham
                              (Denbigh)
Add: Hope St.
Refs: PIG/NCD/28: PIG/NAT/DIR/
   28/9.

GOODISON, *Benjamin*   Manchester
Add: 4 Riding's Court, St. Mary's
   Gate.
Refs: PIG/NCD/24: MAN/DIR/24: PIG/
   CDS/25/6.

GOODWYN, *John Gale*   Tetbury
(Etc, etc).   (Glos.)
Add: Long St (39).
Refs: O.C. ½ blue calf on Maxwell's
   Wild Sports, 2 vol., 1832, labels,
   "Bd by/G/T". ROB/NINE/39.

GORSUCH, *Thomas*   Preston
(& Paper Machine Ruler).
Add: 14 Chapel Yard.
Refs: PRES/DIR/21: LANC/DIR/25:
   PIG/NCD/28: PIG/NAT/DIR/28/9.

GOWLAND, *Thomas*   Bolton
(B S &).
Add: 16 Mealhouse Lane (24): Old
   Shambles (34).
Refs: LANC/DIR/24: PIG/NAT/DIR/
   28/9: BOLT/DIR/29: PIG/SEVEN/
   DIR/34.

GRAFTON & REDDELL
(Etc).   Birmingham
Add: High St.
Refs: BIRM/DIR/97: 00.

GRAHAM, *Charles*   Manchester
Add: 5 Turner St.
Refs: PIG/NCD/28: MAN/DIR/28.

GRAHAM   Alnwick
E D: ca. 11.
Refs: Ticket illustrated in WSM/KC/
   NEW.

GRAHAM, *William*   Preston
(& Machine Ruler).
Add: Main-spit-wend.
Refs: PIG/NCD/28: PIG/NAT/DIR/
   28/9.

GRAINGER, *John*   Worcester
Add: 18 Foregate.
Refs: WOR/DIR/40.

GRANVILLE, *Arthur*   Devonport
Add: 14 Princess St, Fort St
Refs: PIG/NCD/30: PLY/DIR/30.

PLATE V

PLATE VI

GRAPEL, *William* Liverpool
Add: 61 Church St (also label seen with No. 43).
Refs: PIG/LPCD/22.

GRAVE, *Robert* Gt. Yarmouth
Add: Middle St.
Refs: PIG/LPCD/22.

GRAY (or GREY), *Gilbert*
Newcastle-upon-Tyne
Add: Manor Chair (78): Stock Bridge (82): Pandon Gate (87): Pudding Chair.
Refs: NEW/DIR/78: 82: 87: 90: BRI/DIR/91.

GREEN, *W.* Bruton (Somerset)
E D: 20?
Refs: LAB/KNA "W. G/Binder/B": ca. 20. Ticket on 1831 work mentioned in WSM/KC/NEW.

GREGORY & TAYLOR Liverpool
Add: 53 Castle St.
Refs: PIG/18/20.

GREGSON, *J.* Leeds
(Binding manufacturer).
Add: Meadow Lane.
Refs: LEEDS/DIR/07.

GRESSWELL Taunton
E D: 35?
Refs: O.C. ¾ red mor. binding on Button's Description of Lancashire, n.d. Ticket "Gresswell/Binder/Taunton".

GRIFFIN, *John* Devizes (Wilts.)
Add: Buttox.
Refs: ROB/NINE/DIR/39.

GRIFFIN, *John* Norwich
Add: Dove St.
Refs: PIG/HC/39.

GRIFFITH, *Harriet* Swansea
Add: Wind St.
Refs: PIG/NCD/30.

GRIFFITHS, *John* Manchester (Salford)
Add: 76 Bury St, Salford.
Refs: MAN/DIR/32.

GRIFFITHS, *John* Whitby
Add: Market Place.
Refs: PIG/NCD/28: PIG/NAT/DIR/28/29.

GRIFFITHS, *Thomas* Ludlow
(& P R).
Refs: BRI/DIR/91.

GRIGGS, *Thomas* Woodstock
Refs: ROB/SIX/DIR/39.

GRINTER (GRINTON), *Charles Edward* Norwich
Add: Gildengate St (36) (Grinton): Middle St, St. George's, Colegate (39) (Grinter).
Refs: NORF/DIR/36: PIG/HC/39: ROB/NINE/DIR/39: ROB/SIX/DIR/39.

GRISDALE, *William, & Co.*
Whitehaven (Cumberland)
Add: 1 Market Place.
Refs: CUMWES/DIR/29.

GRIST, *William Thomas*   Wells
Add: Bath Road.
Refs: PIG/NCD/30.

GUEST, *James*   Birmingham
Add: 91 Steelhouse Lane.
Refs: PIG/MID/DIR/35: PIG/CDS/37:
PIG/MND/42.

GUMM, *William*   Gloucester
Add: Westgate St.
Refs: ROB/NINE/DIR/39.

GURNER, *William*   Bath
Add: 1 St. Michael's Place (19):
8 Chapel Row, Queen's Sq. (33).
Refs: BATH/DIR/19: 24: 26: 29: 33:
PIG/LPCD/22: PIG/NCD/30.

GUY, *Henry*   Chelmsford
(Etc).
Add: High St.
Refs: PIG/PLCD/32.

HACK, *Robert*   Bishops Stortford
Add: Windhill.
Refs: PIG/LPCD/23.

HACKMAN, *James*   Chichester
(S T, P R &).
Add: Tower St (34): North St (39).
Refs: PIG/LPCD/34: ROB/HOMCO/
DIR/39.

HADDOCK, *J. & J.*   Warrington
E D: 15?
Refs: A. Hobson states two vols.
bd. for Ld. Newton (Lyme Park
Library): JA/4203.

HADDOCK, *Thomas*
Newcastle-upon-Tyne
Add: Bigg-market.
Refs: NEW/DIR/01.

HALBERT, *C.*   Shrewsbury
(See Hulbert).

HALL, *J.*   Wainfleet (Lincs.)
(B S &).
Refs: LAB/KNA/ "Bound by/J.H/
Bookseller/W".
(Doubtfully before 1840).

HALL, *John*   Newcastle-upon-Tyne
Add: Mount, Castleyard (90):
Castlegarth (95).
Refs: NEW/DIR/90: 95: 01.

HALL, *John Vine*   Maidstone

HALL, *John Vine & Son*
(B S, S T &).
Add: High St (23): 83 Bank St (32).
Refs: PIG/LPCD/23: PIG/LPCD/32: 34:
PIG/HC/39 ("& Son").

HALL, *Joseph*   Holbeach (Lincs.)
(P R, B B & S T).
Refs: HOLD/11.

HALL, *Mungo* Berwick-on-Tweed
  Add: Church St.
  Refs: DUR/DIR/27.

HALL, *Philip* Macclesfield
  Add: Market Place.
  Refs: MACC/DIR/25.

HALL, *William Mungo*
                  Berwick-on-Tweed
  Add: 53 Church St.
  Refs: PIG/SIN/20: PIG/NCDS/25: PIG/
    SEVEN/DIR/34: PIG/CDS/37.

HALL, *William* Manchester
  Add: 17 Newmarket.
  Refs: BRI/DIR/91: MAN/DIR/94.

HALL, *William*
            Newcastle-upon-Tyne
  Add: Middle St (20): Burnt House
    Entry, Side (24).
  Refs: PIG/SIN/20: NEW/DIR/24.

HALL & MARSH Newbury
  Add: Speenhamland.
  Refs: PIG/NCD/30.

HALL *& Son* Berwick-on-Tweed
  Add: Church St.
  Refs: BERW/DIR/06.

HALSTEAD, *John* Hebden Bridge
                        (Yorks.)
  Refs: PIG/SEVEN/DIR/34.

HAMILTON, *William Henry*
  (& P R) Guernsey
            (St. Peter's Port)
  Add: Mount-Durand (26): Mill St.
    (39).
  Refs: GUER/G/26: ROB/NINE/DIR/39:
    GUER/DIR/40.

HAMMOND, *Charles* Birmingham
  Add: 4 Minories.
  Refs: PIG/MID/DIR/35: PIG/CDS/37:
    PIG/MND/42. Ticket illustrated in
    WSM/KC/NEW.

HANCOCK, *W.* Guernsey
  (& S T) (St. Peter's Port)
  Add: 19 Pollet St.
  Refs: GUER/G/26: ROB/NINE/DIR/39:
    GUER/DIR/40.

HANDYSIDE(S), *Cuthbert*
            Newcastle-upon-Tyne
  Add: Head of the Side (11): Bell's
    Entry (20): St. Nicholas Square
    (24): Court 52 Side (27): Head of
    the Side (28): 143 Pilgrim St (33):
    Golden Tiger Entry (34): Court
    Head of Side (38).
  Refs: NEW/DIR/11: 24: 33: 38: PIG/
    SIN/20: DUR/DIR/27: PIG/NCD/28:
    PIG/NAT/DIR/28/29: PIG/SEVEN/DIR
    /34: PIG/CDS/37: Ticket illustrated
    in WSM/KC/NEW.

HANKIN, *James* Cambridge
  Add: Petty Cury.
  Refs: PIG/LPCD/23: PIG/HC/39: ROB/
    NINE/DIR/39: ROB/SIX/DIR/39.

HARDING, *B.*   Gosport
ED: 00?.
Refs: AE/COLL/LAB.

HARDING, *George*   Chester
(B S &).
Add: Watergate Row (?25): Bridge
St Row (32).
Refs: Ticket on book on Russian
medallions sold at Sotheby's,
Lot 401, Nov., 50. Two tickets
on 1832/3 bound ($\frac{1}{2}$ calf). Sports-
man's Annual, one "Bd.by/GH/
B.S.R/C" and the other in book
shape "GH/BS & B/C".

HARLAND, *Edward Robinson*   Hull
Add: Prospect St (35): 11 Carlisle
St (38).
Refs: PIG/SEVEN/DIR/34: HULL/DIR/
35: 38: 39: PIG/CDS/37: PIG/MND/
42.

HARLOW, *Isaac*   Birmingham
(Toolmaker).
Add: 186 Livery St.
Refs: PIG/MID/DIR/35: PIG/CDS/37:
PIG/MND/42.

HARMAN, *James*   Dartford
Add: High St.
Refs: PIG/LPCD/34.

HARPER, *John*   Hull
(S T &)
Add: 8 Carr Lane (35): No. 3 (42).
Refs: HULL/DIR/35: 39: PIG/CDS/37:
PIG/MND/42.

HARRIS, *W.*   Dover
ED: 40?
Add: Albion Library.
Refs: Label seen at Fletcher's,
Nov. 50.

HARRIS, *Henry*   Devonport
(P R &).
Add: 80 George St.
Refs: PLY/DIR/30.

HARRIS, *Thomas*   Carlisle
Add: Castle St.
Refs: Ticket on calf binding:
Arthur Roger's Cat. 113: No.384
(ca. 1800).

HARRIS, *Walter*   Bath
Add: 2 St. James's St (29): 7 Prince's
St (30).
Refs: BATH/DIR/29: PIG/NCD/30.

HARRIS, *William*   Halesowen
(P R &).   (Salop)
add: High St.
Refs: PIG/MID/DIR/35.

HARRIS, *William*   Birmingham
Add: 179 High St, Deritend.
Refs: BIRM/DIR/33: 35: 39: PIG/
MID/DIR/35: PIG/CDS/37: PIG/MND
/43.

HARRIS, *Bros.*   Liverpool
Add: 20 Chapel St.
Refs: PIG/SEVEN/DIR/34.

HARRISON, *John* Bingley (Yorks.)
(P R &).
Refs: PIG/NCD/28: PIG/NAT/DIR/28/
29.

HARRISON, *John* Maryport
(Etc). (Cumberland)
Add: Crosby St.
Refs: HOLD/11: CUMWES/DIR/29:
PIG/NAT/DIR/28/9.

HARRISON, *Mary* Maryport
Add: Wood St. (Cumberland)
Refs: CUMWES/DIR/29.

HARRISON, *Robert* North Shields
Add: Church Way.
Refs: PIG/SEVEN/DIR/34.

HARRISON, *Thomas* Leeds
Add: 153 Briggate.
Refs: PIG/MND/42.

HARRISON, *William* Reading
(Under B S, S T & B B heading,
  but marked as B B only).
Add: 45 Minster St.
Refs: READ/DIR/28.

HART, *Joseph* Cambridge
(See Fitkin & Hart).
Add: White Bull Yard.
Refs: PIG/HC/39.

HART & COLE Exeter
Add: Fore St.
Refs: HOLD/11.

HARTLEY, *William* Manchester
Add: 30 New Cannon St.
Refs: PIG/CDS/37: MAN/DIR/38.

HARVEY, *John* Sidmouth
(Etc.)
Refs: SID/DIR/36.

HARVEY, *Robert* Harleston
(Norfolk)
Refs: PIG/NCD/30.

HARWOOD Derby
E D: ?
Add: Market Place.
Refs: Hob/Abb. App. XI, p. 194.

HASLINGDEN, *John* Manchester
Add: Hanging Bridge (73): Cannon
  St (81).
Refs: MAN/DIR/73: 81.

HASTINGS, *John* Watton
(P R &). (Norfolk)
  and East Dereham (Norfolk)
Add: Watton (30): Market Place,
  East Dereham (39).
Refs: PIG/NCD/30: ROB/NINE/DIR/
  39: ROB/SIX/DIR/39.

HATCH, *W.* Exeter
Add: High St (07): South St (16).
Refs: EX/P/J/07: 16: HOLD/11.

HATT (HUTT), *Jun.* (?John or *Jonathan*) Cambridge
(B S, etc & Circulating Library).
E D: 10?
Add: Pease Hill.
Ref: Label (blue) on calf binding, seen at Legueltel, Paris, June, 1952. A binding in the Munby Coll. appears to have been as late as 1835. See also ROB/SIX/DIR/39 which quotes "John Hatt, Peas Hill".

HATTON, *George* Manchester
E D: 25?
Add: Victoria St.
Refs: LAB/KNA. ca. 25.

HATTON, *John* Manchester
Add: 48 Long Millgate (04): 1 Hunt's Bank (08).
Refs: MAN/DIR/04: MAN/DIR/08: 11: 13: 15: PIG/16/17.

HATTON, *Susannah* Manchester

HATTON, *Susannah, & Son* (37).
Add: 1 Hunt's Bank (25): 2 Pool Fold (37 "& Son").
Refs: LANC/DIR/25: PIG/NCD/28: PIG/CDS/37: MAN/DIR/28: 32: 38. There was a Hatton working at 6/7 Greenwood St, Corporation St, about 1852.

HAWKER, *George* Winchester
Add: Square.
Refs: PIG/LPCD/23.

HAWKER, *G. R.* Salisbury
E D: 10?
Refs: LAB/KNA: ca. 10.

HAYDAY & *Co.* Oxford (& London)
E D: (pre) 40.
Refs: See Holloway (Brighton).

HAYES, *Abraham* Burton (Westmorland)
Refs: PIG/NCD/28: PIG/NAT/DIR/28/ 29.

HAYES, *Abraham* Gisburn (Yorks.)
Refs: YORK/DIR/22.

HAYES, *Samuel* Plymouth
Add: Willow St.
Refs: PLY/DIR/22: 23.

HAYES, *Thomas* Worcester
Add: 56 Broad St.
Refs: WOR/DIR/40.

HAY(E)S, *William* Oxford
b. 1756. d. 20.v.22.
(Binding in his name seems to have continued at least till 1835 and the firm apparently worked in Oriel St till about 1939).
Add: St. Mary Hall Lane.

Refs: HOLD/11: PIG/LPCD/23 (*sic*):
PIG/NCD/30: OXF/DIR/35: Timp/
Enc. 42, p. 885: Huth Cat. 5348.
JA/4470: Binder to the Bodleian
from 1789, and occurs in University
accounts as binding stationer,
etc, from 1793 (Information supplied
by I. G. Philip of Bodleian
Library). Hayes also bound for
Oriel College, and a fine binding
in my O.C. executed between
1817 and 1821 is probably his
work.

HAYMAN?   Liverpool
Add: 4 Back Lime St (18): 124
Copperas Hill (34).
Refs: LIV/DIR/18: PIG/SEVEN/DIR/34.
Soth. 22.5.50/No. 80. Vell. gilt,
red and blue inlays; gauffered
edges.

HAYMEN, *John*   Liverpool
Add: 18 Webster St, Everton.
Refs: LIV/DIR/34.

HAYWARD, *Robert*   Canterbury

HAYWARD, *Charles Thomas* (38)
Add: 6 Burgate Lane.
Refs: KENT/DIR/03: HOLD/05: PIG/
LPD/26/27:   PIG/LPCD/32:   34:
KENT/DIR/38: PIG/HC/39: LAB/
JONES (3).

HAYWARD, *Thomas*   Deal
(Etc).
Add: 23 Lower St.
Refs: ROB/HOMCO/DIR/39.

HAYWOOD, *William*   Cirencester
(& S T & Copperplate Printer).
Add: Leuse Lane.
Refs: PIG/NCD/30.

HAZARD   Bath
E D: 1761?
Refs: Hob/Abb. App. XI, p. 194.
There was a Samuel Hazard, P R,
B S, and Circ. Lib. at Cheap St
in 1801 (BATH/DIR/01). Ticket
referred to in WSM/KC/NEW.

HAZARD, G.   Yarmouth
                (?Norfolk or I. of W.)
E D: 17?
Refs: AE/COLL.

HEAP, *Thomas*   Bolton
Add: Independent St (29): Barn St
(34).
Refs: BOLT/DIR/29: PIG/SEVEN/DIR/
34.

HEARD, *Elizabeth*   Truro
Add: Boscawen St.
Refs: PIG/NCD/30.

HEARD, *John*   Truro
Add: 39 Boscawen St.
Refs: PIG/LPCD/23.

HEARN, *John*   Salisbury
   Add: Poultry Cross.
   Refs: ROB/NINE/DIR/39.

HEATON, *James*   Leeds

HEATON, *John* (34).
   Add: 7 Briggate.
   Refs: YORK/DIR/22: PIG/LPCD/22:
     PIG/SEVEN/DIR/34: PIG/CDS/37:
     LEEDS/DIR/34: 39: PIG/MND/42.

HEDGE, *John*   Hull
   (?see EDGE, *John*).
   Add: 9 Market Place.
   Refs: HULL/DIR/06.

HEMSWORTH, *William*
         Gainsborough (Lincs.)
   Add: Lord St.
   Refs: PIG/LPCD/22.

HENDERSON, *John*
         Berwick-on-Tweed
   Add: 5 Hyde Hill.
   Refs: PIG/SEVEN/DIR/34: PIG/CDS/37.

HENDERSON, *William*   Durham
   Refs: BRI/DIR/91.

HENDRY, *Osborn*   Dover
   (& Albion Circulating Library).
   Add: 86 Snargate St.
   Refs: PIG/HC/39.

HENSMAN, *Osborn*   Daventry
   Refs: Born at Harrold, Beds. in
     1812. Apprenticed 27.2.26 to
     Wiles Codgbrook, Northamp-
     ton. Transferred 30.3.30 to
     William Wheeler, Northampton.
     Set up in Daventry in 1832.
     Succeeded by Henry Hensman
     and then by W. Osborn Hens-
     man, who has supplied this
     information.

HER(R)ON, *Thomas*   Sunderland
   Add: 44 George St (27): Coronation
     St (34).
   Refs: DUR/DIR/27: PIG/NCD/28: PIG/
     NAT/DIR/28/9: PIG/SEVEN/DIR/34.

HETHERINGTON   Uxbridge
   E D: 19? or 24?
   Refs: "Hetherington, Binder,
     Uxbridge" printed on inside of
     nice (but very damaged) ¾ calf
     gilt bdg., on Crabbe's Tales of
     the Hall, 1819. Title page bears
     date 29.12.24.

HETHERINGTON, *Robert*
         Newcastle-upon-Tyne
   E D: 15?   (Gateshead)
   Add: Lower Fell (27): Sheriff Hill,
     G. (33): High Fell, Gateshead (34).
   Refs: DUR/DIR/27: PIG/NCD/28: PIG/
     NAT/DIR/28/29: NEW/DIR/33: 38:
     PIG/SEVEN/DIR/34: Ticket illus-
     trated in WSM/KC/NEW: BEP/WM
     dated 1815.

HEWITT, *Charles*   Glastonbury

HEWITT, *Georges* (22).
(Schoolmaster, P R &).
Add: High St (22).
Refs: BRI/DIR/91: PIG/LPCD/22.

HEWSON, *Stephen*   Hull
(& Stationer).
Add: 37 Lowgate.
Refs: PIG/CDS/37.

HEXTALL, *William*   Leicester
(Etc).
Add: High St.
Refs: LEIC/DIR/27.

HEYMAN, *John*   Liverpool
Add: 10 Trowbridge St (18): 12
    Back Lime St (21): 5 White Mill
    St (25): 127 Copperas Hill (29).
Refs: LIV/DIR/18: 21: 25: 29 (Hay-
    man).

HICKLING, *William*   Coventry
(B S, S T, etc &).
Add: High St & Cross Cheaping.
Refs: PIG/MND/42.

HICKS, *George*   Hull
(& Stationer).
Add: 12 Bishop's Lane.
Refs: PIG/NCD/28: PIG/NAT/DIR/
    28/29.

HICKS, *J. G.*   Guernsey
(& Librarian (26): & Optician (40)).
Add: Smith St (26): Bordage St
    (40).
Refs: GUER/G/26: GUER/DIR/40.

HICKSON, *T. H.*   Malvern Link
E D: 25?   (Worcester)
Refs: LAB/KNA.

HIGGINSON, *John*   Preston
Add: 26 Fishergate.
Refs: PIG/NCD/28: PIG/NAT/DIR/
    28/9.

HILL, *Abraham*   Exeter
Add: 75 South St.
Refs: EX/DIR/35.

HILL, *J.*   Liskeard (Cornwall)
(P R &).
E D: ?
Refs: LAB/JONES.

HILL, *Thomas*   Manchester
Add: 9 St. Ann's St.
Refs: MAN/DIR/32.

HILL, *William*   Ballingdon (Suffolk)
E D: ?
Refs: LAB/JONES. (Bound by).

HILL, *William Glenn*   Bath
Add: 18 Green St.
Refs: BATH/DIR/37.

HILLS, *Thomas Addison* Ely
Add: St. Mary's.
Refs: PIG/HC/39.

HILLYARD & MORGAN Bristol
(& B S).

HILLYARD, *W.* (39)
Add: 9 John St (24): Low Maudlin
St (39): 6 Montague St (40).
Refs: PIG/NCD/24: ROB/NINE/DIR/
39: BRIS/DIR/40.

HILTON, *R. & J.* Nottingham
Add: Carlton St.
Refs: NOTT/REG/40.

HIRD, *Robert* Leeds
(See Knight & Hird).
Add: 64 Kirkgate (16): Sherwood's
Yard, Briggate (34).
Refs: PIG/16/17: LEEDS/DIR/17: 34:
PIG/18/20 (Herd).

HIRST, *John* Halifax
Add: Jail Lane.
Refs: YORK/DIR/22.

HITCHCOCK, *Richard* King's Lynn
Add: Purfleet St.
Refs: NORF/DIR/36.

HOBSON, *Frederick* Leeds
(Agent to F. Jacobson, Goldbeater,
London, 26).
(B S, S T &).
Add: 117 Briggate (26): No. 50
(34).
Refs: LEEDS/DIR/26: 34: PIG/CDS/37.

HOBSON & ROBINSON Leeds
(Pocket-book warehouse).
E D: 00?
Add: Under Moothall (?00): Back
of Shambles (22).
Refs: DIR/YORK/22: PIG/LPCD/22:
AE/COLL/LAB.

HOCKER, *John* Oswestry
(Decd. 85).
Refs: JBO/AE.

HOCKNULL (HOCKENBULL) *C.*
Bath
Add: 2 Chatham Bldgs.
Refs: BATH/DIR/19: PIG/LPCD/22.

HODGE, *William* Chichester
(Etc).
Add: East St.
Refs: PIG/LPCD/34: PIG/HC/39: ROB/
HOMCO/DIR/39.

HODGES & MORGAN (Bristol)

HODGES, *B.*
Add: 29 Bridge St (21): 5 St.
Augustine Place (27).
Refs: BRIS/DIR/21: 27.

HODGES, *John* Shrewsbury
E D: 94?
Refs: JBO/AE.

HODGKINS, *Joseph* Birmingham
Add: Aston Road.
Refs: PIG/MID/DIR/35.

HODGSON, *James*　　　Manchester
(& S T).
　Add: 99 Cannon St.
　Refs: PIG/CDS/37.

HODSON, *Edward & Son*　　Ludlow
(Etc).
　Add: Broad St.
　Refs: PIG/MID/DIR/35.

HODSON, *Edward*　　　Nottingham
(& S T)
　Add: St. Peter's Gate, Stamp Office.
　Refs: HOLD/11.

HOGG, *George*　　　　Chatham
　Add: 2 Hammond Place.
　Refs: PIG/LPD/26/7.

HOLDEN, *Robert M.*　　　Bolton
　Add: Mealhouse Lane.
　Refs: BOLT/DIR/29: LAB/KNA:
　　"Bound by/RMH/ML/B": (ca
　　25/30).

HOL(D)GATE, *Thomas*　Manchester
　Add: Edward St (08): 2 Grosvenor
　　St, Piccadilly (13): 4 Grosvenor
　　Ct, Piccadilly (28).
　Refs: MAN/DIR/08: 11 p: 13: 15:
　　PIG/16/17: PIG/NCD/28.

HOLDSWORTH, *William*　　Hull
(Etc).
　Add: Lowgate.
　Refs: HULL/DIR/10.

HOLL, *John* (88).　　　Worcester

HOLL, *J. & T.* (92).
　Add: 54 High St.
　Refs: WORC/DIR/88: 0: 92: 94: 97:
　　HOB/ABB/ App. XI, p. 195:
　　JA/3560: Munby Coll. has charm-
　　ing blue silk bdg. with silk end
　　papers, ca. 1790. Binder's name
　　stamped at foot of frontispiece.
　　John Holl was already Book-
　　binder to H.M. in 1790: By 1792
　　the firm was J. & T. (?Thomas)
　　Holl. I have not been able to trace
　　the firm thereafter. In 1790
　　there was a firm of printers,
　　Chalk & Holl, at 72 High St, and
　　by 1794 a firm of Holl & Bran-
　　dith at the same address, styling
　　themselves "Printers & Book-
　　binders". In 1797 Thomas Holl
　　was working as Printer at 54
　　High St.

HOLLAND, *James*　　Manchester
　Add: 10 Spring Gardens (25): 3
　　Palace St (28): 9 St. Ann's St (32).
　Refs: LANC/DIR/25: PIG/NCD/28:
　　MAN/DIR/32: 28.

HOLLESTER, *Matthew*　　Bristol

HOLLESTER, *William* (30).
　Add: 26 Montague Hill: 3 Beaufort
　　Cottages, Wilson St (33).
　Refs: BRIS/DIR/06: 09: 12: 13: 15:
　　18: 21: 24: 27: 30 ("W"): BRIS/
　　IND/18: PIG/LPCD/22: PIG/NCD/30:
　　PIG/NAT/DIR/28/29.

HOLLOWAY, *George*   Brighton
Add: 19 Trafalgar St.
Refs: Label reported by D. Lincoln
(Oxford), "G. Holloway, estabd.
1840, Bookbinder & account
book mfr. (from Hayday & Co.,
Oxford & London) etc, etc."

HOLLOWAY, *Henry*   Bath
(Successor to Charles Badham,
decd. and late servant to Mr.
Cater of London).
E D: ca. 90?
Add: Wheatsheaf, Stall St.

HOLLOWAY, *W.*   Bampton
E D: 20?   (Devon)
Refs: Communication from J.
Stevenson Cox, of Ilchester (July
1952). Ticket reads: "This work
was bound by W. Holloway,
Bampton, a self-taught printer &
binder". Binding on odd
numbers of "The Scourge".

HOLME, *George*   Blackburn
Add: 32 Queen St.
Refs: LANC/DIR/24.

HOLROYD, *J.*   Halifax
(B S, B B & S T).
E D: 04?
Refs: Label on Shenstone's work,
1804 in B.M. "J.H/BS/B &/S/
Halifax". The Binding is typical
trade calf for this style of edition,
and doubtfully of local produc-
tion, but see PIG/16/17.

HOLT, *Robert*   Manchester
Add: New Cross.
Refs: MAN/DIR/81: 88.

HOOKE, *J.*   Guildford
E D: ?
Refs: LAB/JONES.

HOOKER, *H.*   Exeter
Refs: EX/DIR/31.

HOOKEY, *W.*   Portsea (Hants.)
(& P R).
Add: 108 Queen St.
Refs: PIG/LPCD/23.

HOON, *W.*   Ashborne
(S T).   (Derbyshire)
E D: 25?
Refs: Ticket: "Bd by/W.H/St/
Ashborne" seen at Traylen's on
Tasso. Ger. Lib. London, 1820,
dull half calf.

HOOPER, *William*   Portsmouth
Add: St. Thomas St.
Refs: ROB/HOMCO/DIR/39.

HOPE, *George*   York
Add: 3 Castle Gate.
Refs: WHI/ENR/40: Pigot MND/42.

HOPPER, *George*   Durham
Add: South St.
Refs: PIG/SIN/20: DUR/DIR/27: PIG/
NCD/28: PIG/NAT/DIR/28/9: PIG/
SEVEN/DIR/34.

HOPPER, *Richard*   Durham
     Add: Hallgarth St.
     Refs: DUR/DIR/27: PIG/NCD/28: PIG/
     NAT/DIR/28/9.

HOPPS, *John*   Leeds
     Add: 7 Yard, Lower Head Row
     (34): 3 Lonsdale Yard, Lower
     Head row (37): 41 Bridge St (42).
     Refs: PIG/CDS/37: WHI/WRY/37/8:
     LEEDS/DIR/34: 39: PIG/SEVEN/DIR/
     34: PIG/MND/42.

HORN   Dover
     (B S, P R &).
     Refs: KENT/DIR/07.

HORRIDGE, *George Blake*
                          Liverpool
     Add: 25 Whitechapel & 4 Tithe-
     barne St.
     Refs: LIV/DIR/40.

HOSKINS, *George*   Bath
     Add: 2 St. John's Place (26): 13
     Westgate Bldgs. (41).
     Refs: BATH/DIR/26: 29: 33: 37: 41.

HOUGHTON, *William, & Co.*
     (B S, S T &)   Hull
     Add: 42 Whitefriargate.
     Refs: HULL/DIR/17.

HOWARD, *Henry*   Liverpool

HOWARD, *Mary* (34).
     Add: 22 Addison St (32): No. 21
     (Mary) (34).
     Refs: LIV/DIR/32: 34.

HOWE, *John*   Hull
     (Etc).
     Add: 3 Scale Lane (28): 147 (34): 48
     Blanket Row (37).
     Refs: PIG/NCD/28: PIG/NAT/DIR/28/
     29: PIG/SEVEN/DIR/34: PIG/CDS/
     37: HULL/DIR/21: 38: PIG/MND/42.

HOWE, *Thomas*   Exeter
     (Also B S & P R).
     Add: 217 High St.
     Refs: EX/DIR/31.

HOWE, *W. T.*   Hull
     Add: 48 High St & 33 Lowgate.
     Refs: PIG/CDS/37: HULL/DIR/38.

HOWELL, *William*   Liverpool
     Add: 44 Highfield St (24): No. 46
     (32): No. 45 (34): 1 Moorfields,
     Dale St (40, " & Sons").
     Refs: LANC/DIR/24: PIG/NCD/28:
     LIV/DIR/29: 32: 34: 40: PIG/
     SEVEN/DIR/34.

HOWITT, *John*   Nottingham
     Add: Clumber St.
     Refs: NOTT/DIR/40.

HOWLDEN, *Richard*   Sheffield
     Add: 29 High St.
     Refs: SHEFF/DIR/25.

HUBBARD, *William* Dartford
Add: High St.
Refs: PIG/HC/39.

HUDDLESTON, *William* Preston
Add: Friargate.
Refs: PREST/DIR/21.

HUDSON, *Benjamin* Birmingham
(Etc, etc).
Add: 18 Bull St.
Refs: PIG/NAT/DIR/28/29: WARW/
DIR/30: BIRM/DIR/29: 33.

HUDSON & NICHOLSON Kendal
(Westmorland
Add: Highgate.
Refs: CUMWES/DIR/29.

HUGHES Bath
Add: Wade's Passage
Refs: BATH/DIR/12.

HUGHES, *John* Liverpool
Add: 11 Marshall St.
Refs: LANC/DIR/24.

HUGHES, *John* Llangollen
(& Glass Dealer).
Refs: PIG/MID/DIR/35.

HUGHES, *Robert* Liverpool
Add: 59 Ranelagh (37): 4 Ranelagh
St (40).
Refs: PIG/CDS/37: LIV/DIR/40.
Lesage. Gil Blas. Paris 35,
morocco gilt (GROLIER, Guide
du Bibliophile, 1950, p. 537).
The English Binder, R. HUGHE
(*sic*) may be the same.

HUGHES, *William* Holywell
(& Parish Clerk) (N. Wales)
Add: Well St (28): Greenfield St
(35).
Refs: PIG/NCD/28: PIG/NAT/DIR/28/9:
PIG/MID/DIR/35.

HULBERT, *Charles* Shrewsbury
(S T). (b. 1778. d. 1857).
Add: High St.
Refs: SALOP/DIR/28: Old/Shrew.,
p. 163: JA/2784.

HULME, *William Lang* Shrewsbury
Add: Wyle cop.
Refs: PIG/NCD/28.

HUNT, *James* Canterbury
Add: 8 Burgate St.
Refs: KENT/DIR/38: PIG/HC/39.

HUNT, *Benjamin* Birmingham
(& Pattern-card Maker, 08).

HUNT, *& Son* (? 27).
Add: 20 Navigation St (08): Bartholomew St (15): 86 High St (16): No. 75 (22): and Navigation St (25).
Refs: BIRM/DIR/08: 12: 15: 18: 25: 29: 33: 35: 39: PIG/16/17: PIG/LPCD/22: PIG/NCD/28: PIG/NAT/DIR/28/29: WARW/DIR/30: PIG/MID/DIR/35: PIG/CDS/37: PIG/MND/42. Contemporary label "Bd by/BH & S/St & PR/ 75 H.S/B" seen on ½ mor. bdg. on work dated 1827.

HUNTLEY, *William*   Bristol (& B S).
Add: 4 John St.
Refs: PIG/NCD/24.

HUTCHINGS, *John*   Exeter
Add: 26 South St.
Refs: PIG/LPCD/23: E.P.J/25: 27:30: 33: EX/DIR/28: 31: PIG/NCD/30.

HUTCHINSON, *John*   Hull
Add: 3 Scale Lane (34): 30 (37).
Refs: PIG/SEVEN/DIR/34: PIG/CDS/37: PIG/MND/42.

HUTLEY, *John*   Leeds.
Add: Leadenhall St.
Refs: PIG/CDS/37.

HUTT, *Edward* (?HATT, q.v.)
        Cambridge
Add: Little St. Mary's Lane.
Refs: PIG/HC/39.

HYDE & CREWE
        Newcastle-under-Lyme
E D: 40?
Refs: O.C. Milman, Poetical Works, 3 vol., 40, f.m.g. (ticket).

HYNES, *E.*   Dover
E D: May be after 40?
Add: 7 Townwall St.
Refs: LAB/JONES: LAB/KNA.

ILLINGWORTH & HICKS
E D: 20?   Wakefield
Refs: LAB/KNA: "I & H/Late R. Nichols/Bookbinders, etc/W" ca. 20.

INCHBOLD, *Thomas*   Leeds

INCHBOLD, *Rachel* (34) (S T, B S &).
Add: Back of Shambles (22): 62 Briggate (34).
Refs: YORK DIR/22: PIG/LPCD/22: LEEDS/DIR/34.

INGALL, *Charles*   Reading (Etc, etc).
Add: 7 High St.
Refs: READ/DIR/37.

INGLETON, *Thomas*   Eton
Add: High St.
Refs: PIG/NCD/30. Small silver (paper) shield seen on Shakespeare's Works, 46. May be a binder and/or bookseller. (P) Label about 10, spelt Inglaton.

INGRAM, *William*   Cambridge
  Add: St. Andrew St.
  Refs: PIG/HC/39: ROB/NINE/DIR/39:
    ROB/SIX/DIR/39.

INGRAM & COOKE   Nottingham
  Add: Chapel Bar.
  Refs: NOTT/DIR/40.

INKSON, *Henry*   King's Lynn
  Add: 23 King St.
  Refs: NORF/DIR/36.

IRVING, *John*   Leeds
  (& S T).
  Add: 4 Green's Ct, 66 Briggate.
  Refs: LEEDS/DIR/26.

ISMAY, *John*   Wigton
  (& Circ. Library)   (Cumberland)
  Add: King St.
  Refs: CUMWES/DIR/29.

JACKSON, *Joseph*   Bristol

JACKSON, *Grace* (03).
  Add: Lower Maudlin Lane.
  Refs: BRIS/DIR/97: 99: 01: 03: 06:
    HOLD/11 (Grace).

JACKSON, *Robert*   Manchester
  Add: 155 Gt. Ancoats St.
  Refs: MAN/DIR/04.

JACOB, *Jacob*   Winchester
  Add: Square.
  Refs: PIG/LPCD/23.

JACQUES   Leicester?
  E D: 17?
  Ref: Long-grain morocco binding
    in the Lovejoy style seen on a
    collection of Swiss Costumes at
    Haywood Hill's, March, 51.

JACQUES   Chichester
  Refs : Munby/Coll : red mor.
    gt. on book printed at Chichester
    1812.

JACQUES, *D.*   Chichester
  E D: 16 ?
  Refs: Hob/Abb. App. XI, p. 194,
    LAB/JONES.

JAMES, *John*   Carlisle
  Add: 27 Annetwell St (34):
    Mechanics Arms Inn, 24 Fisher
    St (40).
  Refs: PIG/SEVEN/DIR/34: PIG/CDS/
    37: CARL/DIR/37: 40.

JAMES, *John*   Hexham
  Add: Fore St.
  Refs: DUR/DIR/27: PIG/NAT/DIR/28/
    29.

JAMESON, *J.*   Leeds
  E D: 84?
  Add: Bottom of Boar's Lane.
  Ref: AE/HEAL/LAB.

JARDINE, *John*   Chichester
  (Tobacco, S T &).
  Add: South St.
  Refs: PIG/HC/39: ROB/HOMCO/DIR/
    39.

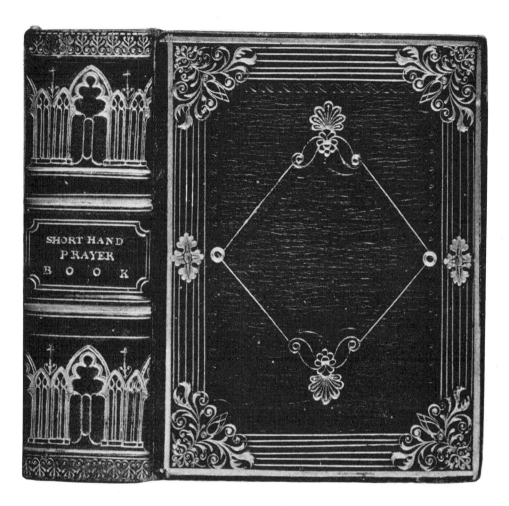

PLATE VII

PLATE VIII

JARMAN, *Stephen* Ramsgate
Add: 76 King St.
Refs: PIG/LPD/26/7.

JARRETT, *William Castle* Bristol
(& S T).
Add: 2 Old Park, St. Michael's.
Refs: BRIS/IND/18: PIG/LPCD/22:
PIG/NCD/30: BRIS/DIR/21: 24: 27:
33: 36: 40: ROB/NINE/DIR/39.

JEFFERIES, *C. T.* Bristol
Add: 69 Redcliff St.
Refs: BRIS/DIR/27: 30: 33.

JEFFERIES, *Leonard* Portsea
Add: 37 St. George's Sq. (Hants.)
Refs: PIG/LPCD/23.

JEFFERIES *& Sons* Bristol
E D: 40?
Refs: B.M. 4400. u. 23. Red Mor.
gilt on Meditations of St. Augus-
tine. Label "J & Son/Style—
/Bristol".

JEFFERSON, *Samuel* Carlisle
Add: 34 Scotch St.
Refs: PIG/CDS/37: CARL/DIR/37: 40.

JEFFERSON, *William* Leeds
Add: Lambert's Yard, Briggate.
Refs: PIG/MND/42.

JEFFERY, *William* Greenwich
(Etc).
Add: Blue Stile.
Refs: PIG/HC/39: ROB/HOMCO/DIR/
39.

JEFFERY, *William, Jun.* Sherburne
Add: Cheap St.
Refs: PIG/NCD/30.

JENKINS, *John* Bristol
Add: 27 Upper Arcade.
Refs: ROB/NINE/DIR/39.

JENKINS, *Robert* Reading
(& P R).
Add: 26 London St (30): No. 23
(39).
Refs: PIG/NCD/30: READ/LIB/37:
ROB/NINE/DIR/39: ROB/HOMCO/
DIR/39.

JENKINS, *William* Birmingham
(& S T, 08).
Add: 22 Philip St (08): Bunney's
Court, High St (18): High St (30):
8 High St (37).
Refs: BIRM/DIR/08: 18: 21: 25: 29:
33: 35: HOLD/11: PIG/18/20: PIG/
LPCD/23: WARW/DIR/30: PIG/MID/
DIR/35: PIG/CDS/37.

JENNER, *Isaac* Tewkesbury
(Etc, etc).
Add: Long St.
Refs: ROB/NINE/DIR/39.

JEW, *T.* Gloucester
  Add: Westgate St.
  Refs: GLOU/DIR/20: MUNBY/COLL/
    ticket.

JOHN, *T.* Cardigan
  E D: 20?
  Refs: AE/f.

JOHNSON, *J.* Dover
  E D: ?
  Refs: LAB/JONES.

JOHNSON, *Joseph* Leeds
  Add: 11 Rotation Office Row,
    Central Market.
  Refs: PIG/CDS/37: WHI/WRY/37/8:
    LEED/DIR/39; PIG/MND/42.

JOHNSON, *Robert* Northampton
  Add: Drapery.
  Refs: PIG/NCD/30.

JOHNSON, *Robert* St. Albans
  (& Paper-hanger).
  Add: Holywell Hill, or Lane.
  Refs: PIG/HC/39: ROB/HOMCO/DIR/
    39.

JOHNSON, *Samuel* Leeds
  Add: 1 Kirkgate.
  Refs: PIG/MND/42.

JOHNSON, *Samuel* Leicester
  Add: Chatham St.
  Refs: PIG/NCD/28: PIG/NAT/DIR/28/
    29.

JOHNSON, *Samuel* Manchester
  Add: 234 G. Ancoats St (28): 88
    Market St (37).
  Refs: MAN/DIR/28: 38: PIG/CDS/37.

JOHNSON, *Samuel* Preston
  (? later in Manchester).
  Add: Strait Shambles & Anchor
    Court (25): Market Place (28).
  Refs: LANC/DIR/25: PIG/NCD/28:
    PIG/NAT/DIR/28/9.

JOHNS(T)ON, *Thomas* Hull
  (& S T).
  Add: 7 Market Place.
  Refs: HOLD/11: HULL/DIR/10.

JOHNSTON, *James* Lincoln
  Refs: BRI/DIR/91.
  Ticket reported by Munby, ca.
    1800.

JOHNSTON, *Robert* Southampton
  Add: Four Posts.
  Refs: PIG/NCD/30.

JOLL, *Edward D.* Plymouth
  (Etc).
  Add: Cornwall St.
  Refs: PLY/DIR/36.

JONES, *Abraham* Llanvylling
  (Grocer &). (Montgom.)
  Refs: HOLD/11.

98

JONES, *Daniel*   Birmingham
(& P R, etc).
   Add: 53 Edgbaston St.
   Refs: BIRM/DIR/35: PIG/MID/DIR/35:
   PIG/CDS/37.

JONES, *Edward*   Birmingham
(Etc).
   Add: 23 Bull St.
   Refs: BIRM/DIR/87: 91: 97: 98.

JONES, *E.*   Llanerchymedd
                  (Anglesey)
JONES, *Owen* (35).
(& P R).
   Refs: Munby Coll.: "E.J., B. & Pr.,
   L.", on 1827 work. PIG/MID/DIR/
   35.

JONES, *H.*   Swansea
   E D: 25?
   Add: 3 Oxford St.
   Refs: LAB/KNA. ca. 25.

JONES, *J.*   Brentford
(Etc).
   Refs: PIG/LPCD/32.

JONES, *James*   Llanidloes
                  (Montgomery)
   Add: Short Bridge St.
   Refs: PIG/NCD/28: PIG/NAT/DIR/
   28/9.

JONES, *John*   Liverpool
(b. 1771. d. 30.10.31).
   Add: 5 Peter St (05): 5 Temple Lane
   (07): Residences: 37 Lime St (13):
   No. 28 (18): No. 35 (21).
   Refs: LIV/DIR/05: 07: 10: 13: 16:
   18: 21: 25: PIG/16/17: 18/20:
   PIG/LPCD/22. The Roscoe Sale
   Cat. 19.8.1810 describes him as
   an expert in removing folds in
   vellum. See HOB/ABB. App. XI,
   p. 194, where examples of his
   work are quoted: also TIMP/ENC/
   42, p. 919, as to his librarianship
   of the Liverpool Athenaeum.
   He probably ceased binding
   about 1825 and was succeeded by
   his son of the same name (q.v.).
   H. Roscoe: "Life of W. Rose",
   II, p. 87, says that he bound for
   Holkham.

JONES, *John, Jun.*   Liverpool
   E D: ca. 25 (when he succeeded his
   father. (q.v.)).
   Add: 5 Temple Lane (ca. 25): 5
   Houghton St (32): No. 24/34):
   Residence: 14 Clarence St (25).
   Refs: LIV/DIR/25: 29: 32: 34: PIG/
   NCD/28: PIG/SEVEN/DIR/34: PIG/
   CDS/37.

JONES, *John, Jun.*   Llanrwst
JONES, *John* (35)   (Denbigh)
   Refs: PIG/NCD/28: PIG/NAT/DIR/
   28/9: PIG/MID/DIR/35.

JONES, *John Thomas*   Liverpool
Add: 2 Seel St & St. George's Place,
     Netherfield Lane, Everton.
Refs: LIV/DIR/40.

JONES, *Robert*   Llanfair (N. Wales)
(Etc).
Refs: PIG/NAT/DIR/28/9.

JONES, *Thomas*   Newcastle Emlyn
(B S, S T &).   (Wales)
(Binder to Archdeacon Milling-
     champ of Llangoedmore).
E D: 20?
Refs: AE/f: PIG/MID/DIR/35.

JONES, *Thomas*   Nottingham
Add: Back Lane (32): Lincoln St
     (34).
Refs: NOTTSH/DIR/32: NOTT/DIR/34:
     PIG/MID/DIR/35.

JONES, *William*   Brentford
Add: Butts.
Refs: PIG/HC/39.

JONES, *William*   Bristol
(See Bolt, & Jones & Bolt).
Add: 19 Denmark St (24): No. 5
     (27): 36 Broad St (36): Adam &
     Eve Passage, Wine St (33 & 39).
Refs: BRIS/DIR/24: 27: 33: 36: ROB/
     NINE/DIR/39.

JONES & BOLT   Bristol
(& S T) (see Bolt & Jones sep-
     arately).
Add: Taylor's Ct, Broad St.
Refs: PIG/NCD/30: BRIS/DIR/30.

JORDAN, *William*   Manchester
Add: Potter St, Gartside St.
Refs: MAN/DIR/28.

JOSCELYNE, *James*   Braintree
Add: High St.   (Essex)
Refs: ROB/HOMCO/DIR/39.

JOSEPH, *W.*   Birmingham
(Etc, etc).
Add: Edgbaston St.
Refs: BIRM/DIR/21.

JUBB, *Joseph*   Hull
(P R, etc).
Add: 17 Bishop Lane (26): 75 Low-
     gate (35).
Refs: LINC/DIR/26: PIG/NCD/28: PIG/
     PIG/NAT/DIR/28/29: PIG/SEVEN/
     DIR/34: HULL/DIR/35: 39: PIG/CDS
     /37: PIG/MND/42.

JUNGIUS, *Joseph*   Norwich
Add: Gregory St.
Refs: PIG/HS/39: ROB/NINE/DIR/39:
     ROB/SIX/DIR/39.

KAY, *John*   Bury (Lancs.)
(Etc).
Add: Fleet St.
Refs: PIG/18/20.

KEATING, *Henry Dundas* Liverpool
Add: 31 Clarendon Buildings, St. John St (29): No. 1 (40): Res: 11 Commutation Row.
Refs: LIV/DIR/29: 32: 34: 40: PIG/SEVEN/DIR/34: PIG/CDS/37.

KEEVIL, *James* Bath
Add: 36 Walcot St (30): 1 Lyncombe Terrace (37).
Refs: PIG/NCD/30: BATH/DIR/37.

KELL, *John* Bolton
(B S &).
Add: 54 Deansgate.
Refs: LANC/DIR/24: PIG/NAT/DIR/28/9.

KELLY, *George*
Newcastle-upon-Tyne
Add: Pilgrim St.
Refs: NEW/DIR/24.

KELLY, *James* Windsor
Add: High St.
Refs: PIG/LPCD/23.

KENDALL, *William* Liverpool
Add: 1 Union Court, Thurlow St.
Refs: LIV/DIR/29.

KENDREW, *James* York
Add: Colliergate.
Refs: PIG/18/20.

KENNARD, *W.* Deal
Refs: KENT/DIR/03.

KENNARD & *Son* Bath
(& Working S T).
Add: 14 Old Bridge Place, Holloway.
Refs: BATH/DIR/33.

KENNEDY, *J. D.* Hawick
E D: ca. 21.
Refs: Tickets on 1821 and 1825 works mentioned in WSM/KC/NEW.

KENNINGTON, *George* Bath
Add: 25 Bennett St (33): 1 Circus Place (37): 33 Morford St: Res. 19 Richmond Pl (41).
Refs: BATH/DIR/33: 37: 41.

KENT, *Charles* Manchester
Add: Bridgewater St (08): Little John St (13): 23 Longworth St (11 P), 12 Peter St (28).
Refs: MAN/DIR/08: 11 P: 13: 28.

KENT, *Sam. & Co.* Liverpool
Add: 87 Paradise St.
Refs: LIV/DIR/40.

KEYMER, *J.* Yarmouth
E D: 11?
Add: King St.
Refs: Ticket "Bound by J. Keymer, King Street, Yarmouth" seen at Marks, June 1951, on 1811 Shakespeare, though binding appears slightly later.

KEYWORTH, *M.* Lincoln
  E D: 28?
  Refs: Munby Coll.: Label "B & S
    by M.K., BS, etc. L", ca. 1828.

KILE, *F.* Oxford
  Refs: Same binder as F.K. of
    London (see BS/HOWE/LBB, p. 54).
    The Oxford and London speci-
    mens in my O.C. resemble each
    other closely.

KILE, *Francis* Oxford

KILE, *Frederick*
  E D: 07?
  Add: Pembroke St (07): St.
    Clements (23).
  Refs: PIG/LPCD/23: PIG/NCD/30
    (Frederick). O.C. Memoirs, Sir
    John Wilmot, 11, f.c.g. (ticket).
    O.C. Pindarus, 2 vol. f. russ. g.
    07 (W.M. 11) (ticket). Both
    bindings appear roughly con-
    temporary—tickets read "Bd
    by/F.K./P.St./0".

KING Brighton
  (Bookseller to the Queen Dowager:
    S T &).
  E D: ?
  Add: 1 North St & 44 East St.
  Refs: P. Labels. (By 1865, the firm
    was H. & C. Treacher (late King
    & Co.) at the same addresses.

KING, *A. M.* Southampton
  (Etc).
  Add: 22 High St.
  Refs: ROB/HOMCO/DIR/39.

KING, *E.* High Wycombe
  (Etc). (Bucks.)
  Add: Market Place.
  Refs: ROB/NINE/DIR/39: ROB/HOMCO
    /DIR/39: ROB/SIX/DIR/39.

KING, *J. P.* Andover
  (B S, etc).
  E D: ?
  Refs: LAB/JONES/("Bound by").

KING, *Robert* Hythe

KING, *Robert William* (39).
  Add: High St (39).
  Refs: PIG/LPCD/23: PIG/LPD/26/27:
    PIG/LPCD/32: 34: PIG/HC/39.
    LAB/Jones.
    Sotheby's Sale 22.V.50, No. 72,
    had an Etruscan style binding on
    Junius 03.

KING, *Thomas* Bristol
  Add: Key St (97): Quay St (99):
    Narrow Wine St (03): Merchant
    St (09): Syms's Alley (11).
  Refs: HOLD/11: BRIS/DIR/97: 99:
    03: 06: 09: 12: 13: 15.

KINGSTON, *H.* ?
Refs: O.C. (Hodgson Cat./2/11/51,
No. 412), contemp. green m.g. on
Westall's Gt. Britain, 30, mor.
ticket "H. Kingston, Bookbinder,
1831".

KINGSTON, *J. B.* Bristol
Add: 9 Bath St.
Refs: BRIS/DIR/30.

KIRBY, *Henry* Liverpool
Add: 17 Freemason's Row.
Refs: LIV/DIR/13.

KIRK, *Thos.* Nottingham
Add: Peter's Gate.
Refs: NOTT/DIR/40.

KIRKCONEL, *James* Workington
Add: Wilson St. (Cumberland)
Refs: CUMWES/DIR/29.

KIRKMAN, *William* Ulverston
Add: Canal St.
Refs: CUMWES/DIR/29.

KNAGGS, *Margaret* Gainsborough
(& P R). (Lincs.)
Add: Lord St.
Refs: PIG/LPCD/22.

KNAPP, *Richard* Faringdon
(P R &). (Berks.)
Add: Bull St.
Refs: PIG/NCD/30.

KNEE, *William* Reading
(Under B S, S T & B B heading,
but marked as B B only).
Add: 45 Munster St.
Refs: READ/DIR/28.

KNIGHT, *James Young* Leeds
(B S, S T &).
Add: 132 Briggate (34): No. 39
(42).
Refs: LEEDS/DIR/34: WHI/WHY/
37/8: PIG/MND/42.

KNIGHT & HIRD Leeds
(see Hird).
Add: 61 Kirkgate.
Refs: YORK/DIR/22 (Bird): PIG/LPCD
/22 (Hird).

LACEY, *Charles* Hull
Add: 2 Little Queen St.
Refs: HULL/DIR/39.

LACY, *Charles* Northampton
(Son of John, ca. 1755).
E D: 80 ?
Refs: JBO/AE.

LAING, *John* Sheffield
(& Ruler).
Add: 3 High St.
Refs: WHI/WRY/37/8.

LAKE Uxbridge
Refs: O.C. Dymond's Essays, 2
vol. 29 (dedication same year).
Blond calf and red labels (ticket
"Bd by L/U").

LAKE, J.   Falmouth
(Later J.H. & R.G.).
Add: Commercial Printing Office,
    opp. Wynn's Royal Hotel.
Refs: LAB/JONES(2). (Seem to have
    started as printers and binders and
    in their later form to have inclu-
    ded bookselling, stationery, etc):
    FALM/DIR/15.

LAMBERT, *Henry*   Hull
(& S T).
E D: 37.
Add: 45 Savile St (34): Res: 27
    Silvester St (35): 51 Savile St
    (37).
Refs: PIG/SEVEN/DIR/34: HULL/DIR/
    35: 38: 39: PIG/CDS/37: PIG/MND/
    42.

LAMBERT, *M. & M. W.*
E D: ?   Newcastle-upon-Tyne
Refs: LAB/JONES: Ticket illustrated
    in WSM/KC/NEW.

LAMBERT, *William*   Bath
(& Working Stationer).
Add: York St (24): 6 Kingston
    Bldgs. (26).
Refs: PIG/NCD/30: BATH/DIR/24: 26:
    29: 33: 37: 41.

LAMBERT, *William*   Newport
(& B S).   (I. of W.).
Add: High St.
Refs: VEC/DIR/39 (pleasing advt.).

LAMBERT, *William*   Stockport
(& P R).
Add: Little Underbank.
Refs: LANC/DIR/25.

LAMPEN   Devonport
E D: ?
Add: Tavistock St.
Refs: LAB/KNA "L/Bookbinder/TS/
    D". Might be just after my
    period.

LANCASHIRE, M.   Rochdale
Refs: Batty: Welsh Scenery, 23,
    ½ calf, ticket "From Entwistle
    Library, Foxholes: Christie sale,
    1.4.53, lot 311.

LANCASTER, *Henry*   Brampton
Add: Market Place. (Cumberland)
Refs: CUMWES/DIR/29.

LANCASTER, *Henry*   Bristol
(Etc, etc).
E D: 23?
Add: 23 Broad St.
Refs: (P) label: ROB/NINE/DIR/39.

LANE, *James*   Lynn Regis
Add: 7 Purfleet St.
Refs: PIG/HC/39.

LANGDALE, *Thomas*   Ripon
(Etc).
Refs: PIG/NAT/DIR/28/29: O.C.
    cont. tree calf binding on Scott's
    Don Roderick, 1811. Label "Bd
    by/T.L/R".

LANGDON, *J. C.*   Bristol
   Add: 3 Dove St.
   Refs: BRIS/DIR/30: 33: 36: 40.

LANGFORD, *Thomas*   Warminster
   Refs: BRI/DIR/91.

LANGLEY, *Edward*   Dorking
   (P R &).
   Refs: BRI/DIR/91.

LANKESTER, *Francis*
             Bury-St.-Edmunds
   Add: 17 Abbeygate St.
   Refs: PIG/NCD/30.

LANSDOWN, *Joseph*   Bristol
   (& S T in 1801).
   Add: Tower Hill (94): Tower Lane
   (97): John St (99).
   Refs: BRIS/DIR/94: 97: 99: 01: 03.

LARGE, *John*   Wolverhampton
   (P R &).
   Add: Stafford St.
   Refs: WOLV/DIR/27.

LARKIN, *John*   Birmingham
   Add: Holt St.
   Refs: BIRM/DIR/39.

LAUDER, *Joseph*
             Berwick-on-Tweed
   Add: Hyde Hill (34): High St (37).
   Refs: PIG/SEVEN/DIR/34: PIG/CDS/
   37.

LAVIN, *John*   Penzance
   Add: East St.
   Refs: PIG/LPCD/23: PIG/NCD/30.

LAW, *James*   Brentford
   (B S, S T &).
   Refs: PIG/LPCD/32.

LAW, *James*   Liverpool
   E D: 36?
   Add: 1 Church Lane, Church St
   (40).
   Refs: AE/f.

LAWRENCE, *Ann*   Carmarthen
   Add: Chapel St.
   Refs: PIG/NCD/30.

LAWRENCE, *John*   Carmarthen
   Add: Cambrian Place.
   Refs: PIG/MID/DIR/35.

LAWRENCE, *Thomas*   Carmarthen
   Add: Red Lion Court.
   Refs: PIG/LPCD/22: PIG/NCD/30.

LAWRENCE, *William Henry*
              Cambridge

LAWRENCE & UNDERWOOD
   (39).
   Add: St. Edward's Passage.
   Refs: PIG/LPCD/23: PIG/NCD/30: PIG/
   HC/39: ROB/NINE/DIR/39: ROB/
   SIX/DIR/39.

LAWSON, *James*   Liverpool
(& Grocer).
Add: 73/4 Strand St.
Refs: LIV/DIR/81: 87: 90.

LAYB(O)URN, *Joshua*   Whitby
Add: Baxter Gate (22): St. Ann's
Staith (28).
Refs: DIR/YORK/22: PIG/NCD/28:
PIG/NAT/DIR/28/29: PIG/SEVEN/
DIR/34.

LEA, *James*   Gloucester
Add: 2 Westgate St.
Refs: ROB/NINE/DIR/39.

LEADBERRY & SMITHSON   Hull
Add: 37 High St.
Refs: LINC/DIR/26: PIG/NCD/28: PIG/
NAT/DIR/28/29.

LEACH, *John Huster*   Leeds
Add: 31 Market Place.
Refs: PIG/18/20.

LEACH, *Robert*   Rochdale
Add: Bank St.
Refs: PIG/SEVEN/DIR/34.

LEADER, *Robert*   Sheffield
(& S T).
Add: 19 Angel St.
Refs: YORK/DIR/22: SHEFF/DIR/25:
PIG/NCD/28: PIG/NAT/DIR/28: 29.

LEAKE, *James*   Manchester
(& Broker in 1808).

LEAKE, *Charles* (28).
Add: Old Bridge St, Salford (88):
Parsonage (04): Blackfriars (08):
5 Half St (28).
Refs: MAN/DIR/88: 04: 08: 11: 13:
15: 28.

LEAKE, *James*   Manchester
(& S T).

LEAKE, *Charles William*
Add: Old Bridge St, Salford (94):
4 Tyson's St, St. Mary's Gate
(24): 5 Half St (25).
Refs: MAN/DIR/94: 24: LANC/DIR/
25: PIG/CDS/25/26: PIG/NCD/28.

LEAREY, *Robert Heley*   Lincoln
Add: Broadgate.
Refs: PIG/NCD/28: PIG/NAT/DIR/28/
29.

LEE, *John*   Newcastle-upon-Tyne
Add: 108 Percy St.
Refs: NEW/DIR/38.

LEE, *Robert*   Manchester
Add: Half St.
Refs: MAN/DIR/88.

LEE, *Samuel*   Loughborough
(Etc).
Add: Baxter Gate.
Refs: PIG/MID/DIR/35.

LEE & Co. (39)   Lewes
  E D: 15?
  Add: 64 High St (39).
  Refs: PIG/HC/39. Munby Coll. has
    a most unusual, and probably
    contemporary calf gilt binding on
    J. G. Spurzheim: Outlines of the
    Physiognomical System, 1815,
    sides decorated with caricatures
    relating to the contents.

LEECH, *Samuel*   Knutsford
  Decd. 1786.   (Cheshire)
  Refs: Notes & Queries, Vol. 153
    (1927), p. 453.

LEEMING, *I.*   Lancaster
  E D: 90?
  Refs: Ticket "Bd by/I.L/Book-
    seller" seen on 1790 book at
    Traylen (1951). Binding seems
    contemporary.

LEF(E)AUX, *Isaac*   Chichester
  Add: St. Pancras.
  Refs: PIG/LPCD/23: PIG/LPCD/34:
    ROB/HOMCO/DIR/39.

LEFEUBRE, *C.*   Jersey
  E D: 81?
  Add: Beresford Library.
  Refs: Wheeler 159: AE/COLL/LAB
    puts him as late as 1820.

LEGG, *Jacob*   Gosport
  Refs: BRI/DIR/91.

LEIGH, *Richard*   Manchester
(& S T).
  Add: 8 Exchange Alley (73): 60
    Port St (91): 22 Blackfriars (00):
    5 Kennedy St (11 P.): Leigh
    Road, Crown Alley (25): Ex-
    change Bldgs., Ducie Place (28)
    & Res: 7 Kennedy St (28).
  Refs: MAN/DIR/73: 94: 00: 11:
    11 P: 21: 24: 28: BRI/DIR/91: PIG/
    16/17: 18/20: PIG/NCD/24: LANC/
    DIR/25; PIG/NCD/28.

LEIGH, *Robert*   Manchester
  Add: Old Church Yd (73): 5
    Kennedy St (91): 32 Back King
    St.
  Refs: MAN/DIR/73: 80: 94: 00: 04:
    BRI/DIR/91: PIG/16/17.

LEIGH & WOOLLEY   Manchester
  Add: Ducie Place.
  Refs: MAN/DIR/32.

LEIGHTON, *John*   Nottingham
(& Wholesale Stationer).
  Add: Lincoln St.
  Refs: NOTTSH/DIR/32: PIG/MID/DIR/
    35: NOTT/DIR/40.

LE LIEVRE CHADWICK
            St. Helier (Jersey)
  Add: 6 Halkett Pl.
  Refs: ROB/NINE/DIR/39.

LEMMON, *James* Norwich
  Add: Elm Hill.
  Refs: PIG/NCD/30.

LEONARD, *Jas.* Rugeley (Staffs.)
  (Bookseller, etc—see below).
  Add: Market Place.
  Refs: The 1835 Staffs. Directory
    quotes Jas. Leonard as bookseller,
    circulating library, newsagent,
    printer, medicine vendor, and
    agent for the Royal Exchange
    Insurance Co.
    O.C. Batty's Italian Scenery,
    1820, 2 vols. green m.g. in Frye
    style, stamp in black ink—
    "Leonard Binder Rugeley".

LEPPERD, *William* Brighton
  (Etc, etc).
  Add: 17 East St.
  Refs: PIG/HC/39: BRIG/DIR/39.

LESLIE, *Robert* Bristol
  Add: 33 College St (18): Somerset
    Sq (24).
  Refs: BRIS/IND/18: BRIS/DIR/24.

LESLIE & PYE Bristol
  Refs: BRIS/IND/18, p. xxx.

LE TANSUR St. Neots
  (B S & Singing Master).
  (b. 1700. d. 83).
  Refs: Notes & Queries: X: XII
    (1909): Buried 9.10.1783: DBP/
    1726/75, p. 242.

LETHE, *William* Hull
  (& S T).

LETHE & MARSHALL (16)
  Add: Humber St (13): 43 High St
    (16): Humber St (workshop) : 43
    High St (shop) (17): Sykes Bldgs.
    (22).
  Refs: HULL/DIR/13: 17: 21: PIG/16/
    17: YORK/DIR/22: PIG/LPCD/22.

LEVETT, *James* Cambridge
  E D: 00?
  Add: Pump Lane (23).
  Refs: PIG/LPCD/23.
    O.C. Barclaii Argenis, 1651.
    Bound in white vellum, decora-
    ted in black with vignettes and
    Etruscan borders. Fore-edge
    painting under marbled edges.

LEVETT, *John* Rochester
  Add: 72 High St.
  Refs: PIG/LPD/26/7.

LEWIN, *David* Coventry
  Add: Cross Cheaping.
  Refs: WARW/DIR/30.

LEWIS, *Thomas* Mold
  (P R &). (Flintshire)
  Refs: HOLD/11.

LEWIS, *Thomas* Worcester
  Add: 69 Broad St.
  Refs: WOR/DIR/40.

LIDDELL, *James*   Bodmin
(P R &).
Refs: BRI/DIR/91.

LIFFEN, *J.*   Norwich
Add: Gildengate St.
Refs: NORF/DIR/36.

LINCHAM, *H.*   Newark (Notts.)
Add: Castle Gate.
Refs: PIG/LPCD/22.

LINDEN, *James (and/or Jun.)*
      Southampton
Add: 29 Above Bar: (S.D.): High
St (Hold).
Refs: SOUTH/DIR/11: HOLD/11.

LINDRIDGE, *George*   Maidstone
Add: 67 Week St (32). In 1823 he
appears to have been a bookbinder and straw hat manufacturer at Tenterden, 16 miles
from Maidstone.
Refs: PIG/LPCD/23: 32: 34: PIG/HC/
39.

LINE, *Henry*   Daventry
Add: St. John's Square.
Refs: PIG/NCD/30.

LINFIELD, *W. Bartley* Wandsworth
Add: West Hill.   (Surrey)
Refs: ROB/HOMCO/DIR/39.

LINNEY, *John D.*   York
Add: 14 Low Ousegate.
Refs: PIG/MND/42.

LISON (or LYSON), *Thomas* Hull

LYSON, *Thomas, Jun.*
Add: White Horse Yard, Market
Place: Myton St (39).
Refs: PIG/16/17: DIR/YORK/22: HULL
DIR/21: 39.

LITTLEWOOD, *J.*   Rochdale
Refs: O.C. Ormerod, County Pala-
tinate, 3 vol. 1819. F. blue mor.
with tickets. Christie Sale, 1.4.53.

LITTON   Teignmouth
(P R, S T, etc. &).
E D: 29.
Refs: Label taken from a date
Calculator at Marks, Jan. 51,
describes his various activities.

LLOYD, *Evan*   Mold
(Etc).
Refs: PIG/MID/DIR/35.

LOFTHOUSE, *John*   Hull
Add: 49 Market Place (22): Spread
Eagle Entry, Market Place (22):
Spinster's Court, Church St (28).
Refs: YORK/DIR/22: PIG/LPCD/22:
PIG/NCD/28: PIG/NAT/DIR/28/29.

LOMAS, *Frederick*   Lewes
Add: 48 West St (P 39): High St
(R 39).
Refs: PIG/HC/39: ROB/HOMCO/DIR/
39.

LOMAS, *James*   Manchester
    Add: Riding's Ct, St. Mary's Gate.
    Refs: PIG/18/20.

LOMAX, *John*   Clitheroe
    (& S T).
    Add: Wellgate.
    Refs: LANC/DIR/24.

LOMAX, *T. G.*   Lichfield
    E D: 30?
    Refs: JBO/AE.

LONDON (LOUDON), *Edward*
    (& S T).   Manchester
    Add: 13 Half Moon St (24): 290
    Deansgate (also 24): Abraham's
    Court (34).
    Refs: MAN/DIR/24: PIG/NCD/24: PIG
    /CDS/25: PIG/SEVEN/DIR/34.

LONG, *James*   Taunton
    (& Copper plate printer).
    Add: Mill Lane, North St.
    Refs: PIG/LPCD/22: PIG/NCD/30.
    O.C. T. Livius, Hist. 6 vol. Basle
    1740, f.c.g. (ticket).

LONG, *Joshua*   Cheltenham
    Add: Well Wall.
    Refs: ROB/NINE/DIR/39.

LONG, *Mary Ann*   Bristol
    Add: Tower Lane.
    Refs: BRIS/DIR/85.

LORAINE, *Fenwick*
    (Etc in 38).   Newcastle-upon-Tyne
    Add: 10 Collingwood St (28): Grey
    St (38).
    Refs: PIG/NCD/28: PIG/NAT/DIR/28/
    29: NEW/DIR/38.

LOVE & BARTON   Manchester
    Add: 10 & 12 Market St.
    Refs: PIG/CDS/37: MAN/DIR/38.

LOVEJOY   Reading
    E D: 25?
    Refs: LAB/KNA.

LOVESY, *J.*   Cheltenham
    E D: 25?
    Add: Imperial Library, Promenade.
    Refs: ROB/NINE/DIR/39.
    Ticket reported by Marks "Bd by/
    J.L/I.L/C" on Waterton's Wan-
    derings, 25, ½ calf.

LOWE, *Edward*   Belper
    (Etc).
    Add: Market St Lane.
    Refs: PIG/MID/DIR/35.

LOWER, *Reuben William*   Lewes
    Add: 43 High St.
    Refs: PIG/HC/39.

LOWREY, *Alexander*   Liverpool
    Add: 3 Cartwright Pl.
    Refs: PIG/NCD/28.

LOWTHER & DOUGLAS
(Etc).   Newcastle-upon-Tyne
Add: 14 High St, Gateshead.
Refs: NEW/DIR/38.

LUBBOCK, *William*
            Newcastle-upon-Tyne
Add: St. Nicholas Churchyard.
Refs: NEW/DIR/11: PIG/SIN/20.
   O.C. Shute. Sermons, 11, f.m.g.
   orange silk end papers (ticket).
   Sch. R. de R. IV, 48: Hob/Abb.
   App. XI. WSM/KC/NEW illustrates
   a ticket, and quotes a PIGOT
   Directory of 1821 which gives
   his address as Church St.

LUCY, *W. W.*   Marlborough
   (P R &).
   E D: 24?
   Refs: Label seen on mor.bdg. on
   Major's Walton, 2nd ed. at
   Thorp's, Dec. 50.
   LAB/JONES.

LUKE, *W. H.*   Plymouth
   E D: 30?
   Add: Bedford St.
   Refs: LAB/KNA: Label "Bd by/W.
   H. Luke/B. St./Plymouth" on
   Eccles Ants. of Devon, by Rev.
   G. Oliver, Exeter, 1840. (Lowe,
   51).

LUSCOMBE, *Richard*
(P R &). Newton Abbott (Devon)
Add: East St.
Refs: PIG/LPCD/23.

LYON   Wigan
   E D: 87?
   Refs: Munby Coll: Label "B. by
   L,W". Marbled calf gilt, 1787.

LYON/S), *Stephen*   Southampton
(See E. Paul).
   E D: 16?
   Add: Near the Theatre (16): French
   St (23): 5 St. Michael's Sq (30).
   Refs: PIG/LPCD/23: PIG/NCD/30:
   Munby Coll. Label "SL, BB,
   N.T.T., S" green mor. gilt, 1816.
   O.C. Moore: Loves of Angels,
   cream m.g. 23. Depping, Even-
   ing Entertainments, Hailes 18,
   same bdg. Rombaldi. 44. G. 50.

McCARTHY, *D. T.*   Bristol
   Add: 1 Bridewell Lane.
   Refs: BRIS/DIR/27: 30: 33.

McCOLL & TATE   South Shields
(B S, etc).
   E D: ?
   Add: 16 Market St.
   Refs: WSM/KC/NEW illustrates a
   ticket.

McCOMB(I)E, *John*   Whitehaven
                        (Cumberland)
Add: 10 Church St (29): 63 Market
    Place.
Refs: CUMWES/DIR/29: PIG/SEVEN/
    DIR/34.

McCRE, *William*   Liverpool
Add: 51 Portland St.
Refs: LIV/DIR/29.

McCREERY, *Jas.*   Burslem
(& Copper-plate printer & machine
    ruler).
Add: Navigation Road.
Refs: STAF/DIR/34: PIG/MID/DIR/35:
    PIG/MND/42.

McCREERY, *James*   Liverpool
Add: 19 Temple Lane (87): No.
    18 (90): 28 John St (96): No. 24
    (00).
Refs: LIV/DIR/87: 90: 96: 00: 03.

McDONALD, *John*   Wooler
(B S, S T &).   (Northumberland)
Refs: PIG/SEVEN/DIR/34.

McDOUGALL, *James*   Liverpool
Add: 40 Baptist St.
Refs: LIV/DIR/29.

McDOWALL, *Charles*   Bristol
Add: 24 High St.
Refs: PIG/NCD/24.

McDOWELL, *Cornelius*   Falmouth
Add: High St.
Refs: PIG/NCD/30:   LAB/KNA:
    "Bound by/CMD/F".

McGAFFIE, *William*   Liverpool
Add: 79 Gerard St.
Refs: LIV/DIR/21.

McNEILL, *William*
            Ashby-de-la-Zouch
Add: Kilwardby St.
Refs: PIG/MID/DIR/35.

MACHELL, *Richard*   Leeds
Add: 7 Newsom's Yard, 135 Brig-
    gate (34): No. 25(39).
Refs: PIG/SEVEN/DIR/34: PIG/CDS/
    37: WHI/WRY/37/8: LEEDS/DIR/
    34: 39: PIG/MND/42.

MACHIN, *Thomas*
            Newcastle-under-Lyme
Add: 2 York St.
Refs: NEW/LYME/36.

MACKAY, *James*   Morpeth
(Etc).
Add: Newgate St.
Refs: PIG/SEVEN/DIR/34.

MACKENZIE, *Joseph*   Exeter
Add: Catherine St.
Refs: BRI/DIR/91.

MACKEY, *Robert*   Liverpool
   Add: 1 Vernon St, Dale St.
   Refs: LIV/DIR/00.
   R.M. seems to have moved to
   Salford by 1804 (see R. M.,
   Salford). He no longer appears in
   LIV/DIR/05.

MACKEY, *Robert*
            (Manchester & Salford)
   Add: 26 Clowes St (04): Queen's St
   (08): Brown's Place, Queen St
   (11): St. Ann's Sq: House, St.
   Ann's Alley, (13): Riding's Ct,
   St. Mary's Gate (16).
   Refs: MAN/DIR/04: 08: 11: 13: PIG/
   16/17. Marks had a plain calf
   binding on Johnson's Works,
   1787, with St. Ann's Sq. Label
   which he dated ca. 00.

MACLEISH, *Archibald*   Sunderland
   Add: Cumberland St, Bishops-
   wearmouth: Bedford St (34).
   Refs: DUR/DIR/27: PIG/NCD/28:
   PIG/NAT/DIR/28/9: PIG/SEVEN/DIR/
   34: WSM/KC/NEW illustrates a
   ticket.

MAGINNIS, *Patrick*   Liverpool
   Add: 21 William St.
   Refs: LIV/DIR/21.

MAJOR, *William & Co.*   Bristol
   (& B S).
   Add: St. John's Step.
   Refs: PIG/NCD/24.

MALE, *Thomas*   Birmingham
   Add: Duke St.
   Refs: BIRM/DIR/35.

MANDERSON, *William*   Brighton
   (Working B B).
   Add: 28 London Rd.
   Refs: BRIG/DIR/39.

MANGER, *Joseph*   Guernsey
                  (St. Peter's Port)
   Add: Constitution Steps.
   Refs: GUER/DIR/40.

MANN, *Alice*   Leeds
   Add: 12 Duncan St & 1 Central
   Market.
   Refs: PIG/MND/42.

MAPLES, *Robert Sewel* Nottingham
   Add: Bridlesmith Gate.
   Refs: NOTT/DIR/40.

MARBROOK, *John*   Sandwich
                        (Kent)
   Refs: KENT/DIR/03: HOLD/11.

MARCHANT, *William* Cheltenham
   Add: Whitcombe Pl.
   Refs: ROB/NINE/DIR/39.

MARSH, *John*   York
   Add: 19 High Peter Gate.
   Refs: PIG/NCD/28: PIG/NAT/DIR/
   28/29.

MARSH, *Thomas*   York
  Add: Minster Gates.
  Refs: PIG/SEVEN/DIR/34.

MARSDEN, *Thomas*   Bungay
  Add: Mill Lane.   (Suffolk)
  Refs: PIG/HC/39.

MARSHALL, *Charles*   Liverpool
  Add: 3 Upper Newington (13):
    52 Ranelagh St (16).
  Refs: LIV/DIR/13: 16 (Apparently
    the same person appears in 1818
    as a straw-bonnet maker and in
    1821 as a bookseller).

MARSHALL, *George*
  Add: Salop St.   Wolverhampton
  Refs: PIG/MID/DIR/35.

MARSHALL, *Matthew*   Hull
  Add: 4 Kingston Ct, Blanket Row
    (17): 152 High St (21): 29 Low-
    gate (22): 3 Stewart's Yard, High
    St (24): 44 Stafford St and 29
    Lowgate (28): Old Dock-end
    (34): 5 Whitefriargate (37): Ct
    58 Whitefriargate (38).
  Refs: DIR/YORK/22: LINC/DIR/24:
    PIG/NCD/28: PIG/NAT/DIR/28/29:
    WHI/WRY/37/38: PIG/SEVEN/DIR/
    34: HULL/DIR/17: 21: 35: 38:
    LAB/JONES: WSM/KC/NEW illus-
    trates a ticket.

MARSHALL, *William*
  (Etc).   Newcastle-upon-Tyne
  Add: 4 Church St.   (Gateshead)
  Refs: PIG/NAT/DIR/28/29.

MARTEN, *Charles*   Canterbury
  Add: 6 Guildhall St.
  Refs: KENT/DIR/38.

MARTIN, *J.*   Walsall
  (& S T).
  Add: Digbeth.
  Refs: Munby Coll.: green printed
    label "J. M., BB. & St., D,W" on
    1820 work.

MARTIN, *James*   Brixton
  Add: Holland St.
  Refs: PIG/LPCD/32: 34.

MARTIN, *James*   Maidstone
  Add: 40 Stone St.
  Refs: PIG/LPD/26/7.

MARTIN, *John*   Plymouth
  (& Paper-ruler).
  Add: Treville St.
  Refs: PLY/DIR/36.

MARTIN, *Susannah*   Birmingham
  (P R &).

MARTIN, *Susannah & Thomas*.
  Add: Ann St.
  Refs: BIRM/DIR/00: 03: 08: HOLD/
    05.

MARTIN, *Thomas*   Birmingham
Add: Duke St (28): 39 Oxford St:
    Res: Bradford St (33).
Refs: PIG/NCD/28: PIG/NAT/DIR/28/
    29: WARW/DIR/30: BIRM/DIR/29:
    33.

MARYSON, *Francis* Gt. Yarmouth
Add: 101 Row.
Refs: NORF/DIR/36: PIG/HC/39.

MASON, *Thomas*   Canterbury
    (& Newsvendor).
Add: 54 Broad St.
Refs: KENT/DIR/38: PIG/HC/39.

MASTERS, *I.*   Shepton Mallet
    E D: 17?   (Somerset)
Refs: Munby Coll.: Label "IM,
    BB, SM" ½ calf, 1817.

MASTERS, *John*   Bristol

MASTERS, *J. F., Jun.* (40).
Add: 26 Hill St (33): No. 20 (36):
    Bridge Parade (40).
Refs: BRIS/DIR/33: 36: 40.

MATE, *Charles*   Dover
Add: Market Place.
Refs: PIG/LPCD/23: PIG/LPD/26/7.

MATHER, *William*
            Newcastle-upon-Tyne
Add: Bigg-market.
Refs: NEW/DIR/95.

MATHIAS, *Daniell*   Cardiff
Add: Running Camp, Crockherb-
    town (29): Smith St (30).
Refs: CARD/DIR/29: PIG/NCD/30.

MATTACKS, *U. B.*   Colchester
    (B B, S T & P R).
Add: Head St.
Refs: ROB/HOMCO/DIR/39.

MATTACKS, *U. W.*   Colchester
Add: Short Wyre St.
Refs: ROB/HOMCO/DIR/39.

MATTHEWS, *Thomas*   Bristol
    (B S &).

MATTHEWS & BESLES
Add: Quay.
Refs: BRIS/DIR/87: (M. & B.): 97
    (Thomas).

MAUD, *William*   Andover
    (S T, B S & B B).
Refs: HANTS/DIR/84.

MAUGHAM, *Frances*   Spalding
Add: Church St.
Refs: PIG/MID/DIR/35.

MAURICE, *J. W.*   Birmingham
Add: 57 Snow Hill.
Refs: WARW/DIR/30: BIRM/DIR/29.

MAWSON, *William*   Leeds
(& Ruler).
Add: 33 Vicar Lane.
Refs: WHI/WRY/37/8.

MAY, *George*   Barnstaple
Add: Boutport St.   (Devon)
Refs: PIG/NCD/30.

MAY, *George*   Evesham
E D: 30.
Refs: Label in O.C. taken from ¼
calf cont. binding on book dated
1830.

MAY, *J.*   Dover
(Etc).
Add: King St.
Refs: ROB/HOMCO/DIR/39.

MAYBURY, *Randall* (91)   Bath

MAYBURY, *William* (00).
Add: Green St (91): 1 Quiet St (00).
Refs: BRI/DIR/91: BATH/DIR/00: 01:
05.

MAYOR, *Thomas*   Liverpool
Add: 18 Temple St.
Refs: LIV/DIR/07: 10.

MAYNARD, *Thomas*   Truro
Add: 66 Kenwyn St.
Refs: PIG/NCD/30.

MEAD, *John*   Leeds
Add: Wood's Court, Vicar Lane
(22): 21 Dickinson Ct, Boar
Lane (26): 2 Crown Court (30).
Refs: YORK/DIR/22: 30: PIG/LPCD/
22: LEEDS/DIR/26.

MEAN, *Robert*   Berwick-on-Tweed
Add: Church St.
Refs: PIG/NCD/28: PIG/NAT/DIR/28/
29.

MEDLEY, *John*   Romsey
Add: Mid Bridge St.
Refs: ROB/HOMCO/DIR/39.

MELLOR, *J. B.*   Blackburn
(B S &).
Add: 45 Salford.
Refs: LANC/DIR/24.

MELROSE, *Thomas*
(Etc).   Berwick-on-Tweed
Add: 67 High St.
Refs: PIG/SEVEN/DIR/34: PIG/CDS/37.

MEPHAM, *Samuel*   Dorchester
E D: 20?
Refs: LAB/JONES: LAB/KNA: O.C.
Ticket.

MEPHAM, *Samuel*   Dorchester
Refs: Dubois d'Enghien quotes a
blue ½ calf binding with ticket on
Mérimée: Mosaique: 33.

MERRIDEW, *John* Leamington Spa
(& High St, Warwick)
Add: 34 Bath St. (30): No. 35 (33).
Refs: LEAM/DIR/30: 33: 37.

MERRILL, *Thomas* Cambridge

MERRILL, *T. & J.* (1758-75).

MERRILL, *J. & J.* (1775-95)*.
(B S, Publisher &).
Add: Regent Walk.
Refs: DBP/1726/75, p. 168.
 * Appears to have been suc-
 ceeded in 1794 by J. Bowtell as
 binder to King's College. (See
 Camb. Ant. Soc. Proc., Vol. XI,
 p. 359).

MICHAEL, *William* Westbury
(Etc). (Wilts.)
Add: Edward St.
Refs: ROB/NINE/DIR/39.

MIDLANE, *James* Newport
(I. of W.)
Add: South St (30): also near the
 P.O. (ca. 1830).
Refs: PIG/NCD/30. Ticket on lot
 245 in Sotheby's Sale, Nov. 25,
 1952.

MILLER, *John* Lancaster
Add: Chapel St.
Refs: PIG/SEVEN/DIR/34.

MILLER, *Richard*
Newcastle-upon-Tyne
Add: 31 Mosley St.
Refs: NEW/DIR/11: PIG/NAT/DIR/28/
29.

MILLER, *William*
Newcastle-upon-Tyne
Add: Beehive Entry, Fleshmarket
 (78): Fleshmarket (82): Groat-
 market (87).
Refs: NEW/DIR/78: 82: 87.

MILLET, *Brid(?get)*
(Etc). Newcastle-upon-Tyne
Add: 68 Pilgrim St.
Refs: NEW/DIR/38.

MILLETT, *William* Liverpool
Add: 4 Islington Row.
Refs: LIV/DIR/29.

MILLIGAN, *Peter*
Newport (I. of W.)
Refs: HANTS/DIR/84.

MILLMAN, *J.* Stonehouse (Devon)
Add: Chapel St.
Refs: PLY/DIR/14.

MILLS, *Benjamin* Birmingham
(& Clerk of St Bartholomew
 Chapel (29).
Add: Bartholomew Row (11):
 Square (16).

Refs: HOLD/II: PIG/16/17: 18/20:
PIG/LPCD/22.
BIRM/DIR/38: 12: 18: 21: 29: 35:
PIG/NCD/28: PIG/NAT/DIR/28/29:
WARW/DIR/30: PIG/MID/DIR/35:
PIG/CDS/37.

MILLS, *Thomas*   Newport Pagnell
Add: Tickford End.   (Bucks.)
Refs: ROB/SIX/DIR/39.

MILLS, *Thomas*   Bristol
Add: Wine St.
Refs: BRIS/DIR/85: 87.

MILLS, *William*   Bath
Add: Wade's Passage (91): 3 Kings-
mead St (09): 22 St James's
Parade (19): 3 Abbey Green (22).
Refs: BRI/DIR/91: BATH/DIR/00: 01:
05: 09: 12: 19: PIG/LPCD/22.

MILNER, *John*   Halifax

MILNER, *Susan* (28).

MILNER, *William* (30).
Add: Fox Alley (22, John): 4
Smithy Stake (28, Susan): 4
Causeway (30, William).
Refs: PIG/LPCD/22: PIG/NCD/28:
YORK/DIR/30: PIG/NAT/DIR/28: 29.

MILLSON, *Richard*   Scarborough
Add: Cross St.
Refs: YORK/DIR/22.

MILSON, *Joseph*   Scarborough
Add: Cross St.
Refs: PIG/NAT/DIR/28/29.

MILSON, *Joseph*   Scarborough
Add: Cross St.
Refs: PIG/NCD/28.

MILTON, *James*   Exeter
Add: Paul St.
Refs: EX/P/J/16.

MINOR, *Thomas*   Manchester
(& S T).
Add: 13 Wright's Ct.
Refs: PIG/CDS/37: MAN/DIR/38.

MINSHALL, *Richard*   Oswestry
(P R &).
Add: Salop Rd.
Rep: PIG/MID/DIR/35.

MINSHULL, *T.*   Shrewsbury
(P R &).
Add: College Hill (03).
Refs: SHREW/DIR/03: JBO/AE.

MINTORN, *John*   Bristol
(B S, S T &).
Add: Drawbridge.
Refs: BRIS/DIR/97: 99: WSM/KC/NEW
illustrates a ticket.

MITCHELL, *James*   Helston
Refs: BRI/DIR/V/98.   (Cornwall)

MOFFAT, *Francis* Manchester
Add: 14 St Ann's Alley.
Refs: MAN/DIR/11 P.

MOIR, *George* Sunderland

MOIR, *Jane* (34).
Add: Lombard St.
Refs: PARS/WHI/27: PIG/NCD/28: PIG/NAT/DIR/28/9: PIG/SEVEN/DIR /34.

MOLLISON, *John* Liverpool
(& Secondhand books*).
Add: 10 Earle St (05): 32 Whitechapel (07): No. 43 & 51 Lord St BB. shop 12 Williamson St. (13).
Refs: LIV/DIR/05: 07: 10: 13: 16: 18: PIG/16/17: 18/20.
* In 10 he is not listed as a binder at all.

MOLLOY, *James* Liverpool
(& Paper ruler).
Add: 30 Castle St (37): No. 58 (40).
Refs: PIG/CDS/37: LIV/DIR/40.

MONRO, *William* Plymouth
Add: Princess St. (Dock)
Refs: PLY/DIR/22.

MONTGOMERY, *Benjamin* Hull

MONTGOMERY, *Mary* (38).
Add: 23 Lowgate (26).
Refs: LINC/DIR/26: HULL/DIR/38.

MONTGOMERY & PERFECT(03).
(B S &). Hull

MONTGOMERY, *John*
(& Victualler in 06).
Add: Wincolmlee (03): 21 Robinson Row, 26 (06): No. 18 (10): 5 Dagger Lane (28).
Refs: HULL/DIR/03: 06: 10: 17: 21: PIG/16/17: 18/20: YORK/DIR/22: PIG/LPCD/22: PIG/NCD/28: PIG/NAT/DIR/28/29.

MOODY Alresford (Essex)
E D: 32?
Refs: Munby Coll.: grey lithographed label "M.B.A." on 1832 work.

MOODY, *Charles* Liverpool
Add: 34 Bold St.
Refs: LIV/DIR/18.

MOODY, *William* Winchester

MOODY, *Robert* (23)
Add: High St (11): Southgate St (30).
Refs: HOLD/11: PIG/LPCD/23: PIG/NCD/30.

MOODY, *Samuel* Leeds
Add: Central Market.
Refs: PIG/MND/42.

MOON, *Robert* Lewes
E D: 00?
Refs: AE/COLL/LAB.

MOON, *Samuel*   Bristol
    Add: Temple St.
    Refs: BRIS/DIR/21.

MOORE, *George*   Leek (Staffs.)
    Refs: BRI/DIR/V/98.

MO(O)REHOUSE, *Thomas*
    Add: Warser Gate.   Nottingham
    Refs: NOTT/DIR/34: PIG/MID/DIR/35.

MORGAN, *John* Bury-St.-Edmunds
    Refs: BRI/DIR/91.

MORGAN, *Robert*   Norwich
    Add: St. Gregory's (30): Pottergate
    St (39).
    Refs: PIG/NCD/30: PIG/HC/39.

MORGAN, *Thomas*   Bristol
(& S T).

MORGAN *& Son* (36).

MORGAN, *W.* (40).
    Add: 15 John St (12): 14 Broad St
    (21): 16 High St (22 & 27): No. 10
    (24): 1 Clare St (& Son) (36).
    Refs: BRIS/DIR/12: 21: 24: 27: 30:
    36: 40: BRIS/IND/18: PIG/LPCD/22.

MORLEY, *David*   Ipswich
    Add: Upper Brook St.
    Refs: PIG/NCD/30. O.C. Clarke's
    History of Ipswich, 1830, ½ c.g.
    leather label inside corner.

MORRIS, *Charles*   Newport
    Add: Pyle St.   (I. of W.)
    Refs: ROB/HOMCO/DIR/39.

MORRIS, *David*   Carmarthen
    Add: Lammas St.
    Refs: PIG/LPCD/22: PIG/MID/DIR/35.

MORRIS, *David*   Newport
    Refs: BRI/DIR/V/98.   (Shropshire)

MORRIS, *Seth Newland*   Bath
(S T &).
    Add: 3 Bath St.
    Refs: BATH/DIR/33.

MORRIS, *William*   Shrewsbury
    E D: 92?
    Refs: JBO/AE.

MORTON, *J.*   Windsor
(To Their Majesties).
    E D: 30?
    Refs: Sch. S. de R. IV, 61: Hob/
    Abb. App. XI, p. 195. Mumby
    Coll. Label "JM, BS, S & B to
    their Majs., W" Green m.g. 1830.

MOSS, *John*   Lane End (Potteries)
    Add: Cornhill.
    Refs: PIG/STAF/28/9: PIG/NCD/28:
    PIG/NAT/DIR/28/29.

MOSS, *William*   Carlisle
    Add: Peascod's Lane, English St.
    Refs: CARL/DIR/11.

MOWATT, *William*   Hull
     Add: Market Place.
     Refs: HULL/DIR/03: 10.

MOWBRAY, *George*   Manchester
     Add: 2 Bailey's Court (25): St.
     Ann's St (28).
     Refs: LANC/DIR/25: PIG/NCD/28.

MUDGE, *John*   Plymouth (Dock)
     (P R &).
     Add: James St.
     Refs: TCG/PLY/23.

MUIR, *George*   Woolwich
     Add: Mulgrave Place.
     Refs: PIG/LPCD/23.

MULLINGER, *J. M.*
     (& S T, P R).   Bishop's Stortford
     Add: North St.
     Refs: ROB/HOMCO/DIR/39.

MULLINS, *William*   Manchester
                             (Salford)
     Add: 17 Gravel Lane (08): 5 Garden
     Lane (11): 1 Crown St, York St,
     Salford, when Librarian at the
     College (28).
     Refs: MAN/DIR/08: 13: 11 P: 15:
     21: 28: PIG/16/17: 18/20.

MUNCASTER, *Thomas*   Liverpool
     Add: Baptist Lane, Circus St.
     Refs: LIV/DIR/07: 10.

MUNDY, *Thomas*   Oxford
     Add: 88 High St.
     Refs: ROB/SIX/DIR/39.

MURGETROYD, *Joseph*
     Add: Bradford St.   Birmingham
     Refs: BIRM/DIR/08.

MURRAY, *Courtney*   Bath
     (& S T).
     Add: 35 Horse Parade.
     Refs: BATH/DIR/09.

MURRAY, *John*   Liverpool
     Add: Hackin's Hey, Dale St.
     Refs: LIV/DIR/03.

MUSGRAVE, *Robert*
     E D: 11.   Newcastle-upon-Tyne
                        (Gateshead)
     Add: King St (N) (11): Bottle Bank
     (27): Bridge St (28).
     Refs: NEW/DIR/11: DUR/DIR/27: PIG
     /NCD/28: PIG/NAT/DIR/28/29.

MUSKETT, *Charles*   Norwich
     Add: Bridewell   Alley,   St.
     Andrew's.
     Refs: ROB/NINE/DIR/39: ROB/SIX/
     DIR/39.

MYHILL, *Richard*   Norwich
     Add: St. Andrew's Hill.
     Refs: PIG/LPCD/22: PIG/NCD/30:
     Hob/Abb. App. XI, p. 194.

NALL, *George*   Gt. Yarmouth
    Add: 182 King St.
    Refs: NORF/DIR/36.

NEALD, *Mark* Ashton-under-Lyne
    Add: Soup St.
    Refs: LANC/DIR/24.

NEEDHAM, *Joshua*   Gloucester
    (B S &).
    Add: Westgate St.
    Refs: ROB/NINE/DIR/39: JA/3065.

NESBIT, *Alexander*
              Berwick-on-Tweed
    Add: Church St.
    Refs: BERW/DIR/06.

NETTLEFORD, *Edward* Plymouth
    (Etc, etc).
    Add: Whimple St.
    Refs: PLY/DIR/36: JA/4924.

NETTLETON, *W.*   Plymouth
    (Probably only incidentally a
      binder).

NETTLETON *& Son* (pre 1822).

NETTLETON, *Edward* (1822).
    Add: 2 Pike St (?05): 57 Market St
    (22).
    Refs: PLY/DIR/22: Hob/Abb. App.
    XI, p. 194: Soth. Cat. 27.11.50/
    No. 213: ABB/CBS.

NEWLANDS, *Thomas*
            Newcastle-upon-Tyne
    Add: 61 Head of the Side.
    Refs: PIG/SEVEN/DIR/34: PIG/CDS/
    37: NEW/DIR/38.

NEWMAN, *H. P.*   Cambridge
    Add: Bridge St.
    Refs: PIG/LPCD/23.

NEWMAN, *William*   Newport
    Add: Pentonville   (Mon.)
    Refs: PIG/MID/DIR/35.

NEWTON, *John*   Whitehaven
              (Cumberland)
NEWTON, *Joseph* (29).
    Add: 9 Plumblands-lane.
    Refs: PIG/SIN/20: PIG/NCD/28:
    CUMWES/DIR/29:   PIG/NAT/DIR/
    28/9.

NICHOLLS, *Richard* Sittingbourne
    Add: Green St.
    Refs: PIG/LPCD/32: 34: PIG/HC/39.

NICHOLS   *Farnham*
    Refs: Ticket "Bd by/N/F" seen at
    Marks, Sept., 52, on very nice
    ½ russia binding with distinctive
    Herring-like tooling. Date of
    book 1824, and binding probably
    contemporary.

NICHOLLS, *John* (oo)   Leeds

NICHOLLS, *John & Isaac* (oo).

NICHOLLS, *Isaac* (17).
(Etc).
Add: St. George's St (J. 00): Rose
& Crown Yard, Cross Parish (J.
& I. 00): R. & C. Y., Market
Place (J. & I. 07): 34 Back of
Shambles (I. 17).
Refs: LEEDS/DIR/00: 07: 17.

NICHOLLS, *R.*   Wakefield
Refs: See Illingworth & Hicks.

NICHOLS, *William*   Cambridge
Add: Blackbear Yard.
Refs: PIG/NCD/30.

NICHOLSON   Leeds
(? Same as Samuel Nicholson).
Refs: HOLD/11.

NICHOLSON, *John*   Hull
Add: 15 Bishop Lane.
Refs: PIG/MND/42.

NICHOLSON, *John & Son*
          Cambridge

*NICHOLSON (Binder to the Uni-
versity, 85).
Add: Trinity St.
Refs: PIG/LPCD/23.
   *Camb. Ant. Soc. Proc., Vol.
XI, p. 359.

NICHOLSON, *Samuel*   Leeds
Add: Hunslet Lane (09): 87
Meadow Lane (16): No. 86 (18):
No. 37 (26).
Refs: PIG/16/17: 18/20: LEED/DIR/
09: 17: 26: 34: 39: YORKS/DIR/
22: 30: PIG/NCD/28: PIG/NAT/DIR/
28/29: PIG/SEVEN/DIR/34: PIG/
CDS/37: WHI/WRY/37: PIG/MND/
42.

NICHOLSON, *Samuel*   Manchester
Add: 6 Back George St (8): 4
Fountain St: Res: 9 Back George
St (11 P).
Refs: MAN/DIR/08: 11 P.

NICHOLS'S   Leeds
Add: Market Place.
Refs: LEEDS/DIR/98.

NIDDERY, *D.*   Watford (Herts.)
(Etc).
Add: High St.
Refs: ROB/HOMCO/DIR/39.

NISBET, *David*   Newcastle
E D: 80?
Refs: AE/f.

NOBBS, *Abraham*   Hungerford
(& S T, 30).
Add: Charnham St (30).
Refs: PIG/LPCD/23: PIG/NCD/30.

123

NOBLE Boston (Lincs.)
(P R &).
E D: 14.
Add: Market Place (14).
Refs: LAB/KNA. "Bound by/N/B"
ca. 25. Spec. in Munby Coll.:
Similar labels on "Heads of the
People", 1840/41. (E. C. Lowe,
51). Seen at Marks: cont. calf
binding on 1814 work with
ticket "Bound at/Noble's/Print-
ing Office/Market Place/Boston".

NORMAN, *Benjamin* Norwich
Add: Haymarket.
Refs: NORF/DIR/36.

NORRIS, *Ann & Son* Uttoxeter
(B S, S T, B B & Stamp Office).
Add: Market Place.
Refs: PIG/MID/DIR/35: PIG/MND/42:
Mr. A. Hobson reports ticket on
Curtis: Botanical Mag. 28, tree
calf.

NORTON, *John* Bristol
(& B S).
E D: 75?
Add: Milton's Head, Wine St (75?):
5 Corn St (24).
Refs: PIG/NCD/24. O.C. Holy Bible,
2 vol., 1768, f.m.g., with label
"Made and sold by/J. Norton/
Book & Printseller/at ye Milton's
Head/Wine Street/Bristol". M.S.
note "Bristol, Aug. 7, 1775".

NOSWORTHY, *Ambrose*
Plymouth (Dock)
Add: 70 Prince St (Ply. Dock) (14):
Princess St (30).
Refs: PLY/DIR/14: 23: PIG/NCD/30.

NUTE, *William* Brighton
Add: 38 Agremont Place.
Refs: BRIG/DIR/32: ROB/HOMCO/
DIR/39.

OGLE, *John* Bolton
(B S &).
Add: Market St (24): New Market
St (28.
Refs: LANC/DIR/24: PIG/NAT/DIR/
28/9.

OLDINGS, *James & Nathaniel*
Wincanton (Somerset)
Add: High St.
Refs: PIG/LPCD/22.

OLDLAND, *Henry* Bristol
Add: 28 Corn St.
Refs: ROB/NINE/DIR/39.

OLIVER, *J.* Bristol
Add: 20 Broad St.
Refs: BRIS/DIR/40.

OLTON, *J.* Bristol
(See OTTON).

ORAM, *Chas.* Bristol
(& B S).
Add: 57 Quay.
Refs: PIG/NCD/24.

ORTON, *Thomas* Sheffield
(& Pattern card manufacturer).
Add: Snig Hill (18): 32 High St
(22).
Refs: PIG/18/20: YORK/DIR/22:
SHEFF/DIR/25.

OSBORNE, *Edward C.* Birmingham
Add: 14 Temple Row.
Refs: PIG/MID/DIR/35: PIG/CDS/37.

OSBORNE, *Henry* Hastings
(P R, S T &).
Add: 55 George St.
Refs: ROB/HOMCO/DIR/39.

OSBORNE, *William* Liverpool
Add: 2 Milton St (18): 6 Brown St
(21).
Refs: LIV/DIR/18: 21.

OSMOND, *Benjamin* Bath
Add: 3 St. Michael's Place.
Refs: BATH/DIR/29.

OSTLER, *C.* Leamington Spa
Add: 11 Church St.
Refs: LEAM/DIR/33.

OSTLER, *Charles* Maidstone
Add: 13 Union St.
Refs: PIG/HC/39: MAID/DIR/39: ROB/
HOMCO/DIR/39.

OSWALD, *John* Liverpool
Add: 28 Pall Mall (10): 12 Cropper
St (13).
Refs: LIV/DIR/10: 13.

OSWELL, *Geo.* King's Lynn
Add: 20 Broad St.
Refs: NORF/DIR/36.

OTTAWAY, *Henry* Maidstone
Add: High St.
Refs: PIG/LPCD/32: 34: PIG/HC/39.

OTTON, *John* Bristol
(& Ironmonger in 1813).
Add: 10 Old Market St.
Refs: HOLD/11: BRIS/DIR/12: 13:
15: 18: 21: 24: BRIS/IND/18: PIG/
LPCD/22.

OTTY, *Philip* Norwich
Add: Orford Hill.
Refs: NORF/DIR/36.

OVERTHROW, *Samuel*
Add: Dyer St. Cirencester
Refs: ROB/NINE/DIR/39.

OVISTON (or OVERTON), *John*
Newcastle-upon-Tyne
Add: St. Nicholas Church Yard
(11): No. 2 (27): Amen Corner
(20).
Refs: NEW/DIR/11: 24: 33: 38: PIG/
SIN/20: DUR/DIR/27: PIG/NCD/28:
PIG/NAT/DIR/28/29: PIG/SEVEN/
DIR/34: PIG/CDS/37.

OWENS, *Thomas* Liverpool
(& Paper ruler in 1825).
Add: 7 Skelborne St (21): 41
Bispham Place (25).
Refs: LIV/DIR/21: 25.

OXLEY, *James*   Bristol
   Add: 15 Frogmore St (21): Old
     King St (24).
   Refs: BRIS/DIR/21: 24.

PADBURY, *Francis*   Oxford
   Add: St. Mary Magdalen's (30).
   Refs: BRI/DIR/91: PIG/NCD/30
   (Francis).

PADBURY, *John*   Oxford
   (Decd. Jan., 1826, aged 69).
   Add: Facing Dolphin Inn, Mag-
    dalen Parish.
   Refs: Advt. in Jackson's Oxford
   Journal, 8.10.85, where he states
   he was late foreman to Mr.
   Wingrove, Red Lion Ct, Lon-
   don. Figures as binder in Bod-
   leian Accounts, 1785/9.

PAGE, *Martin*   Cambridge
   Add: Jesus Lane.
   Refs: PIG/HC/39: ROB/NINE/DIR/39:
   ROB/SIX/DIR/39.

PAGE, *Edward*   Hammersmith
   (Etc).
   Add: King St.
   Refs: PIG/LPCD/32.

PAGE, *Mrs. Mary*   Cambridge
   Add: Market St.
   Refs: PIG/LPCD/23. Munby Coll.:
   red printed label "P,BS,B,etc.C"
   on 1822 work.

PAGE, *William*   Cambridge
   Refs: BRI/DIR/91.

PAINE, *T.*   Oxford
   Add: Gravel Walk.
   Refs: PIG/LPCD/23.

PAINE & *Co.*   Cheltenham
   Add: 127 High St.
   Refs: CHELT/DIR/39.

PAINTER, *John*   Helston
   (P R &).   (Cornwall)
   Refs: BRI/DIR/V/98.

PAINTER, *J.*   Wrexham
   Add: High St.
   Refs: Wheeler 162, on Goldsmith's
   Works, 1751. (Pre-period ?).

PARDON, *R.*   Plymouth
   Add: Higher Broad St.
   Refs: PLY/DIR/14.

PARKE, *William*   Wolverhampton
   Add: High St.
   Refs: PIG/MID/DIR/35: PIG/MND/42.

PARKER, *John*   Cheltenham
   Add: 8 St. James St.
   Refs: PIG/NCD/30.

PARKER, *Joseph*   Bristol
   Add: Griffin Lane (21): 4 Thornhill
   Place, Upper Maudlin Lane (30):
   6 Maudlin St (36).

Refs: PIG/LPCD/22: PIG/NCD/30:
BRIS/DIR/21: 24: 27: 33: 36: 40:
ROB/NINE/DIR/39.

PARKER, *Joseph*   Ipswich
Add: St. Stephen's Lane.
Refs: PIG/HC/39: LAB/KNA (slightly
earlier).

PARKER, *Thomas* Chorley (Lancs.)
(P R &).
Add: St. Thomas Sq.
Refs: PIG/16/17: 18/20.

PARKER, *Thomas*   Oxford
(Decd. June, 1805, aged 83).
Refs: MAT/OX/9.7.45: Succeeded
Thomas Sedgley as principal
Bodleian binder. Figures in a/cs.
1749/94. Grandson of Bishop
Parker.

PARKER, *Mrs.*   Cheltenham
Add: 8 St. James's St.
Refs: CHELT/AN/37 to 40: CHELT/
DIR/39.

PARKINSON, *William* Liverpool
Add: 27 Sawney Pope St & 62 Lord
St (shop) (13): 6 Leather Lane (18).
Refs: LIV/DIR/13: 18: 21. By the 25
Directory he seems to be only a
bookseller and stationer. PIG/18/
20: YORK/DIR/22: PIG/LPCD/22.

PARRY, *John*   Chester

PARRY, *John & Son* (40).
(B B, B S & S T).
Add: Upper Bridge St (28): East-
gate St (40).
Refs: PIG/NCD/28: PIG/NAT/DIR/28
/9: CHEST/DIR/40.

PARRY, *John*   Liverpool
Add: 126 Duke St.
Refs: LIV/DIR/16.

PARSLOW, *S. & Co.*   Bristol
Add: 1 Narrow Wine St.
Refs: BRIS/DIR/30.

PARSON, *William*   Bristol
Add: Upper Arcade.
Refs: ROB/NINE/DIR/39.

PARSONS, *James*   Norwich
Add: Pottergate St.
Refs: PIG/NCD/30.

PARTRIDGE, *Benjamin*
E D: 93?   Shrewsbury &
Refs: JBO/AE.   Bridgnorth

PARTRIDGE, *James*   Brecon
Refs: PIG/NCD/30.

PARTRIDGE, *John*   Rugby
(B S, S T &).
Refs: PIG/MND/42.

PARTRIDGE, *W.*   Nailsworth
E D: 25?   (Glos.)
Refs: LAB/KNA.

127

PATTINSON, *John*   Alston
(& S T).   (Cumberland)
Refs: HOLD/11: CUMWES/DIR/29:
   He was parish clerk, and included
   bookbinding among his numer-
   ous literary activities. PIG/NAT/
   DIR/28/9.

PAUL, *Edward*   Southampton
(Successor to S. Lyon).
Add: 24 French St.
Refs: SOUTH/DIR/36: ROB/HOMCO/
   DIR/39: LAB/PEARSON: LAB/OC.

PAUL, *Thomas*   Gt. Yarmouth
(Vellum binder).   (Norfolk)
Add: 181 Gaol St.
Refs: PIG/NCD/30: NORF/DIR/36: PIG
   /HC/39.

PAYN, *Philip*   St. Helier (Jersey)
(Publisher of the Royal Almanack,
   1837, describes himself as "B S,
   S T, P R & B B").
Add: Royal Saloon, facing the
   Royal Square.
Refs: Information supplied by the
   St. Helier Public Librarian.

PEARCE, *A.*   Bristol
Add: 23 Narrow Wine St (36): 136
   Redcliff St (39).
Refs: BRIS/DIR/36: 40: ROB/NINE/
   DIR/39.

PEARCE, *John*   Frome
Add: Gentle St.
Refs: SOM/DIR/40.

PEARCE, *Joseph*   Sheffield
(Etc).
Add: 32 Gibraltar St (34): No.
   37 (37): No. 188 (42).
Refs: PIG/SEVEN/DIR/34. PIG/CDS/37:
   PIG/MND/42 (& Son).

PEARCE, *L. N.*   Bristol

PEARCE, *L. N. & Co.* (30).
E D: 25?
Add: 10 Bath St.
Refs: BRIS/DIR/30: Soth. Cat.,
   19.2.51, ½ calf on Syntax.

PEARCE, *William*   Bristol
(Also account book maker and in
   1812 also stationer).
Add: 3 Temple St (12), 25 Bath St
   (18): ? Res: Durdham Down (30
   PIG): Union Ct, Corn St (24).
Refs: BRIS/DIR/12: 13: 15: 18: 24:
   27: 30: 33: 36: 40: PIG/LPCD/22:
   PIG/NCD/30: ROB/NINE/DIR/39.

PEARSON, *Lawrence*
          Newcastle-upon-Tyne
Add: Gates-head (20): near the
   P.O., Market Place (27).
Refs: PIG/SIN/20: DUR/DIR/27.

PEARSON, *Samuel* Portsea (Hants.)
Add: 37 North St.
Refs: PIG/LPCD/23: PIG/NCD/30: ROB
   /HOMCO/DIR/39.

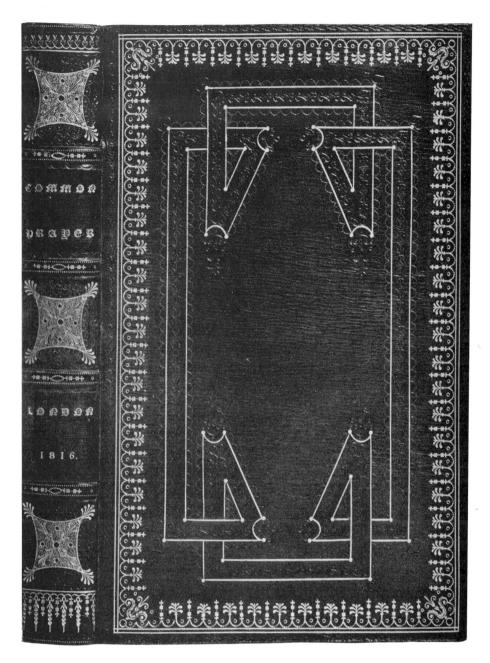

PLATE IX

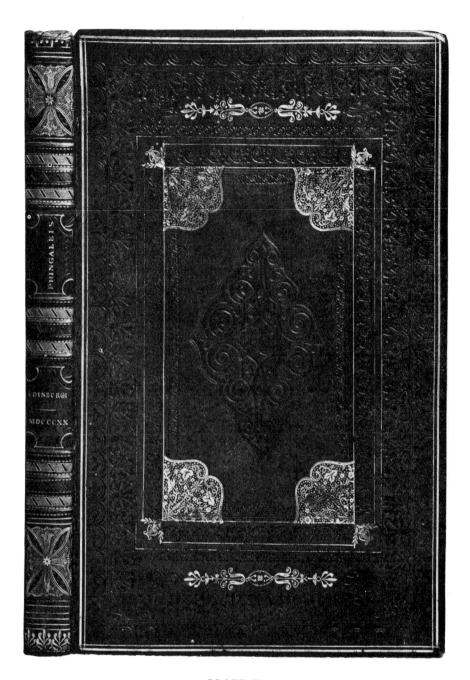

PLATE X

PEART, *Richard*   Birmingham
  (& S T).

PEART, *& Son* (18).

PEART, *Richard & Son* (42).
  Add: Temple St (00): Top of
  Spiceal St (03): 38 Bull St (08).
  Refs: BIRM/DIR/00: 01: 03: 08: 12:
  18: 25: 29: 33: PIG/18/20: PIG/
  NPCD/22: WARW/DIR/30: PIG/MND
  /42. O.C. Hayley's Life of Cow-
  per, 4 vol. 06: m.g. label "Bd by
  RP/B, BS etc./BS/B."

PEART, *W.*   Retford
  E D: 96?
  Refs: Sch. S. de R. IV, 24: Hob/
  Abb/App. XI, p. 194.

PEATY   Tredegar
  E D: 45?
  Refs: Label seen at Fletcher, 1850.
  The book is dated 23, but the
  very ordinary half calf binding
  can hardly date earlier than 1845-
  60.

PECK, *Michael*   Hull
  (Etc).
  Add: 43 Lowgate.
  Refs: HULL/DIR/39.

PECK, *Thomas*   Liverpool
  Add: 6 Dansie St.
  Refs: LIV/DIR/18.

PECK, *William*   Lincoln
  (Etc).
  Add: Steep Hill.
  Refs: LINC/DIR/26: PIG/NAT/DIR/28/
  29: PIG/MID/DIR/35.

PECK & SMITH   Hull
  Add: 38 Lowgate.
  Refs: PIG/SEVEN/DIR/34.

PEEL, *William*   Shrewsbury
  E D: 00?
  Refs: JBO/AE.

PENALUNA, *William*   Helston
  (P R, B B & S T).   (Cornwall)
  Refs: HOLD/11.

PENDRELL, *J. A.* Walsall (Staffs.)
  Add: Digbeth.
  Refs: STAFF/DIR/18.

PENN, *Joseph*   Barking
  (P R &).
  Add: High St.
  Refs: PIG/HC/39.

PENROSE, *Elizabeth*   Hull
  Add: 35 Bond St (34): 25 (37): 58
  Carr Lane (40).
  Refs: PIG/SEVEN/DIR/34: PIG/CDS/
  37: WHI/WRY/37/8: HULL//DIR/
  38: WHI/ENR/40.

PENROSE, *John*   Hull
    Add: Whitefriargate (10): 1
    Hewitt's Yard, Whitefriars (13):
    26 Saville St (18): No. 21 (24).
    Refs: HULL/DIR/10: 13: 17: 22:
    PIG/16/17: 18/20: YORK/DIR/22:
    PIG/LPCD/22: PIG/NCD/28: PIG/
    NAT/DIR/28/29.

PERFECT, *John*   Derby
    Add: City Row (29): 44 Nuns St
    (35).
    Refs: COUNT/DER/29: PIG/MID/DIR/
    35.

PERFECT, *John*   Grantham
    Add: Castlegate.
    Refs: LINC/DIR/36.

PERFECT, *John*   Grantham
    Add: Back Lane.
    Refs: LINC/DIR/26: PIG/NCD/28: PIG/
    NAT/DIR/28/29.

PERFECT, *William*   Bedford
    Add: Clapham St (30): Conduit St
    (39).
    Refs: PIG/NCD/30: ROB/NINE/DIR/
    39: ROB/SIX/DIR/39.

PERFECT, *William*   York
    Add: Stonegate.
    Refs: YORK/DIR/87: BRI/DIR/91.

PERRY, *Francis*   York
    Add: 73 Walmgate.
    Refs: PIG/MND/42.

PERRY, *John*   Bristol
    Add: 4 Clark St, Milk St.
    Refs: PIG/NCD/30: BRIS/DIR/30: 33.

PERRY & METCALF   Liverpool
    Add: Lord St Chambers.
    Refs: LANC/DIR/24.

PEWTERS, *Thomas*   Bristol

PEWTERS, *K* (33).
    Add: 16 Clare St.
    Refs: PIG/LPCD/22: BRIS/DIR/30.

PHELAN, *Michael*   Manchester
    Add: 47 Clarendon St, Chorlton
    Row.
    Refs: MAN/DIR/32.

PHILIPS, *John*   Ruthin (Denbigh)
    Add: Clwyd St.
    Refs: PIG/NCD/28: PIG/NAT/DIR/
    28/9.

PHILLIPS, *John*   Birmingham
(Bookbinders' presses, etc).
    Add: Square.
    Refs: HOLD/11.

PHILLIPS, *John*   Narberth
    Refs: PIG/MID/DIR/35. (Pembroke)

PHILLIPS, *William*   Exeter
    Add: 126 Fore Street Hill (PIG):
    South St (E.P.J.30): Waterbeer
    St (35).
    Refs: PIG/NCD/30: E.P.J. 30: 33: 36:
    40: EX/DIR/31: 35.

PHILP & EVANS   Bristol
    Add: 29 Clare St.
    Refs: ROB/NINE/DIR/39.

PICKARD, *Thomas Morris*
                     Birmingham
    (Bookbinders' tools).
    Add: 75 Bull St.
    Refs: PIG/MID/DIR/35: PIG/CDS/37.

PICKEN, *William*   Plymouth (Dock)
    (P R &).
    Add: Tavistock Lane.
    Refs: PLY/DIR/22: 23: 30.

PICKERING, *George*   York
    Add: 19 Shambles.
    Refs: WHI/WRY/37/8: WHI/ENR/40:
      PIG/MND/42.

PICKERING, *T.*   Bristol
    Add: 25 Lower Arcade.
    Refs: BRIS/DIR/33.

PIERCE, *Pierce*   Aberystwyth
    Add: C/o Samuel Williams,
      Printer, etc, Bridge St.
    Refs: ABERY/DIR/16.

PIERCY, *Edward*   Birmingham
    (P R, S T &).
    Add: 96 Bull St (oo): & Calthorpe
      St (15).
    Refs: BIRM/DIR/00: 01: 08: 12: 15:
      HOLD/11.

PIGGE   Lynn (Norfolk)
    E D: oo?
    Refs: AE/COLL/LAB.
    Circular Labels, black on yellow,
      seen on booksa bout 1800 with
      bookplate of Sir Martin Brown
      ffolkes, reading "P/B/L".

PIGOTT, *Walter*   Derby
    Add: 9 Bridge Gate.
    Refs: PIG/MID/DIR/35.

PIGOT, *James & Son*   Manchester
    Add: 55 Fountain St.
    Refs: PIG/CDS/37: MAN/DIR/32: 38:
      PIG/SEVEN/DIR/34.

PIKE, *Walter & William*   Derby
    (P R &).
    Add: Derby Reporter News Office,
      Corn Market.
    Refs: DERBY/DIR/23/4.

PINSON, *Henry*   Norwich
    Add: Pottergate St.
    Refs: NORF/DIR/36.

PITMAN, *Charles Henry*   Salisbury
    Add: Fisherton St.
    Refs: PIG/NCD/30.

PLAMPIN, *Major*   Birmingham
    Add: 72 Newhall St.
    Refs: PIG/MND/42.

PLATT, *Joseph*   Plymouth (Dock)
(P R &, etc).
Add: Duke St.
Refs: HOLD/11.

PLAYER, *John*   Bristol
Add: Clare St.
Refs: ROB/NINE/DIR/39.

PLAYER, *Joseph*   Exeter
Add: 14 Fore St (23): High St (07
& 25).
Refs: EPJ/07: 25: HOLD/11: PIG/
LPCD/23.

POLLARD, *William*   Hastings
Add: 21 High St.
Refs: ROB/HOMCO/DIR/39.

POLYBANK, *William*   Truro
Add: 8 High Cross.
Refs: PIG/LPCD/23: PIG/NCD/30.

POMEROY, *Thomas*   Birmingham
E D: 00.
Add: 7 Lower Temple St (00):
Little Colmore St (16).
Refs: BIRM/DIR/00: 01: 08: 12: 15:
PIG/16/17: 18/20: PIG/LPCD/22.

PONDER, *William*   Manchester
Add: Back of 43 Booth St, Tib
Lane.
Refs: MAN/DIR/08.

POOLE, *John*   Taunton
Add: Fore St.
Refs: PIG/LPCD/22.

POOLE, *T.*   Chester
(Etc, etc, etc).
Add: Eastgate Row.
Refs: Munby Coll: engraved label
"Sold by T.P., BS, B & St., etc.,
etc., etc." on 1789 Chester pub-
lication.

POOLE & BOULT   Chester
Refs: Viaggio ai tre Laghi, Milan,
1818 cloth (ticket). Sotheby, 18.
XII. 50. No. 242. O.C. Mundy,
Life of Ld. Rodney, 2 vol., 1830
(ticket): WSM/KC/NEW.

POOLE & HARDING   Carnarvon
(S T &).
E D: 17?
Refs: Munby Coll: Label "P & H,
S & BB, C". Diced Russia, 1817:
A.BB/CBS/LAB. (20).

POOLE & HARDING   Chester
(& S T, 42).
Add: Eastgate St Row.
Refs: PIG/NCD/28: PIG/NAT/DIR/28
/9: LAB/JONES: JA/5003. Soth.
Cat. Oct. 30/Nov. 1950, No. 386
(about 1842).

POPE, *James*   Hackney
Add: Church St.
Refs: PIG/LPCD/23.

PORTBURY, *George*   Exeter
Add: North St.
Refs: BRI/DIR/91: JA/4541.

PORTBURY, *Henry*   Exeter
  Add: Waterbeer St.
  Refs: BRI/DIR/91.

PORTER, *John*   Chatham
  (Etc).
  Add: High St.
  Refs: ROB/HOMCO/DIR/39.

PORTER, *W.*   Cheltenham
  Add: 7 & 8 Arcade.
  Refs: Munby Coll.: yellow en-
    graved label "WP, BS & B, 7 &
    8 A, C" on 1823 work.

PORTER, *William*   Maidstone
  Add: Week St.
  Refs: PIG/LPCD/23.

POTE, *Joseph*   Eton
  (b. 1703: d. 3.3.87. Printer and
    bookseller. He employed Roger
    Payne, but was doubtfully a
    bookbinder himself).
  Refs: TIMB/ENC: 42/760. Re-
    searches in the Eton College
    Library might yield further
    results.

POTTER, *Jesse*   Brighton
  Add: 13 Marshall's Row.
  Refs: BRIG/DIR/24.

POTTER, *William* (also *& Co.*).
               Carnarvon
  Add: Turf Square.
  Refs: PIG/MID/DIR/35: Soth. Cat.
    Oct. 30/Nov. 1, 1950. Nos. 389
    & 400. LAB/KNA "Bound by/W.P.
    & Co./C." ca. 30: JA/5002:
    O.C. f.c.g. binding on Marryatt's
    Pirate, 1836: label "Bd by/W.P.
    & C./Carnarvon".

POT(T)S, *Thomas*
           Newcastle-upon-Tyne
  (& publican in 82).
  E D: 78.
  Add: end of Byker-chair (78):
    Unicorn, Byker-chair (82):
    Byker-chair (binder only 87):
    Pandon (90).
  Refs: NEW/DIR/78: 82: 87: 95:
    BRI/DIR/91.

POTTS, *William*   Banbury
  Add: Parsons St.
  Refs: ROB/SIX/DIR/39.

POUNTNEY, *John S. & Co.*
  (S T &).   Bristol
  Add: Redcliff St.
  Refs: BRIS/DIR/09.

POVER, *Edward*   Chester
  Add: Exchange, Northgate St.
  Refs: PIG/NCD/28: PIG/NAT/DIR/
    28/9.

POVEY   Wotton
    E D: 02?   (Bucks)
    Refs: Ticket "Bd by/P/W" seen
      on cont. ½ calf binding on book
      dated 1802.

POWELL, *Charles*   Chester
    (& machine ruler).
    Add: Custom-house   tavern,
      Watergate St.
    Refs: PIG/NCD/30.

POWELL, *Robert*   Newbury
    Refs: BRI/DIR/91.

POWIE, *Benjamin*   Ross
                (Monmouth)
    (doubtfully a bookbinder).
    Refs: ROSS/DIR/25.

PRATT, *John Slater*   Stokesley
    (Etc).   (Yorks.)
    Add: Market Place.
    Refs: PIG/SEVEN/DIR/34.

PREECE, *R. M.*   Carnarvon
    (?primarily stationers).
    E D:?
    Refs: Soth. Cat. Oct. 30/Nov. 1,
      1950. No.387.

PRENTICE, *Sam*   Canterbury
    Add: 3 & 20 Guildhall St.
    Refs: KENT/DIR/38.

PRICE   Wells
    Refs: LAB/KNA: ca. 35.

PRICE, *William* (05)   Bath
PRICE, *Joseph*
    (& stationer) succeeded by W.
      Evans about 1829.
    Add: 23 Kingsmead St (05): 24
      Kingsmead St (?06): London
      Terrace (12): 3 Wade's Pass (19).
    Refs: Label seen in Dublin (Aug.,
      1950) on an 1812 ed. of the
      Gull's Hornbook. PIG/LPCD/22:
      BATH/DIR/05: 12: 19: 24: 26:
      O.C. Life of Sir W. Jones, 2 vol.
      06. Label: "J.P, B, 24 Kings-
      mead St, etc".

PRICE, *Matthew*   Newbury
    Add: Market Place.
    Refs: PIG/NCD/30.

PRICE, *T.*   Dartmouth
    E D: 20?   (Devon)
    Refs: LAB/KNA: "T.P/D/Binder"
      ca. 20.

PRICE, *Thomas*   Maidstone
    Add: 49 King St.
    Refs: PIG/LPD/26/7: PIG/LPCD/32:
      34: PIG/HC/39: ROB/HOMCO/
      DIR/39.

PRICE, *W.*   Oswestry
    (Etc).
    Add: Cross St (28): Beatrice St
      (35).
    Refs: SALOP/DIR/28: PIG/MID/DIR/
      35: LAB/KNA "Bound by/W.P/
      O": ca. 30.

PRICE & CO.   Bristol
  Add: 29 Bridge St.
  Refs: ROB/NINE/DIR/39.

PRICE & WATSON   Birmingham
  Add: 4 Peck Lane.
  Refs: PIG/CDS/37.

PRITCHARD, *J.*   Carnarvon
  Add: Bangor St.
  Refs: For this family, see Soth.
  Cat. Oct. 31/Nov. 1, 1950, Nos.
  386/400. All their work is rather
  rough, and they were primarily
  stationers in all probability. JA/
  4998.

PRITCHARD, *T.*   Bristol
  Add: 23 Maryport St.
  Refs: BRIS/DIR/33.

PRITCHARD, *W.*   Carnarvon
  E D: 28 or 33?
  Add: High St.
  Refs: Soth. Cat. Oct. 30/Nov. 1,
  1950, Nos. 386/400. O.C.
  Keepsake, 28, signed by Ld.
  Newborough. (Label).

PRITCHARD, *W. & J.*
                     Carnarvon
  E D: 30?
  Refs: Soth. Cat. Oct. 30/Nov. 1,
  1950, Nos. 386/400.

PROCTOR, *Samuel*   Hull
  Add: 4 Bowl Alley Lane.
  Refs: PIG/SEVEN/DIR/34: PIG/CDS/
  37: WHI/WRY/37/8: HULL/DIR/38:
  WHI/ENR/40: PIG/MND/42.

PROSSER, *Evan*   Pontypool
  (Etc).
  Add: Commercial St.
  Refs: PIG/MID/DIR/35.

PROVAN, *James*   Manchester
  Add: 149 Longmill Gate.
  Refs: BRI/DIR/91: MAN/DIR/94:
  MAN/DIR/04 (Provin).

PRUDDEN, *William*   Brighton
  Add: 14 Spring Gardens (?25): 192
  Western Rd. (39).
  Refs: LAB/JONES: LAB/KNA: "W.P/
  Binder/14 S.G/B" (ca. 25):
  BRIG/DIR/39.

PRYSE, *Ann*   Shrewsbury
  E D: 84?
  Refs: JBO/AE.

PUNCHARD, *Charles*   Ipswich
  E D: ?
  Add: Button Market.
  Refs: Hob/Abb. p. 194.

PURDEY, *E.*   Hythe
  Add: High St.
  Refs: ROB/HOMCO/DIR/39.

PURDON, *James*   Hull
   Add: 65 Market Place.
   Refs: PIG/CDS/37: PIG/MND/42.

PURDON & BROWN (34)   Hull
PURDON, *William*
   (Etc).   Published 1839 Directory
   Add: 43 Whitefriars (35): Old Corn
     Exchange (37): 47 Market Place
     (37): No. 43 & 19 Old Bridge St.
     (42).
   Refs: PIG/SEVEN/DIR/34: HULL/DIR/
     35: 38: 39: PIG/CDS/37: WHI/
     WRY/37/38: WHI/ENR/40: PIG/
     MND/42.

PURSEY, *William*   Saffron Walden
   Add: East St.
   Refs: PIG/HC/39.

PURVIS, *Archibald*
          Newcastle-upon-Tyne
   Add: Sandgate.
   Refs: NEW/DIR/90: 95: 01.

PYE, *Samuel*   Bristol
   (See Leslie & Pye).
   Add: 16 Cumberland Bldgs (24):
     3 Little John St (33): No. 2 (40).
   Refs: ROB/NINE/DIR/39: BRIS/DIR/
     24: 33: 40.

PYE, *William*
          Newcastle-under-Lyme
   (& Victualler, 36).
   Add: Penkhull St (22): 61 Iron-
     market (36).
   Refs: NEW/LYME/DIR/22: 36.

PYE, *S.*   Bristol
   Add: 2 Little John St.
   Refs: BRIS/DIR/36.

QUINTON, *James*   Norwich
QUINTON, *James & William*
                (39 PIG)
QUINTON, *William & George*
                (39 ROB)
   Add: London Lane (22): Pottergate
     St (36).
   Refs: NORF/DIR/36: PIG/HC/39 (&
     William): ROB/NINE/DIR/39 (W.&
     G.): ROB/SIX/DIR/39 (W. & G.):
     Munby Coll: Label: "Q,BB,LL,
     N": $\frac{1}{2}$ m.g., 1822: JA/4184.

RADCLIFFE, *W. & T.*
               Birmingham
   (Engravers, Printers &).
   Add: Edmund St.
   Refs: BIRM/DIR/21.

RAINES, *Thomas*   Bath
   Add: 3 Lower Borough Walls (09):
     4 James St (19): 7 Kingston
     Bldgs (24): No. 19 (29): Res:
     17 York St (30): ditto & 9
     Kingston Bldgs (33).
   Refs: BATH/DIR/09: 19: 24: 26: 29:
     33: 37: PIG/LPCD/22: PIG/NCD/30.

RALPH, *Barnaby*   Birmingham
RALPH, *Elizabeth*
   (85, P R, B B & Victualler).
   Add: 10 Bell St: New Meeting
     St (91).
   Refs: BIRM/DIR/81: 85: 87: 91
     (Victualler only).

RANSOM, *William*   Hastings
   (P R &).
   Add: 60 George St.
   Refs: ROB/HOMCO/DIR/39.

RATCLIFFE, *James*   Haslingden
   Refs: BRI/DIR/V/98.   (Lancs.)

RATCLIFFE, *William*   Faversham
   (Etc).   (Kent)
   Add: Court St.
   Refs: ROB/HOMCO/DIR/39.
   O.C. Herodotus. 2 vol. Oxford
     24. f.c.g. (?35/40). (Knatchbull
     Book Plate).

RAWLINGS, *John*   Harwich
   (Etc).
   Add: Market St.
   Refs: PIG/LPCD/32: 34: PIG/HC/39:
     ROB/HOMCO/DIR/39.

RAWLINGS, *Thomas*   Andover
   (P R, B B & S T).
   Refs: HANTS/DIR/84.

RAWSON & RODFORD   Hull
   (See also Rodford)
   (B S, S T &).
   Add: Lowgate.
   Refs: HULL/DIR/03.

RAYNER, *John*   Hull
   Add: 15 Lowgate (34): 17 (37).
   Refs: PIG/SEVEN/DIR/34: PIG/CDS/
     37: HULL/DIR/38: PIG/MND/42.

REA, *John*   Northampton
   Add: Bridge St.
   Refs: PIG/NCD/30.

READ, *William*   Exeter
   (Law Stationer &).
   Add: North St (27): Paris St (28):
     144 Fore St Hill (33): Heavitree
     (35).
   Refs: EX/P/J: 27: 33: EX/DIR/28:
     31: 35.

READHEAD, *John Simpson*
   Add: 11 New Sq.   Cambridge
   Refs: PIG/HC/39.

REDFERN, *George*   Shrewsbury
   Refs: JBO/AE.

REES, *J.*   Bristol
   E D: 28?
   Add: 53 Centre of Wine St.
   Refs: Munby Coll: Label "JR,
     BS, S, B. Pat. Medicine Ware-
     house, 53 C.W.S., B". Calf
     gilt, 1828.

REID, *Andrew*   Berwick-on-Tweed
    Add: Bridge St.
    Refs: PIG/CDS/37.

REID, *F. W. B.*   Bristol
    Add: 43 Park St.
    Refs: ROB/NINE/DIR/39.

REID, *James*   Bristol
    (B S, S T &).
    Add: 7 Corn St.
    Refs: Munby Coll: engraved label
    "J.R, BS, ST & B, 7 C.S, B."
    on 1824 work.

RENNIE, *E.*
    Refs: Gilhofer Cat. June 20/21,
    1933, No. 203. Handsome mor.
    binding on Bible, with ticket,
    and ded. to Alexander I. ca. 1813.

RESTON, *James*   Liverpool
    Add: 42 St. Thomas Buildings.
    Refs: LIV/DIR/10: (Had ceased to
    list himself as a bookbinder by
    1813).

REWCASTLE, *James*
        Newcastle-upon-Tyne
    (Etc).
    Add: 103 Side.
    Refs: NEW/DIR/38.

REYNARD, *John*   Leeds
    Add: Lambert's Yard, 163 Brig-
    gate: also 5 Lambert's Court in
    1830, possibly the same address.
    Refs: PIG/NCD/28: PIG/NAT/DIR/28/
    29: YORK/DIR/30: PIG/SEVEN/DIR/
    34: PIG/CDS/37: WHI/WRY/37/6:
    LEEDS/DIR/34: 39: PIG/MND/42.

REYNOLDS, *George*   Chatham
    (Etc).
    E D: 39.
    Add: Military Road.
    Refs: ROB/HOMCO/DIR/39.

REYNOLDS, *J.*   Redruth
    Refs: AE/HEAL/LAB.   (Cornwall)

REYNOLDS, *Samuel*   Liverpool
    Add: 6 Pool Lane (05): 9 Drury
    Lane (07).
    Refs: LIV/DIR/05: 07.

RICHARDS, *Thomas*   Liverpool
    Add: 72 Brownlow Hill (25): 19
    Russell St (29).
    Refs: PIG/NCD/28: LIV/DIR/25: 29:
    32.

RICHARDSON   King's Lynn
    E D: 90?
    Refs: Hob/Abb. App. XI. p. 194:
    JA/2392.

RICHARDSON, *Bezaleel*
  E D: 22.   Peterborough
  Add: Market Place.
  Refs: PIG/LPCD/22: PIG/NCD/30.

RICHARDSON, *Henry Samuel*
                    Greenwich
  Add: Stockwell St.
  Refs: PIG/HC/39.

RICHARDSON, *John*   Bristol
  (S T &).
  Add: 6 Clare St.
  Refs: BRIS/DIR/03: 06: 09: 21 (John
    & William: etc): ROB/NINE/DIR/
    39.

RICHARDSON, *M. A.*
  (Etc.).   Newcastle-upon-Tyne
  Add: 101 Pilgrim St.
  Refs: NEW/DIR/38.

RICHARDSON, *Robert*
                Berwick-on-Tweed
  Add: Church St.
  Refs: BERW/DIR/06: PIG/SIN/20.

RICHARDSON, *W.*   Bristol
  (See *John* above).
  E D: ?
  Add: 6 Clare St.
  Refs: Heber's Poems. 1st Ed. seen
    at Seligman.

RICHARDSON & HANDFORD
  (P R &).   Derby
  Add: Market Place.
  Refs: DERBY/DIR/23/4.

RICHER, *Richard*   Norwich
RICHER, *Nicholas*
  Add: 39 London Lane (83): Broad
    St (91. N.).
  Refs: NORW/DIR/83: BRI/DIR/91.

RICKARD, *Thomas*   Burnley
  (Bookseller &).
  Add: 6 Mill St (24): Blucher St
    (28).
  Refs: LANC/DIR/24: PIG/NAT/DIR/
    28/9.

RIDER, *Nicholas*   Norwich
  Add: 6 St. Giles', Broad St.
  Refs: NORW/DIR/02.

RIDGE, *S. & I.*   Newark
  E D: 11?   (Notts.)
  Refs: O.C. f.c.g. on Shakespeare's
    Works, 1811. Ticket. "S. & I.
    Ridge/BB/& Printers/Newark."

RIDGE, *S.*   Grantham
  E D: 80? L D: 34?
  Refs: Sch. S. de R. 59. Bound for
    Syston Park. V. & A. Museum,
    Sermonetta Rer. Gest. Milan.
    Zarotti, 1486, f.m.g. 87. B.
    An. 85/244. (Label). LAB/JONES.

RIDGE, *George* (25)   Sheffield

RIDGE & JACKSON (37)

RIDGE, *George* (42)
Add: 3 King St.
Refs: SHEFF/DIR/25: PIG/SEVEN/DIR/
34: PIG/CDS/37: PIG/MND/42
(George).

RIGDEN, *Thomas*   Dover
Add: 66 Snargate St.
Refs: PIG/HC/39: Munby Coll:
Label "B by TR, BS, S & P,D"
$\frac{1}{2}$ calf gilt, 29.

RILEY, *J. H.*   Sudbury (Suffolk)
Refs: BRI/DIR/91.

RIPLEY, *James*   York
Add: College St (22): Garden
Place (34).
Refs: YORK/DIR/22: PIG/LPCD/22:
PIG/NCD/28:   PIG/SEVEN/DIR/34:
PIG/NAT/DIR/28/29.

RIPPON, *John*   Sidmouth
(Etc).
Refs: SID/DIR/36.

RIVIERE, *Robert*   Bath
(Bookseller &).
Add: 24 Union St.
Refs: BATH/DIR/37: 41.

ROACH, *John*   Plymouth
Refs: BRI/DIR/91.

ROALFE, (or ROULFE), *William*
(& S T).   Canterbury
Add: Mercery Lane (23): 54 St.
Peter's St (26): 77 Northgate St
(32) as WM. *TAYLOR* R.
Refs: PIG/LPCD/23:   PIG/LPD/26/7:
PIG/LPCD/32:   34:   PIG/HC/39:
ROB/HOMCO/DIR/39:   LAB/JONES
(3): KENT/DIR/38 (W.T.R. &
Librarian).

ROBBINS & WHEELER
(B S &).   Winchester
Add: College St.
Refs: ROB/HOMCO/DIR/39.

ROBERT, *James*   Bristol
(& B S).
Add: Newfoundland St.
Refs: PIG/NCD/24.

ROBERTS   Helston (Cornwall)
E D: 19?
Refs: Hob/Abb. App. XI. 194:
Sotheby Cat. 22.5.50. No. 80:
P. Ticket. 20. Munby Coll:
Label "R, BB, H" Diced Russia
1819.

ROBERTS, *David*   Bangor
Add: Castle St.   (N. Wales)
Refs: PIG/NCD/28.

ROBERTS, *Edward*   Carnarvon
Add: Pool St.
Refs: PIG/NCD/28: PIG/NAT/DIR/28/
9.

ROBERTS, *Henry*　　　Holyhead
　Add: Stanley St.
　Refs: PIG/MID/DIR/35.

ROBERTS, *John*　　　Truro
　Add: St. Clements St.
　Refs: PIG/NCD/30.

ROBERTS, *Isaac*　　　Bristol
　Add: 54 Broad St (27): 1 Taylor's
　　Ct, Broad St (30).
　Refs: PIG/NCD/30: BRIS/DIR/27: 30:
　33.

ROBERTS, *I.*　　　Chesterfield
　(& Bookseller).
　E D: 40?
　Refs: O.C. W. H. G. Kingston,
　　Circassian Chief, Vol. I, 43, ½
　　c.g. Label reads "Bound by/
　　I. Roberts/Bookseller/Chester-
　　field". Similar label on 3 vols.
　　dated 1840, seen Aug., 51.

ROBERTS, *William*　　　Carnarvon
　Add: Pool St.
　Refs: PIG/MID/DIR/35.

ROBERTSON, *George*
　　　　Newcastle-upon-Tyne
　Add: 27 Pilgrim St.
　Refs: DUR/DIR/27: PIG/NCD/28:
　PIG/NAT/DIR/24: 28/29.

ROBERTSON, *Henry*　　　?
　E D: 06.
　Refs: Name signed in full with date
　　on edge of inside border (side) of
　　each vol. of 10 vol. edition of
　　Shakespeare's Works with Fuseli
　　Illns. of same date. V. handsome
　　dark blue mor. bdg. with rich
　　gilding on back, sides and deep
　　inside borders, cream silk end
　　papers. Name may be that of
　　owner, and not of the binder.

ROBERTSON, *James*　　Canterbury
　Add: 2 St. George's Place (23):
　　Bridge St (32).
　Refs: PIG/LPCD/23: PIG/LPD/26/7:
　PIG/LPCD/32: 34: LAB/JONES.

ROBINSON　　　　Liverpool
　(& pocket-book maker).
　Add: 19 Lumber St.
　Refs: LIV/DIR/96.

ROBINSON, *Edward Briggs*
　　　　　　Nottingham
　Add: Long Row.
　Refs: PIG/NCD/28: PIG/NAT/DIR/28
　/29: NOTT/DIR/40.

ROBINSON, *Francis, Jun.*
　　　　　　Manchester
　Add: 109 Piccadilly.
　Refs: PIG/CDS/37: MAN/DIR/38.

ROBINSON, *George H.*
　Add: 30 Park St.　　Leamington
　Refs: PIG/MND/42.

ROBINSON, *George & Joseph*
Add: 57 Castle St.   Liverpool
Refs: PIG/SEVEN/DIR/34: PIG/CDS/37.

ROBINSON, *John*
                        Bury-St.-Edmunds
Add: 7 Traverse
Refs: PIG/NCD/30.

ROBINSON, *John*   Whitehaven
(& P R).   (Cumberland)
Add: 61 Lowther St.
Refs: CUMWES/DIR/29: PIG/NAT/
DIR/28/9: AE/COLL/LAB (?"S").

ROBINSON, *Joseph*   Liverpool
Add: 47 Lumber St, Tythebarn St
(00): 15 Covent Garden (05):
10 Richmond Row (13): 30
London Rd & 35 Sweeting St
(shop) (21).
Refs: LIV/DIR/00: 05: 13: 16: 18:
21.

ROBINSON, *Robert*   Manchester
Add: 7 St. Ann's Place.
Refs: PIG/SEVEN/DIR/34: PIG/CDS/37.

ROBINSON, *William*   Liverpool
Add: 34 John St (90): No. 26 (91).
Refs: LIV/DIR/90. (G. & W.):
BRI/DIR/91.

ROBINSON, SON &
HOLDSWORTH (18)   Leeds

ROBINSON & CO. (22)

ROBINSON, *Mary*
(B S, S T &) (34)
Add 14 Commercial St (22): No.
18 (34).
Refs: YORK/DIR/22: PIG/LPCD/22:
LEEDS/DIR/34.

ROBINSON & ELLIS   Manchester
(Bookseller &).
Add: 7 St. Ann's Place.
Refs: PIG/SIN/20.

ROCKLIFF & ELLIS   Liverpool
E D: 35?
Add: 50 Castle St.
Refs: Munby Coll: Label "R & E,
P, BB & ST, 50 CS, L": Calf
gilt 1835.

RODD, *Thomas*   Exeter
Add: 23 Holloway St.
Refs: PIG/NCD/30: E.P.J/27: 28: 30:
33: EX/DIR/31.

RODFORD, *John*   Hull
(Etc). (See Rawson & Rodford).
Add: 54 Lowergate.
Refs: HULL/DIR/10: 17: 22: O.C.
Elaborately tooled maroon mor.
gilt bdg. on MS Shorthand
Prayerbook dated 1824. Plainish
red mor. gilt binding on 4 vol.
Don Quixote, dated 1801, seen
at Francis Edwards, Sept. 1952.
It has an 1806 ded. and the style
is of that period, so Rodford may
have been already binding

between 1801 and 06. Both bindings have circular light yellow tickets "R/B/H".

RODWELL, J.   Oxford
  Add: St. Clement's (17): St. Mary's (23).
  Refs: PIG/LPCD/23. O.C. Scott's Border Antiquities, 2 vol. 14/17. f. russia g. ticket.

ROE, *Henry*   Portsea (Hants.)
  (P R &).
  Add: North St.
  Refs: ROB/HOMCO/DIR/39.

ROGERS & CLARKE
  E D: 20?   Newmarket
  Refs: AE/COLL/LAB.

ROOK, H. J.   Faversham
  E D: ?
  Refs: LAB/JONES/("Bound by").

ROOKE, *Edward*   Wigton
  (Etc).   (Cumberland)
  Add: Market Place.
  Refs: CUMWES/DIR/29: PIG/NAT/DIR/ 28/9.

ROPER, C.   Leicester
  Add: Swine Market.
  Refs: PIG/NPCD/22.

ROSE, *Jacob*   Manchester
  Add: 16 New Market Buildings.
  Refs: LANC/DIR/25: PIG/NCD/28.

ROTHENBURG, *Daniel* Mortlake
  Add: East Sheen Lane.
  Refs: PIG/HC/39.

ROTHERA, *John*   Nottingham
  Add: Parliament St (18): Clare St (32).
  Refs: PIG/18/20: PIG/LPCD/22: NOTT/DIR/18: 25: 34: PIG/NCD/28: PIG/NAT/DIR/28/29: NOTTSH/DIR/ 32: PIG/MID/DIR/35: NOTT/DIR/40: PIG/MND/42.

ROTHERY, *William*   Lancaster
  Add: St. Mary's, Friarage.
  Refs: PIG/LPCD/22.

ROTHERY, *William*   Liverpool
  Add: 48 Lord St Chambers (28): 55 Cable St (32): 15 Dale St (34): 14 Button St (37).
  Refs: PIG/NCD/28: LIV/DIR/29: 32: 34: PIG/SEVEN/DIR/34: PIG/CDS/37.

ROWDON, *James*   Newport
  (Etc, etc).   (I. of W.)
  Add: High St.
  Refs: ROB/HOMCO/DIR/39.

ROWE, *Edward*   Penzance
  Add: Market Place.
  Refs: PIG/LPCD/23.

ROWE, *Samuel*   Plymouth
  (P R, B B, etc).
  Add: Market Place.
  Refs: PLY/DIR/14.

ROWE, *William*   Cullompton
(P R &).   (Devon)
Add: Fore St.
Refs: PIG/NCD/30.

RUDKIN, *John*   Colchester
Add: Crouch St.
Refs: ROB/HOMCO/DIR/39.

RUSHER, *John Golby*   Banbury
Add: Market Place: also at Bridge
St in 1837: Cornhill (39).
Refs: BAN/DIR/32 onwards: ROB/
SIX/DIR/39.

RUSSELL   Guildford
(Etc, etc).
Refs: Munby Coll: printed label
listing him as "R, BS, ST, PR,
B, Cutler, Silversmith, Jeweller,
etc". About 1825 on a sheep
binding.

RUSSELL, *Joseph*   Birmingham
Add: 6 Court, Moor St.
Refs: PIG/MID/DIR/35.

RUTTER, *John*   Wincanton
Add: High St.   (Somerset)
Refs: PIG/LPCD/22.

RYLEY, *William*   Wolverhampton
Add: Dudley St.
Refs: PIG/16/17.

SAFFERY, *James*   Canterbury
E D: ?
Refs: LAB/JONES.

SAILMAN, *Moss*   Portsea (Hants.)
Add: 31 St. James's St (23): 52
Hanover St (30).
Refs: PIG/LPCD/23: PIG/NCD/30.

SALTER & ATKINSON   Oxford
Add: Carter's Passage, High St.
Refs: OXF/DIR/35.

SA(U)NDERS, *John*   Oxford
Add: High St (23): Amsterdam
Ct, High St (30): Bear Lane (39).
Refs: PIG/LPCD/23: PIG/NCD/30:
ROB/SIX/DIR/39.

SANDERSON, *Thomas*
            Newcastle-upon-Tyne
SANDERSON, *F.*
Add: Thompson's Entry (37): 14
Cloath Market (38).
Refs: PIG/CDS/37: NEW/DIR/38:
WSM/KC/NEW illustrates a ticket.

SANFORD, *L.*   Bristol
Add: Upper Arcade.
Refs: BRIS/DIR/33.

SANKY, *Samuel Hurst*   Liverpool
(& Printer, 1832-4).
Add: 12 Concert St (16): 13 Dance
St (18): 16 Renshaw St (21):
No. 12 (24): No. 14 (28): Vine
Place, Lord St (32): 19 Cable St
(34: printer only). Residence:
1 Beresford St (32).

PLATE XI

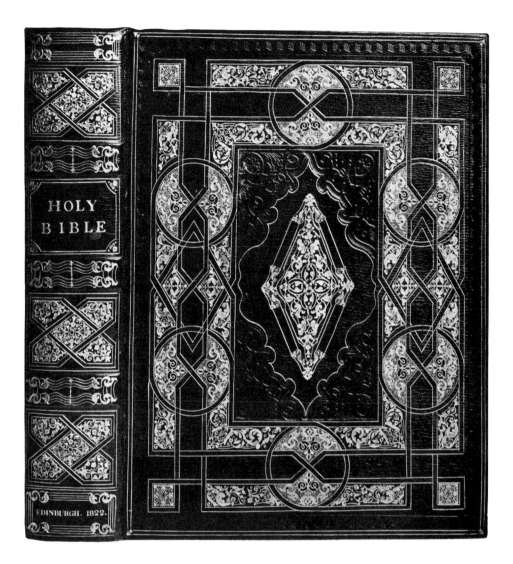

PLATE XII

Refs: LIV/DIR/18: 21: 25: 29: 32:
PIG/16/17: 18/20: YORK/DIR/22:
PIG/LPCD/22: LANC/DIR/24: PIG/
NCD/28: PIG/CDS/37.

SANTLEY, *William*   Liverpool
(& Stationer).
Add: 13 Gloucester St (13): 9
Church Alley, Church St (18):
No. 10 (21): 13 Berry St (25):
No. 14 (29): No. 17 (34): 13
North John St (37): No. 19 (40).
Refs: LIV/DIR/13: 16: 18: 21: 25:
29: 34: 40: PIG/18/20: PIG/LPCD/
22: PIG/SEVEN/DIR/34: PIG/CDS/
37: B. Franklin's Memoirs, 6 vol.
1818. f. russ. gt. with label, at
C. Richardson, Dec., 50.

SAPSFORD, *Thomas*   Cambridge
Add: St. John St.
Refs: PIG/HC/39: ROB/NINE/DIR/39:
ROB/SIX/DIR/39.

SAUNDERS, *John*   Bristol
Add: 5 Portwall Lane.
Refs: BRIS/IND/18.

SAUNDERS, *T. A.*   Salisbury
Add: Winchester St & Bedwyn St.
Refs: ROB/NINE/DIR/39.

SAWYER, *George*   Brighton
Add: 36 Middle St.
Refs: PIG/LPCD/32: 34: BRIG/DIR/39.

SAXTON, *William*   Sheffield
Add: 46 Campo Lane (21): No. 35
(22): 29 High St (34): No. 39
(37): No. 5 (42).
Refs: YORK/DIR/22: SHEFF/DIR/25:
PIG/SEVEN/DIR/34:   PIG/CDS/37:
PIG/MND/42.

SCARRAT, *John*   Liverpool
Add: 5 Cook St, Castle St (87).
Refs: LIV/DIR/87: 90 (G. & W.):
96: 00.

SCAUM, *George*   Beverley
(Etc.).   (Yorks.)
Add: North Bar St within.
Refs: PIG/NAT/DIR/28/29.

SCHOFIELD, *Charles*   Glossop
(B S, P R, S T &).
Add: Howard's Town.
Refs: PIG/MND/42.

SCHOFIELD, SUTCLIFFE   Leeds
(& Law Stationer).
Add: 4 Green's Ct, 66 Briggate.
Refs: PIG/NCD/28: PIG/NAT/DIR/28/
29.

SCHOLFIELD, *Samuel*   Manchester
Add: Coldhouse St.
Refs: MAN/DIR/88.

S(C)HRIMPTON, *John*   Oxford
  Add: Pembroke St (23): St. Ebbs
    (30): Church St, St. Ebbs Lane
    (39).
  Refs: PIG/LPCD/23: PIG/NCD/30:
    OXF/DIR/35: ROB/SIX/DIR/39.

SCRIMPTON, *Thomas*   Oxford
  Add: 13 St. Aldates St.
  Refs: ROB/SIX/DIR/39.

SCONCE, *Robert G.*   King's Lynn
  Add: 19 Union St.
  Refs: NORF/DIR/36.

SCOTT, *Benjamin*   Carlisle
  (See Scott, Hudson).
  Add: English St.
  Refs: CUMWES/DIR/29: O.C.
    Cottin: Elizabeth: London 14:
    Shell Etruscan calf binding:
    T. Campbell: Gertrude of Wyo-
    ming, 1819, f.m.g. ticket. See
    also BM. 1465. C. 1.

SCOTT, *Daniel*   Burslem
  Add: Church St.
  Refs: PIG/LPCD/22: NEW/LYME/DIR/
    22.

SCOTT, *Hudson*   Carlisle
  (?successor of B. Scott).
  (P R, S T &).
  Add: 11 English St.
  Refs: PIG/CDS/37: CARL/DIR/37: 40.

SCREETON, *William*   Hull
  Add: 21 St. Anne's Place, Sykes St.
  Refs: HULL/DIR/39.

SCROGGIE, *William*   Woolwich
  Add: Hare St.
  Refs: PIG/LPCD/23.

SEACOMBE, *John*   Chester
  (& B S, S T).
  Add: 25 Bridge St Row (28).
  Refs: PIG/LPCD/28: PIG/NAT/DIR/28/
    9: CHEST/DIR/40. O.C.
    Test. Goschen. 03/4. 2 vol. f.m.g.,
    silk end papers. (Label).

SECKERSON, *Jas.*   Tunstall
  Add: Market Place.
  Refs: PIG/MND/42.

SEELEY, *John*   Buckingham
  (Etc).
  Refs: HOLD/11.

SELKIRK, *William*   Birmingham
  (Bookbinders' tools).
  Add: 59 Constitution Hill (35):
    Loveday St (37).
  Refs: PIG/MID/DIR/35: PIG/CDS/37.

SELLICK, *Benjamin*   Bristol
  (& S T).
  Add: St. James's Back.
  Refs: BRIS/DIR/99: 01: 03.

SETH, *William*
Newcastle-upon-Tyne
(& Copper Plate Printer).
Add: Quay Side (87): Burnthouse
Entry side (90): St. Nicholas'
Churchyard (91).
Refs: NEW/DIR/87: 90: BRI/DIR/91.

SEVER, *Matthew John*   Beverley
(Yorks.)
(Engraver, P R, B B & B B tool-
cutter).
Add: Butcher Row.
Refs: PIG/SEVEN/DIR/34.

SEWELL, *Thomas*   Appleby
Add: Cloisters.   (Westmorland)
Refs: CUMWES/DIR/29.

SHALDERS, *John*   Norwich,
Gt. Yarmouth & Holt
Add: Regent St (22): Bethel St
(39).
Refs: PIG/LPCD/22: PIG/HC/39:
LAB/JONES (Holt): Two bindings
in the Holkham Collection have
Gt. Yarmouth tickets "Bd by/
S/Y" & BS & ST in the surround.
See article by H. M. Nixon in
B.M. Quarterly, 1952.

SHARP, *William Elsey*   Newark
Add: Farndon Rd.
Refs: PIG/MID/DIR/35.

SHARP(E), *John*   Warwick
E D: 69? L D: 28?
Refs: Name noted on a Bible dated
1760, seen at Joseph's in 1948.
AE/COLL/LAB (28).

SHARPE   Warwick
Refs: Oval label "S, BB, W" on
purple calf binding, ca. 1798 in
Munby/Coll.

SHARROCK, *W. B.*   Curry Rivel
(P R &).   (Somerset)
Refs: SOM/DIR/40.

SHAVE, *John*   Ipswich
Refs: DPB/1724/75.

SHAW, *James* Penrith (Cumberland)
Add: Nether End.
Refs: CUMWES/DIR/29.

SHAW, *John*   Liverpool
Add: 11 Temple St, St. Catherine's.
Refs: LIV/DIR/00.

SHAW, *Joseph*   Nottingham
Add: Carlton St.
Refs: NOTT/DIR/40.

SHAW, *William*   Huddersfield
(& S T).
Add: Beast Market.
Refs: PIG/16/17.

SHEARDOWN, *W.*   Doncaster

SHEARDOWN, *& Son*
  Refs: Munby Coll: Two labels,
  both "Bound by" on works ca.
  1800 & 1820.

SHELDON, *John*   Birmingham
  Add: 15 Moor St.
  Refs: BIRM/DIR/33: 35: 39: PIG/
  MID/DIR/35: PIG/CDS/37: PIG/
  MND/42.

SHEPPARD, *Abraham*   Glossop
  (S T &).   (Derbyshire)
  Refs: COUNT/DER 29.

SHEPHERD, *John*   Salford
  Add: 13 York St.
  Refs: MAN/DIR/08.

SHERRIFF, *H. T.*   Gainsborough
  (& S T).
  Add: Hickman St.
  Refs: PIG/MID/DIR/35.

SHERRINGTON, *William*   Preston
  Add: Midsprit Wend (21): Main-
  sprit Wend (25).
  Refs: PREST/DIR/21: LANC/DIR/25:
  PIG/NCD/28: PIG/NAT/DIR/28/9:
  PIG/SEVEN/DIR/34.

SHIELDS, *J.*   Hetton-le-Hole
                          (Durham)
  (B S & Circulating Library).
  E D: 28?

Refs: Munby reports yellow engraved ticket on ½ calf binding
on 1828 work.

SHIERS (or SHIRES), *Joseph*   Leeds
  Add: St. Ann's St (17): 2 Coach
  Lane (22): 3 Charles St (28):
  10 St. Peter's St (34).
  Refs: LEEDS/DIR/17: 26: 34: PIG/
  18/20: YORK/DIR/22: 30: PIG/
  LPCD/22: PIG/SEVEN/DIR/34: PIG/
  CDS/37: WHI/WRY/37/38.

SHIPP, *John*   Blandford
  (Stamp Office, Printer, Stationer,
  Bookseller &).
  Refs: Green oval ticket noted on
  Lodge's Portraits 35. Binding
  probably 10 years later. AE/COLL/
  LAB (13): Another ticket on a 06
  vol. seen at Fletcher's (Nov., 51).
  Munby Yellow Label "Books
  Bound/on the most/reasonable
  terms/by/John Shipp. B". ?ca.
  00/10.

SHIRES, *Joseph*   Leeds
  (See Shiers).

SHORT, *John*   Guernsey
  (& B S).   (St. Peter Port)
  Add: 20 States Arcade.
  Refs: ROB/NINE/DIR/39: GUER/DIR/
  40.

SHUTE, *John* Liverpool
Add: 3 Redcross St (28): 71 Hill
St, Harrington (34).
Refs: PIG/NCD/28: LIV/DIR/29: 32:
34.

SHUTTLEWORTH, *Samuel*
Add: Almshouse Lane. Wakefield
Refs: PIG/MND/42.

SILBURN & *Co.* Manchester
(& S T, P R).
Add: 24 Abraham's Court.
Refs: MAN/DIR/28.

SIMCOCK, *Esther* Liverpool
(& Stationer in 1825).
Add: 36 Highfield St.
Refs: YORK/DIR/22: PIG/LPCD/22:
LIV/DIR/21 - 25: LANC/DIR/24.

SIMCOCK, *Robert* Liverpool
(& S T in 1816).
Add: 37 Byrom St (13): 34 Moor-
fields (18).
Refs: LIV/DIR/13: 16: 18: PIG/18/20.

SIMM'S LIBRARY Bath
Add: 12 George St. (There was a
Samuel Simms working as BS,
ST, PR, etc, at North Parade as
early as 1801. See BATH/DIR/01).
Refs: Munby Coll: pink engraved
label "Bd at SL, 12 G.S., Bath"
on 1822 work.

SIMPSON, *George* Nottingham
Add: 50 Parliament St.
Refs: PIG/MID/DIR/35.

SIMPSON, *John* Leeds
(& lithographic printer).
Add: 29 Land's Lane (18): top of
Wood St (28).
Refs: PIG/18/20: PIG/NCD/28:
PIG/NAT/DIR/28/29.

SIMPSON, *Thomas*
(Etc). Newcastle-upon-Tyne
Add: 2 Side.
Refs: NEW/DIR/38.

SIMPSON, *Thomas* Wolverhampton
Add: High Green (16): High St
(42).
Refs: PIG/16/17: PIG/MID/DIR/35:
PIG/MND/42.

SIMSON (Bookseller) Hertford
*SIMSON & GROOMBRIDGE
(Printers & Binders).
E D: ?
Add: *Market Place.
Refs: LAB/JONES (2).

SINCLAIR, *John* Maidenhead
Add: High St.
Refs: PIG/NCD/30: ROB/NINE/DIR/
39: ROB/HOMCO/DIR/39.

SLATER, *John* (22) Sheffield

SLATER, *S. & E.* (25)
Add: 98 Fargate.
Refs: YORK/DIR/22: SHEFF/DIR/25.

SLATER, *Thomas*   Darlaston
(& schoolmaster, etc).   (Staffs.)
Refs: STAFF/DIR/18.

SLEE, *John*   Carlisle
(& Ruler).
Add: Lowther St (28): 2 East
    Tower St (34).
Refs: PIG/NCD/28: PIG/NAT/DIR/28/
    29: CUMWES/DIR/29: PIG/SEVEN/
    DIR/34: CARL/DIR/37: 40.

SLOCOMBE & SIMMS   Leeds
Add: 18 Commercial St.
Refs: PIG/MND/42.

SMART, *George*   Liverpool
(B S, S T &).
Add: 18 Pool Lane (90): 54 Paradise
    St: 2 Church Alley (18).
Refs: LIV/DIR/90(W): 94: 18: 21.

SMART, *Joseph*   Wolverhampton
Add: High St.
Refs: PIG/16/17.

SMART, *Thomas*   Bristol
Add: Orange St (18): 16 Somerset
    St, Cathay (36).
Refs: BRIS/IND/18: BRIS/DIR/36: 40.

SMART, *W.*   Southampton
(Etc, etc).
E D: 20?
Add: 154 High St.
Refs: ROB/HOMCO/DIR/39: Label in
    O.C. off Butler's Hudibras. 2
    vol. 06. Binding about 1820.
    "Bound by, etc". Similar label
    in pale yellow LAB/KNA.

SMART, *William*   Stockport
Add: Carr Brook.
Refs: PIG/16/17.

SMITH, *Abraham*   Royston (Herts.)
Add: Kneesworth St.
Refs: ROB/HOMCO/DIR/39.

SMITH, *Edmund*   Bath
Add: 1 North Parade.
Refs: BATH/DIR/12: 19: 24: 26: 29:
    33: PIG/LPCD/22: PIG/NCD/30:
    LAB/JONES.

SMITH, *F.*   Bristol
Add: 11 Welsh Back.
Refs: BRIS/DIR/30.

SMITH, *Gains*   Bath
Add: 30 Southgate St.
Refs: BATH/DIR/41.

SMITH, *George*   Bungay (Suffolk)
Add: Earsham St.
Refs: ROB/NINE/DIR/39: ROB/SIX/
    DIR/39.

SMITH, *George*   Enfield (Middlesex)
   Refs: PIG/LPCD/32: 34.

SMITH, *George Milward*
   Add: 19 Ann St.   Birmingham
   Refs: PIG/CDS/37.

SMITH, *Henry*   Cirencester
   Add: Market Place.
   Refs: ROB/NINE/DIR/39.

SMITH, *James*   Bicester
   Add: Market End.
   Refs: ROB/SIX/DIR/39.

SMITH, *James*   Derby
   Add: Summer Hill.
   Refs: PIG/MND/42.

SMITH, *James*   Manchester
   Add: 51 Piccadilly.
   Refs: MAN/DIR/24:   PIG/NCD/24:
   PIG/CDS/25/26: PIG/NCD/28.

SMITH, *J.*   York
   Add: 20 Goodramgate.
   Refs: YORK/DIR/30.

SMITH, *J. R.*   Holbeach (Lincs.)
   (B S & B B).
   E D: 15?
   Refs: O.C. Ticket taken from a
   cont. ½ calf binding on book
   dated 1815. "JRS/BS/& B/H".

SMITH, *John*   Bristol
   (Papermaker, S T &).
   Add: Nicholas St.
   Refs: BRIS/DIR/09.

SMITH, *John*   Leeds
   (B S, B B & S T).
   Add: Briggate.
   Refs: LEEDS/DIR/00.

SMITH, *John*   Maidstone
   (Etc).
   Add: High St (23): 10 Week St
   (32).
   Refs: PIG/LPCD/23: PIG/LPCD/32:
   34: PIG/HC/39: Marks reported
   April 1951 a ticket on a cloth
   binding, ca. 1830/40.

SMITH, *John*   Manchester
   Add: Cheetham Cottage-town.
   Refs: MAN/DIR/13.

SMITH, *John*   Oxford
   Add: George St, St. Clements.
   Refs: PIG/NCD/30.

SMITH, *John*   Gt. Yarmouth
   Add: George St.   (Norfolk)
   Refs: ROB/NINE/DIR/39:   ROB/SIX/
   DIR/39.

SMITH, *Michael*   Birmingham
   Add: 2 St. Peter's Row, Broad St.
   Refs: PIG/CDS/37.

SMITH, *Robert*   Leeds
(Etc).
Add: Briggate.
Refs: LEEDS/DIR/00: 07: HOLD/11.

SMITH, *T.*   Dover
(Etc).
Add: High St.
Refs: ROB/HOMCO/DIR/39.

SMITH, *Thomas*   Exeter
Add: Little South Lane (27):
Southernhay Lane (28).
Refs: EX/P/J/27: EX/DIR/28.

SMITH, *Thomas*   Liverpool
Add: 43 Dunkenfield St (32):
No. 52 (34).
Refs: LIV/DIR/32: 34.

SMITH, *Thomas*   Louth (Lincs.)
Add: Market Place.
Refs: PIG/NCD/28: PIG/NAT/DIR/28/
29.

SMITH, *W.*   Ironbridge (Salop)
(& Paperhanger).
Refs: Sch. S. de R. IV. 46:
Hob/Abb/111, p. 156 where a
full account of his career is given.
O.C. T. Chambers: Discourses
Astronomy 17, g. c. Label "Sold
by W. Smith, Paperhanger, etc,
Iron Bridge, Salop".

SMITH, *William*   Bedford
(& Stationer).
Refs: BED/DIR/85.

SMITH, *William S.*   Bristol
Add: Hillgrove St.
Refs: BRIS/DIR/13: 15: 17.

SMITH, *William*   Bristol
(& marbled paper maker).
Add: 6 Terril St (13): 11 Charles St
(15): 41 College Green (24):
12 Denmark St (33): Nos. 8 &
41 (36).
Refs: BRIS/DIR/13: 21: 24: 27: 30:
33: 36: 40: BRIS/IND/18: PIG/
LPCD/22: PIG/NCD/30: ROB/NINE/
DIR/39: LAB/JONES.

SMITH, *William*
(P R &).   Newcastle-under-Lyme
Add: Ironmarket.
Refs: NEW/LYME/DIR/22.

SMITH, *William*   Gt. Yarmouth
Add: Howard St.   (Norfolk)
Refs: PIG/NCD/30:   PIG/HC/39:
ROB/NINE/DIR/39: ROB/SIX/DIR/39.

SMITHER, *William*   Chichester
(& Stationer).
Add: North St.
Refs: PIG/LPCD/34.

SMITHSON, *Richard*   Hull
Add: 30 Lowgate (34): 35 (35).
Refs: PIG/SEVEN/DIR/34: HULL/DIR/
35.

SNARE & *NEPHEW* (37)   Reading
SNARE, *J.* (39)
   (Etc).
   Add: 16 Minster St.
   Refs: READ/DIR/37: ROB/NINE/DIR/
   39: ROB/HOMCO/DIR/39.

SNOW, *Richard W.* Norton (Yorks.)
   Refs: PIG/NCD/28: PIG/NAT/DIR/28/
   29: PIG/SEVEN/DIR/34.

SNOWDEN, *Herbert Kennedy*
   Add: Scotch St.   Carlisle
   Refs: CUMWES/DIR/29.

SNOWDON, *James*   Durham
   (& B S).
   Add: Silver St.
   Refs: PIG/SEVEN/DIR/34.

SNOWDON, *William*
                  Newcastle-upon-Tyne
   (& Paper Ruler).
   Add: Groat Market (24): Todd's
   Ct, Groat Market (28).
   Refs: DUR/DIR/27: PIG/NCD/28:
   PIG/NAT/DIR/28/29: NEW/DIR/24:
   33: 38: PIG/CDS/37.

SOMAN & HOWES   Norwich
   Add: St. Andrew's Hill.
   Refs: NORF/DIR/36.

SOMERSCALE, *William Ewart*
   Add: 75 Briggate.   Leeds
   Refs: PIG/MND/42.

SOMERVILLE, *Jas.* (20)   Carlisle
SOMERVILLE, *Joseph* (29)
   Add: Peascod Lane (20): Green
   Market (29).
   Refs: PIG/SIN/20: CUMWES/DIR/29:
   LAB/JONES.

SOULBY, *J.*   Ulverston
   E D: 99?
   Refs: Hob/Abb. App. XI. p. 195.

SOUTHWARD, *Jackson*   Liverpool
   Add: 37 Cornwallis St, Duke St
   (37): No. 22 (40).
   Refs: PIG/CDS/37: LIV/DIR/40.

SOWLER, *T.*   Manchester
   (Propr. *Manchester Courier &
   Manchester Herald*, 1828).
   E D: 18? or 25?
   Add: All Nos. in St. Ann's Square.
   The Nos. include 4, 13, 15 & 22.
   Refs: MAN/DIR/28: 32: 38: PIG/
   SEVEN/DIR/34: PIG/CDS/37.   See
   AE/COLL/LAB. O.C. Common
   Prayer, dated 1816, but plates
   dated 1.1.18, full dark blue mor.
   gt., stippled gold ornaments on
   back and also on deep inside
   dentelles; green silk end-papers
   and gild gauffered edges. Ticket
   "Bd. by/T. S./15 St. A. S./M".
   Kirk White: Life & Remains:
   1825: st. gr. mor. g. Ticket "Bd.
   by/T. S./22 St. A. S./M". Dedication dated New York, Aug.
   1825, which seems to fix 1825 as

date for the No. 22 St. Ann's Sq. address.　See also Sotheran, 14.3.51, No. 18 & 24.7.51. No. 23.

SPARK, *Joseph*
　　　　　Newcastle-upon-Tyne
Add: 42 High Bridge, Groat Market (27): Park St, Gateshead (38).
Refs: DUR/DIR/27: PIG/NCD/28: PIG/NAT/DIR/28/29: NEW/DIR/38.

SPARK, *Robert*　　　　　Exeter
Add: Cathedral Yard.
Refs: PIG/LPCD/23.

SPARK, *Wm.*　　　　　Exeter
(& Librarian).
Add: Cathedral Yard.
Refs: EPJ/25: 27: EX/DIR/28: 31: 35: PIG/NCD/30: LAB/KNA.　Ca. 25.

SPENCE, *John*　　　　　Leeds
(Etc).
Add: Briggate.
Refs: LEEDS/DIR/07.

SPENCE & BURDEKIN　　　York
Add: Pavement.
Refs: PIG/18/20.

SPENCER, *Charles*
　　　　　Bury-St.-Edmunds
Add: 48 Churchgate St.
Refs: PIG/NCD/30: ROB/NINE/DIR/39: ROB/SIX/DIR/39.

SPENCER, *James*　　　Luddenden
Refs: PIG/SEVEN/DIR/34.　(Yorks.)

SPENCER, *John*　　　　Bradford
Add: Bolton Road.
Refs: WHI/WRY/37/8.

SPINK, *Henry*　　　　　Leeds
Add: 36 Briggate (22): No. 37 (25).
Refs: YORK/DIR/22: PIG/LPCD/22: W. Sabine, of Hollis, reports a calf binding on an 1825 work: also that there was a firm of Spink & Thackeray at Trinity Chambers, Boar Lane, at least as late as 1882.

SPONG　　　Biggleswade (Beds.)
E D: 36?
Refs: AE/COLL/LAB.

SPRANGE, *I.*　　Tunbridge Wells
E D: 98?
Refs: Hob/Abb. App. XI. p. 195.

SPREAT, *John*　　　　　Exeter
Add: 92 Sidwell St (33): New Market (35): Gandry St (39).
Refs: EX/DIR/35: EX/P/J/33: 36: 39: 40.

SPURWAY, *James*　　　　Honiton
(P R, B B & S T).
E D: 11?
Add: High St.

Refs: PIG/NCD/30: Soth/Cat/17/ 10/51. No. 741. Diced calf on Knight's Pomona Herefordiensis 11. Label calls him "Printer, Bookbinder & Stationer".

SQUIRE, *Joseph*   Liverpool
(P R &).
Add: Res: 13 Lorton St, Windsor: Shop: 13 N. John St.
Refs: LIV/DIR/34.

STABBACK, *John*   Exeter
Add: College (35): 8 South St (39).
Refs: EX/DIR/35: EX/P/J/36: 39: 40.

STACEY, *John*   Norwich
E D: 21?
Refs: Hob/Abb. App. XI. p. 194.

STAFFORD, *C.*   Bedford
E D: 25?
Add: St. Mary's.
Refs: Munby Coll: Label "B. by C. S/S.M/Bedford". Grained calf, ca. 1825.

STANLEY, *Robert*   Liverpool

STANLEY, *Anne* (32)
Add: 4 George Ct, Fontenoy St. (24, when he also describes himself as working ST.): 31 Sawney Pope St (28): No. 39 (32).
Refs: LANC/DIR/24: PIG/NCD/28: LIV/DIR/29: 32.

STAVELEY, *John*   Nottingham
Add: Smithy Row.
Refs: NOTT/DIR/40.

STEBBING, *J.*   Ipswich
Add: Upper Brook St.
Refs: BRI/DIR/91.

STEELE, *Samuel*   Shrewsbury
E D: 59?   L D: 17?
Refs: Hob/Abb. p. 194: JBO/AE.

STEPHENS, *William*   Chepstow
Add: Church St.   (Mon.)
Refs: PIG/MID/DIR/35.

STEPHENSON, *William*
(Etc.)   Newcastle-upon-Tyne
Add: 8 Bridge St, Gateshead.
Refs: NEW/DIR/38.

STEWART, *Samuel*   Norwich
Add: Prince's St.
Refs: NORF/DIR/36.

STEWARDSON, *W. H.*   Norwich
STEWARDSON, *George Nathaniel*
(39)
Add: Bedford St (36): Magdalene St (39 G. N.).
Refs: NORW/DIR/36: PIG/HC/39.

STEWART, *Robert*   Douglas
Add: Church St.   (I. of M.)
Refs: PIG/CDS/37: JEFF/IM/40.

STEWART, *Robert S.* Liverpool
(& Paper Ruler in 1825).
  Add: 6 Bakehouse Lane (21): 20
    Temple St (24).
  Refs: LIV/DIR/21: 25: LAN/DIR/24.

STEWART & MOLLOY
  Add: 31 Castle St. Liverpool
  Refs: PIG/SEVEN/DIR/34.

STEVENS, *John* Bruton
  Add: Coombe St. (Somerset)
  Refs: PIG/NCD/30.

STEVENS, *Joseph* Manchester
  E D: 24.
  Add: 119 Deansgate.
  Refs: PIG/NCD/24: MAN/DIR/24:
    PIG/CDS/25/6: LANC/DIR/25.

STEVENS, *William* Tunstall
  Add: High St.
  Refs: PIG/MND/42.

STEVENSON, *Thomas* Sheffield
  Add: 39 Westbar St (34): Hicks
    Lane (42).
  Refs: PIG/SEVEN/DIR/34: PIG/CDS/
    37: WHI/WRY/37/8: PIG/MND/42.

STOCK, *H.* Folkestone
(Bookseller, etc).
  E D: ?
  Add: High St.
  Refs: LAB/JONES ("Bound by").

STOCKBRIDGE, *W.* Chatham
  Add: Hammond Place.
  Refs: ROB/HOMCO/DIR/39.

STODDART, *Thomas* Beverley
(Etc).
  Add: Market Place (22): Dyer
    Lane (24).
  Refs: YORK/DIR/22: LINC/DIR/26:
    PIG/NAT/DIR/28/29.

STOKES, *Richard* Worcester
(Bookseller &).
  Add: New St (20): Sidbury (35).
  Refs: WOR/DIR/20: 37: 40: PIG/
    DIR/WORC/35.

STOKES, *William* Gloucester
  Add: College St.
  Refs: ROB/NINE/DIR/39.

STONE, *Richard Peach* Birmingham
(Etc, etc).
  Add: 5 Cherry St (28): 36 Bull St
    (35).
  Refs: PIG/NCD/28: PIG/NAT/DIR/28/
    29: BIRM/DIR/29: 33: WARW/DIR/
    30: PIG/MID/DIR/35: PIG/CDS/37.

STONE, *Robert* Exeter
  Add: Gandy St (27): 10 New
    Bridge St (35).
  Refs: EPJ/27: 30: EX/DIR/28: 31:
    35: PIG/NCD/30.

STONES, *John*   Manchester
(& S T).
  Add: 70 Portland St & 7 Market
    St (28): 7 Old Churchyard (32):
    1 Bailey's Ct, Market Place (34).
  Refs: PIG/NCD/28: MAN/DIR/28: 32:
    38: PIG/SEVEN/DIR/34.

STOREY, *James Everett* Manchester
  Add: 61 Market St.
  Refs: MAN/DIR/38.

STOREY, *Joseph*   Leeds
  Add: 122 Briggate.
  Refs: YORK/DIR/30.

STORR, *R.*   Grantham
(bound for Syston Park).
  E D: 20?
  Refs: Sch. S. de R. 60: Hobb/Abb.
    App. XI. p. 194. O.C. Dangeau,
    Memoirs, 25. 2 vol. Ex-libris Sir
    Charles E. Kent, 2nd Bart.,
    Poynton House, nr. Grantham.
    Phillips: Cultivated Vegetables,
    2 vol. 22: f.c.g. ticket.

STOTT, *R.*   Coventry
(Periodical B S &).
  Add: New Buildings.
  Refs: PIG/18/20.

STOW, *John*   Ipswich
  Add: Tower-ditches.
  Refs: HOLD/11.

STOW, *John*   Margate
  Add: St. John St.
  Refs: PIG/HC/39.

STRATFORD, *Thomas* Worcester
  Add: The Cross.
  Refs: WOR/DIR/40.

STRATTON, *John*
    Prince's Risborough (Bucks.)
  Refs: PIG/LPCD/23.

STRONG, *William*   Bristol
(B S &).
  Add: 26 Clare St.
  Refs: ROB/NINE/DIR/39:   O.C.
    Homer's Works (in Greek) 2 vol.
    01, f.m.g. ticket "Bound by, etc".
    Property of Rev. W. B. de
    Moleyns, Grandson of 1st Ld.
    Ventry.

STUART, *William*   Whitehaven
               (Cumberland)
  Add: 42 Market Place.
  Refs: CUMWES/DIR/29.

STUDDART, *Amos*   Liverpool
  Add: 36 Gt. Crosshall St. (22):
    No. 28 (28): No. 59 (40): Res:
    42 Trueman St. (29).
  Refs: PIG/LPCD/22: LANC/DIR/24:
    PIV/DIR/25: 29: 32: 34: 40: PIG/
    NCD/28: PIG/SEVEN/DIR/34: PIG/
    CDS/37.

SUFFIELD, *William*   Birmingham
(Etc).
  Add: Bull St. (21): 107 Park St. (25).
  Refs: BIRM/DIR/21: 25.

SUGG, *Charles*   Bath
  Add: 39 Walcot St. (00): Slippery
    Lane (26).
  Refs: BATH/DIR/00: 01: 05: 09: 26:
    29.

SUMMERS, *Ann*   Birmingham
  Add: 6 Worcester St.
  Refs: BIRM/DIR/85.

SUMNER, *James*   York

SUMNER, *James & Oliver* (?28)

SUMNER, *Oliver* (?30)

SUMNER, *George*

SUMNER, *William* (d. 7.8.62)
  Add: Various Nos. in Ogleforth:
    No. 5 (30): No. 23 (34).
  Refs: PIG/DIR/18/20: YORK/DIR/22:
    30: PIG/LPCD/22: PIG/NCD/28:
    PIG/NAT/DIR/28/29: PIG/SEVEN/
    DIR/34: WHI/WRY/37/8: WHI/
    ENR/40: PIG/MND/42.
  According to the York City
  Librarian, the firm was founded
  in 1810.
  Oliver seems to be the binder
  favourably referred to by Dibden
  in his Northern tour (I.pp.218-9)

which took place in 1837. W.
Sabine, of Hollis, N.Y., reports
a f.c.g. binding by him on a
1786 quarto.

George was probably his "meri-
torious hardworking son" referred to by Dibden. I saw in
1948 in Paris an excellent binding
by George S. with wide morocco
doublures. The last member of
the family, William, died 7.8.62,
aged 67. The business was then
continued by the Potter family
till about 1914. The machinery
etc, was then transferred to the
firm of Henry Trendall. J. G.
Trendall is still (Oct. 1952) in
business at the age of 81 at Little
Stonegate.

SUNDERLAND, *James*   Sheffield
(& P R).
  Add: New Church St (25):
    Devonshire St & Fleur de Lis
    Yd, Angel St (37).
  Refs: SHEFF/DIR/25: 28: PIG/NCD/28:
    PIG/NAT/DIR/28/29: PIG/CDS/37:
    WHI/WRY/37/8.

SURTEES, *John*   Liverpool
  Add: 7 Spitalfields (13): 7 Ben
    Jonson St (18): 49 Cable St (21):
    Clarendon Bldgs, Lord St (29):
    2 South John St (32). Residence:
    81 Gerard St (29).
  Refs: LIV/DIR/13: 18: 21: 29: 32:
    34.

SUTCLIFFE, *Thomas*   Burnley
  (S T &).
  Add: 32 St. James St.
  Refs: LANC/DIR/24.

SUTHERLAND, *Peter*   Hull
  Add: 30 Grimsby Lane (22): Dog
  Leap (28).
  Refs: YORK/DIR/22: PIG/NAT/DIR/
  28/29.

SUTHERLAND, *Peter*
  (Etc.).   Newcastle-upon-Tyne
  Add: Dog Leap Stairs (27): 18
  Low Bridge.
  Refs: DUR/DIR/27: PIG/NCD/28:
  NEW/DIR/38.

SUTTON, *George*   Liverpool

SUTTON, *John George*
  (John George seems to have taken
  over control about 1828).
  Add: 2 School Lane (13): 30
  Manesty Lane (18): 13 Paradise
  St (21): Stationers' Ct, Manesty
  Lane (34).
  Refs: LIV/DIR/13: 18: 21: 29: 32:
  34: 40: PIG/16/17: 18/20: YORK/
  DIR/22: PIG/LPCD/22: LANC/DIR/
  24: PIG/NCD/28: PIG/SEVEN/DIR/
  34: PIG/CDS/37.

SUTTON, *Richard*   Nottingham
  Add: Bridlesmith Gate.
  Refs: NOTT/DIR/40.

SUTTON, *Robert*   Liverpool
  Add: 29 Paradise St.
  Refs: LIV/DIR/40.

SWA(I)NE, *Henry Edward*   Brighton
  Add: 7 Gardener St (22): 18 West
  St (32).
  Refs: BRIG/DIR/22: 24: 32: 39:
  PIG/LPCD/32: 34: PIG/HC/39.

SWEET, *Edward & John*
  (P R &).   Trowbridge
  Add: Fore St (30).
  Refs: BRI/DIR/91: PIG/NCD/30 (John)

SWINBANK, *Henry*   York
  Add: Petergate.
  Refs: YORK/DIR/22.

SWINNERTON, *James* Macclesfield
  (doubtfully a bookbinder).
  Add: Market Place.
  Refs: MACC/DIR/25.

SYERS, *Alban*   Salford
  Decd. 1799.
  Refs: Notes & Queries: Vol. 153
  (1927) p. 453.

TALBOYS, *David Alfonso*   Oxford
  Add: High St.
  Refs: PIG/NCD/30.

TAMLYN, *W.*   Bristol
  Add: 19 Montague St.
  Refs: BRIS/DIR/36.

TAYLOR   Norwich
Add: Market Place.
Refs: NORW/DIR/11.

TAYLOR, *E. A. W.*   Bradford
(Bookseller, etc).
E D: 38?
Refs: O.C. Thomas Moore, Lalla
  Rookh, 38, (18th Ed.) 1838,
  f.m.g. ticket.

TAYLOR, *Edmund*   Bath
Add: 10 Abbey Churchyard.
Refs: BATH/DIR/33.

TAYLOR, *Edward*   Birmingham
Add: 10 Upper Priory.
Refs: PIG/MID/DIR/35: PIG/CDS/37.

TAYLOR, *Edwin*   Bath
Add: 9 Farmers Bldgs, Pulteney
  Road, (29): 1 Barton Ct (37):
  18 Beauford Sq (41).
Refs: BATH/DIR/29: 37: 41.

TAYLOR, *Elias*   Brighton
Add: 59 Western Road.
Refs: PIG/HC/39: JA/2474.

TAYLOR, *James*   Lowestoft
Add: High St.
Refs: PIG/HC/39: ROB/NINE/DIR/39:
  ROB/SIX/DIR/39.

TAYLOR, *James*   Yarmouth
                         (Norfolk)
Add: Excise Office Row.
Refs: PIG/NCD/30.

TAYLOR, *Philip*   Brighton
Add: 26 Little Castle Square.
Refs: BRIG/DIR/24: Mor. binding,
  elab. vine clusters on 1824 work,
  dedicated to Duke of Cumberland, seen at G. Fletchers, March,
  1951: AE/COLL/LAB.

TAYLOR, *Richard*   Bedale (Yorks.)
(Etc).
Refs: WHI/ENR/40.

TAYLOR, *Richard*   Liverpool
Add: 4 Langthorne Place: shop, 12
  Lower Castle St.
Refs: LIV/DIR/07.

TAYLOR, *Thomas*   Liverpool
(& Machine Ruler).
Add: 1 Paradise St.
Refs: PIG/18/20.

TAYLOR, *William*   Bath
E D: 33.
Add: 10 Abbey Churchyard (33):
  10 Trim St (37).
Refs: BATH/DIR/33: 37: 41: LAB/
  KNA "Bound by" ca. 20/30.

TAYLOR, *William*   Manchester
Add: 30 Red Bank.
Refs: MAN/DIR/04.

TAYLOR, *Wm.*   Nottingham
Add: Chapel Bar.
Refs: NOTT/DIR/40.

TEAL(E), *George*   Huddersfield
  Add: Castlegate.
  Refs: PIG/16/17: YORK/DIR/22: 30:
  PIG/NCD/28: PIG/SEVEN/DIR/34.

TEASDALE, *John*   York

TEASDALE, *Joseph* (42)
  Add: 1 Collier Gate (28): 11
  Copper Gate (37).
  Refs: PIG/NCD/28: PIG/NAT/DIR/28/
  29: YORK/DIR/30: PIG/SEVEN/DIR/
  34: WHI/WRY/37/8: WHI/ENR/40:
  PIG/MND/42: Munby Coll: Label
  'Bd by J. T., Collier G., Y".

TEPPER, *A.*   South Molton
  E D: 10?   Devon
  Refs: O.C. Beckford. Hunting. 10,
  ½ vellum: Munby Coll: 1811.

THIRLWAY, *Henry*   Ripon
  (Etc).
  Add: Market Place.
  Refs. PIG/NAT/DIR/28/29.

THISELTON, *J.*   Faversham
  (Etc).   (Kent)
  Add: Market Place.
  Refs: ROB/HOMCO/DIR/39.

THOMAS, *Charles*   Gloucester
  (& Book & Music Seller).
  Add: 31 Westgate St.
  Refs: ROB/NINE/DIR/39: LAB/JONES
  ("Bound by").

THOMAS, *Francis*   Truro
  Add: 14 Boscawen St.
  Refs: PIG/LPCD/23: PIG/NCD/30:
  AE/COLL/LAB.

THOMAS, *James* H(?artlepool) West
  (P R, B & B S).   (Durham)
  E D: 12?
  Refs: O.C. Rejected Addresses,
  12. Ticket: "Bound by/Jas.
  Thomas / Printer / Binder / Book-
  seller/&/Stationer/H. West".

THOMAS, *John*   Penzance
  Add: East St.
  Refs: PIG/LPCD/23.

THOMAS, *John*   Winchester
  (Etc).
  Add: 43 High St.
  Refs: ROB/HOMCO/DIR/39.

THOMAS, *Owen*   Haverfordwest
        (S. Wales)
  Add: Gloster Terrace (30): St.
  Martin's (35).
  Refs: PIG/NCD/30: PIG/MID/DIR/35.

THOMAS, *Samuel*   Plymouth

THOMAS, *Jenkin* (36)
  (Etc).
  Add: Whimple St. (22): 9 Corn-
  wall St (36).
  Refs: PLY/DIR/22: 23: 36.

THOMAS, *W.* Reading
(S T & P R 37: B B 42).
Refs: READ/DIR/37: 42 (Snare's).

THOMAS, *William* Weymouth
(Library &).
Add: Charlotte Row.
Refs: WEY/DIR/28.

THOMPSON, *C. & W.* Sheffield
Add: 61 Westbar (22): & 3 Market
Place (25).
Refs: YORK/DIR/22: SHEFF/DIR/25.

THOMPSON, *Ebenezer*
(Printer &). Waltham Abbey
Add: High Bridge St.
Refs: PIG/LPCD/34.

THOMPSON, *Edward* Preston
Add: 43 Lune St.
Refs: PIG/SEVEN/DIR/34.

THOMPSON, *G.* Wells
(Bookseller &).
E D: 11?
Refs: Ticket seen at Traylen's
(1951) on a book dated 1811.

THOMPSON, *George* Liverpool
(P R &).
Add: 22 Shawhill St (16): 37
Whitechapel (18): 3 Lawton St
(21).
Refs: LIV/DIR/16: 18: 21.

THOMPSON, *John*
Newcastle-upon-Tyne
Add: Entry above Queen's H,
Groatmarket (78): Groatmarket
(87).
Refs: NEW/DIR/78: 87: 90.

THOMPSON, *Matthew* Manchester
(?same as TOWNSON).
(Bookseller, Bookbinder &
Publisher).
E D: 72/3.
Add: St. Mary's Gate.
Refs: MAN/DIR/1772/3: DPB/1726/75.

THOMPSON, *Samuel* Newport
Refs: BRI/DIR/91. (I. of W.)

THOMPSON, *Samuel* Peckham
(B S &).
Add: Shard's Terrace.
Refs: PIG/LPCD/32.

THOMPSON, *William* Manchester
Add: Spinning-field (00): 41 Deans-
gate (04).
Refs: MAN/DIR/00: 04.

THOMSON, *David* Exeter
Add: Martin's Lane (32): 39 South
St (33).
Refs: EX/DIR/35: EX/P/J/32: 33: 36:
40: EX/DIR/35: JA/4047.

THOMSON Exeter
E D: 36?
Refs: ABB/CBS.

THOMSON, *James & Joseph*
                              Manchester
Add: 39 Market St (37): 15
  Parsonage (38).
Refs: PIG/CDS/37: MAN/DIR/38:
  Munby Coll: Label "JJT, BS &
  BB, 20 MS, M". Vellum gilt
  binding.

THOMSON, *John*   Manchester
Add: Barns St.
Refs: MAN/DIR/04.

THOMSON & WRIGHTSON
                              Birmingham
(See Wrightson).   (Etc, etc).
Add: 73 New St.
Refs: AE/COLL/LAB: BIRM/DIR/12.

THORBRAN, *John*   Bristol
(B S &).
Add: Corn St.
Refs: BRIS/DIR/85.

THORNTON, *Samuel*   Burnley
(& S T).   (Lancs.)
Refs: HOLD/11.

THORPE, *William*   Ely
Add: Waterside.
Refs: PIG/HC/39.

THROSBY   Leicester
E D: 90?
Refs: Hob/Abb. App. XI. p. 194.

THROWER, J.   Norwich
Add: St. Stephen's Alley.
Refs: NORF/DIR/36.

THURGAR, *Thomas*   Norwich
Add: 1 Bethell St.
Refs: NORW/DIR/02.

THURNAM, *Charles*   Carlisle
(Etc).
Add: 5 English St.
Refs: CUMWES/DIR/29: PIG/SEVEN/
  DIR/34: CARL/DIR/37: 40: PIG/
  CDS/37: LAB/JONES "Bound &
  Sold by".

TIBBUTT, *Richard*   Leicester
(Etc).
Add: High St (15): Haymarket (27).
Refs: LEIC/DIR/15: 27.

TICEHURST, *Francis William*
Refs: PIG/LPCD/34.   Battle

TICKELL, *William*   Douglas
(Etc).
Add: Parade St.
Refs: PIG/NCD/24.

TITE, *W.*   Coleshill
Refs: Pickering Cat. 343, No. 59,
  mentions a book dated 1814 as
  printed, published and bound in
  red morocco by W. T.

TODD, *Edward*   Birmingham

163

TODD, *Thomas* (18)
Add: 19 Stafford St. (81. No initial): 15 New Meeting St (00).
Refs: BIRM/MAGN/DIR/00: 08: BIRM/DIR/81: 00: 03: 08: 12: 15: 18: 21 (Thomas): PIG/16/17: 18/20 (T): HOLD/11 (E).

TODD, *J. & G.*   York
(Etc).
Add: Stonegate.
Refs: PIG/SEVEN/DIR/34.

TODD, *James & Sons*   Easingwold
(& P R).   (Yorks.)
Add: Long St.
Refs: PIG/NAT/DIR/28/29.

TOMKINSON, *Joseph*   Uttoxeter
(Etc).
Add: Market Place.
Refs: PIG/NAT/DIR/28/29.

TOMLINSON, *James*   Liverpool
(& Shopkeeper in 1805).
Add: 17 William St, Dale St (00): No. 13 (07): 21 John St (10): 23 William St (13): No. 24 (16): 5 Tempest Hey (18): 5 Harrington St (25): 13 Richmond Fair (32): 9 Duke's Place (34): 30 Castle St (37): No. 58 (40).
Refs: LIV/DIR/00: 03: 05: 07: 10: 13: 16: 18: 21: 25: 29: 32: 34: 40: PIG/LPCD/22: PIG/18/20: LANC/DIR/24: PIG/NCD/28: PIG/CDS/37.

TOMLINSON, *William*   Liverpool
Add: Moorfields: No. 33 (25): No. 29 (29): 32 (34).
Refs: LIV/DIR/21: 25: 29: 34: PIG/NCD/28.

TOMS, *John*   Chard
(Etc).
Add: Market Place.
Refs: SOM/DIR/40.

TOMSON, *Percy C.*   St. Neots
E D: ?
Refs: O.C.: Fairfax, Thos. Complete Sportsman, n.d. f.m.g., with sporting emblems.   (Label).

TOOLE, *C.*   Bath
Add: 2 Chatham Row.
Refs: BATH/DIR/24.

TOPPING & DAWSON   Hull
Add: 47 Lowergate.
Refs: PIG/16/17: 18/20.

TOTHAM, *William*   Colchester
Add: North Hill.
Refs: ROB/HOMCO/DIR/39.

TONGUE, *Richard*   Bath
(Leather Binding Mfr.).
Add: 5 St. John's Court.
Refs: BATH/DIR/01.

TOWNSEND, *William*   Sheffield
(& Ruler).
Add: 1 New Church St. (34):
Surrey Ct (42).
Refs: PIG/SEVEN/DIR/34: PIG/CDS/37:
WHI/WRY/37/8: PIG/MND/42.

TOWNSON, *Matthew*   Manchester
(See Thompson, Matthew).

TRANTER, *Enoch*   Ledbury
Refs: PIG/NCD/30.   (Herts.)

TRATHAN, *J.*   Falmouth
E D: 20?
Refs: LAB/KNA "Bound by/J.T./F"
ca. 20.

TREGONING   Falmouth
E D: 25?
Refs: Munby Coll: yellow en-
graved label "Bd. by T.F.".

TREUBATH, *Benj.*   Penzance
Add: Green Market.
Refs: PIG/LPCD/23.

TREWMAN & *Co.*   Exeter
(P R, B S, B B & S T).
Add: 226 High St.
Refs: EX/P/J/25: 27, etc: EX/DIR/
28: 31: 35.

TRINDLE, *Charles*   Harwich
Add: Market St.
Refs: ROB/HOMCO/DIR/39.

TROOD, *Thomas*   Taunton
Add: High St.
Refs: PIG/LPCD/22.

TUFT, *Charles*   Manchester
Add: 8 Halliwell's Bldgs.
Refs: MAN/DIR/13.

TURNER, *George*   Hull
(Etc).
Add: 62 Market Place.
Refs: HULL/DIR/10.

TURNER, *Joseph*   Rastrick (Yorks.)
Refs: PIG/SEVEN/DIR/34.

TURPIN, *John William*   Bristol

TURPIN, *John William* & *Co.* (21)

TURPIN,   PICKERING   &
LANGDON (36)
Add: Broad St (18): 5 Small St
(21).
Refs: PIG/LPCD/22   PIG/NCD/30:
BRIS/DIR/18: 21: 24: 27: 30: 33:
36: 40.

TYRER, *Thomas*   Liverpool
Add: 30 Hackins Hey (77): 16
Thomas St (81).
Refs: LIV/DIR/77: 81.

TYSON, *S.*   ?
E D: 15?
Refs: Label (without any location)
seen on Walton's Angler, 1815,
at Fletcher's at Guildford (1951).

UNDERHILL, *John*   Liverpool
  Add: 68 London Road.
  Refs: LIV/DIR/40.

UPCROFT, *Wm.*   Norwich
  Add: Fishgate St (36): St.
  Magdalene St (39).
  Refs: NORF/DIR/36: PIG/HC/39:
  ROB/NINE/DIR/39: ROB/SIX/DIR/39.

UPHAM'S LIBRARY   Bath
  E D: 21?
  Refs: O.C. Cosmo III's Tour. 21,
  f.m.g.   Ticket "Bound / at /
  Upham's Library/Bath".

UTLEY, *John*   Leeds
  (& Machine Ruler).
  Add: Corn Exchange Bldgs (34):
  3 Fleet St (37): 2 Turk's Head
  Yard, Briggate (42).
  Refs: LEEDS/DIR/34: WHI/WRY/37/8:
  PIG/MND/42.

VARDY, *Richard Elliott* Warminster
  (Etc, etc).   (Wilts.)
  Add: Market Place.
  Refs: ROB/NINE/DIR/39.

VAUGHAN, *Thomas*   Denbigh
  Add: High St (28): Hennlan St
  (35).
  Refs: PIG/NCD/28: PIG/NAT/DIR/28/
  9: PIG/MID/DIR/35.

VERNEY, *John*   Southampton
  Add: St. George's Place.
  Refs: SOUTH/DIR/11.

VICARY, *J.*   Plymouth (Dock)
  Add: Market St.
  Refs: PLY/DIR/14.

VICKERS, *Joseph Cockern*   Leeds
  (& S T)
  Add: 4 Birch's Yard, Lowerhead
  Row.
  Refs: LEEDS/DIR/26: PIG/NCD/28:
  PIG/NAT/DIR/28/29.

VIGURS, *Thomas*   Penzance
  Add: Chapel St.
  Refs: PIG/LPCD/23.

VINCENT, *George*   Brighton
  Add: 18 Brunswick Place North.
  Refs: PIG/HC/39: ROB/HOMCO/DIR/
  39 (J).

VINCENT, *J.*   Oxford
  (Publisher, B S &).
  Add: Radcliffe Sq.
  Refs: OXF/DIR/35 (published by
  Vincent).

VOWELL   Cambridge
  Refs: This binder is only known
  by a fine contemporary Russia
  binding with gilt spines and
  coloured inlays on Chamber's
  Cyclopaedia, 4 vol. 1786, signed
  "Bound by V., C" at base of
  spines, in the possession of
  Admiral Sir Cecil Harcourt,
  K.C.B.

WADE, *Henry*   Liverpool
Add: 9 Temple Lane.
Refs: LIV/DIR/18.

WADE, *Edward*   Cambridge
Add: Petty Cury.
Refs: PIG/HC/39.

WADE, *John*   Sheffield
Add 33 Bridge St (21): No. 43 (28).
Refs: SHEFF/DIR/21: PIG/NCD/28:
PIG/NAT/DIR/28/29.

WADE, *Whitehouse*   Sheffield
Add: Church St.
Refs: SHEFF/DIR/25: 28.

WADSWORTH, *W. M.*   Hull
Add: 2 Clarkson's Court, West St.
Refs: HULL/DIR/39.

WAGSTAFF, *Elijah*   Worcester
(& S T).
Add: New St.
Refs: PIG/NAT/DIR/28/29.

WAGSTAFF, *J.* Upton-upon-Severn
Add: Old St.
Refs: WOR/DIR/20.

WAIGHT, *George* Melksham (Wilts.)
(& machine ruler & paper hanger).
Add: Church St.
Refs: ROB/NINE/DIR/39.

WAINMAN, *Samuel*   Hull
Add: William's Sq., High St.
Refs: HULL/DIR/39.

WALDEN, *William*   Gloucester
Add: Northgate St.
Refs: GLOU/DIR/20.

WALKER, *George*   North Shields
(Etc).
Add: Tyne St.
Refs: PIG/NAT/DIR/28/29: PIG/
SEVEN/DIR/34.

WALKER, *J.*   Plymouth

WALKER, *Robert* (22)
Add: East St (14): Frankfort St
(22): Finewell St (36).
Refs: PLY/DIR/14: 22: 23: 36.

WALKER, *Mark*   York
Add: Fossbridge.
Refs: PIG/16/17: 18/20.

WALKER, *Robert*   Grimsby
(P R &).
Add: Bull Ring.
Refs: PIG/LPCD/22.

WALLACE, *James*   Putney
Add: High St.
Refs: PIG/LPCD/32: 34.

WALLACE, *William*   Liverpool
(& Victualler).
Add: 7 High St.
Refs: LIV/DIR/77: 81.

WALLIS, *James*   Cambridge
Add: Sidney St.
Refs: PIG/LPCD/23.

WALMSLEY, *Joshua*   Liverpool

WALMSLEY, *Joshua, Jun.*
  (The latter seems to have taken
  over about 1821).
  Add: 60 Lord St (16): 62 Lord St
  (21): 29 Church St (29): No. 51
  (40). Residences: 12 Harrington
  St (16): 24 Wolfe St (25):
  1 Basnett St (29).
  Refs: LIV/DIR/16: 18: 21: 25: 29:
  40: PIG/16/17: 18/20: PIG/LPCD/
  22: LANC/DIR/24.

WALTERS, *John*   Swansea
  Refs: BRI/DIR/91.

WALTERS, *S. E.*   Madeley
  E D: 15?   (Shropshire)
  Refs: JBO/AE.

WALTON, *John*   Dudley
  Add: Flood St.
  Refs: PIG/MID/DIR/35.

WANDLIS, *James*   Kirkham
  Refs: BRI/DIR/V/98.   (Lancs.)

WANSBROUGH & SAUNDERS
                    Bristol
WANSBROUGH, *John* (27)
  Add: 143 Redcliff St (24): No. 12
  (27): No. 124 (33).
  Refs: BRIS/DIR/24: 27: 30: 33:
  ROB/NINE/DIR/39: On two small

vols. in f.m.g. I have seen the
binder's ticket of "J. W., 142
Redcliff St/B". Nice quality.

WANT, *Edward*   Birmingham
  (& S T. Machine Ruler in 1829).
  Add: 15 Court, High St (28):
  74 High St (35).
  Refs: PIG/NCD/28: PIG/NAT/DIR/28/
  29: WARW/DIR/30: BIRM/DIR/29:
  33: 35: PIG/DIR/MID/35: PIG/
  CDS/37: PIG/MND/42.

WARD   Stratford-on-Avon
  E D: 30?
  Refs: Ticket "W/BB, etc/S-on-A"
  seen on Roger's Italy, 1830, at
  Traylen's: Cont. Inscription.
  Gilt. mor. with blind stamping.

WARD, *Christopher*   Oxford
  Add: St. Ebbs.
  Refs: PIG/NCD/30.

WARD, *Edward*   Nottingham
  Add: Upper Parlt. St.
  Refs: NOTT/DIR/40.

WARD, *Horatio Frederick*
  Add: 27 Cannon St.   Birmingham
  Refs: PIG/NCD/28: PIG/NAT/DIR/28/
  29: WARW/DIR/30: BIRM/DIR/29:
  33.

WARD, *Henry*   Canterbury
  Add: 8 Mercery Lane.
  Refs: KENT/DIR/38: PIG/HC/39.

WARD, *John*   Plymouth
  (& Paper Ruler in 1836).
  Add: Treville St (23): St.
  Catherine's St (30).
  Refs: PLYM/DIR/22: 23: 30: 36:
  PIG/NCD/30.

WARDLAW, *William*   Norwich
  (B B & Circulating Library).
  Refs: Decd. 20.8.97. For 30 years
  proprietor of a circulating library
  (Cambridge Chronicle & Journal,
  26.8.97).

WARMAN   Malvern (Worcs.)
  E D: 40?
  Add: Wilton Road.
  Refs: LAB/KNA: ca. 40.

WARNE, *William*   Newport
                          (I. of W.)
  Add: St. James's St (23): Holyrood
  St (39).
  Refs: PIG/LPCD/23: VEC/DIR/39:
  PIG/NCD/30: ROB/HOMCO/DIR/39.

WARREN   Royston
  E D: 33?
  Refs: Munby Coll: lithographed
  label "W,PR,BB & BS,R".
  Cloth binding ca. 1833.

WARREN, *Nathaniel*   Winchester
  Add: High St.
  Refs: ROB/HOMCO/DIR/39.

WARREN, *William*   Exeter
  (& B S & Librarian).
  Add: 65 Fore Hill St (28): No. 95
  (31): Bedford St (35).
  Refs: E.P.J./16: 25: PIG/LPCD/23:
  EX/DIR/28: 31: 35.

WARRICK (or WARWICK),
  William   Barton-upon-Humber
  Add: Market Place.   (Lincs.)
  Refs: LINC/DIR/26: PIG/NCD/28:
  PIG/NAT/DIR/28/29: Munby Coll:
  Label: "B. by W.W., B". Mor.
  gilt, 25; JA/4921.

WARWICK, *Francis*   Leeds
  Add: Old Infirmary Yard, Kirkgate.
  Refs: PIG/16/17: LEEDS/DIR/17.

WARWICK, *William*   Hull
  Add: 21 Bishop Lane.
  Refs: PIG/SEVEN/DIR/34.

WATERSON, *John*   Liverpool
  Add: 65 Peter St.
  Refs: LIV/DIR/16.

WATKINS, *T. B.*   Hereford
  (& S T).
  ED: 04?
  Add: High St.

Refs: O.C. Napleton: Sermons: 04. f.c.g.: (green label) "T.B. Watkins / Binder & Stationer / High St./Hereford". Same ticket occurs on a 1815 work, and he must therefore have been working at least till that date.

WATSON, *Ann*   Manchester
Add: Travis Court, Long Millgate (18): 149 Long Millgate (28).
Refs: PIG/18/20: MAN/DIR/21: 24/28: PIG/NCD/24: LANC/DIR/25: PIG/CDS/25/6.

WATSON, *James*   Manchester
Add: 16 Blackfriars (18): No. 12 (21): 12 Parsonage (25): No. 14 (37).
Refs: PIG/18/20: MAN/DIR/21: 24: 28: 32: PIG/NCD/24: PIG/CDS/25/26: LANC/DIR/25: PIG/NCD/28: PIG/SEVEN/DIR/34: PIG/CDS/37.

WATSON, *Peter*   Manchester
Add: 10 Travis Court, Long Millgate.
Refs: MAN/DIR/08: 13/ PIG/DIR/16/17.

WATSON, *Robert*   Halifax
Add: Woolshops: Petticoat Lane. (PIG).
Refs: YORK/DIR/22: PIG/LPCD/22.

WATSON, *Robert*   Nottingham
Add: Upper Parlt. St.
Refs: NOTT/DIR/40: PIG/MND/42.

WATT, *Robert*   Birmingham
Add: 25½ Anne St.
Refs: PIG/MND/42.

WATTS, *Israel*   Sherburne
Add: Long St.
Refs: PIG/LPCD/23.

WATTON, *William*   Birmingham
Add: 87 New St (35): 25 Church St (37).
Refs: PIG/MID/DIR/35: PIG/CDS/37.

WATTS, *Charles*   Lane End
Add: Gt. Charles St.
Refs: PIG/MID/DIR/35.

WAYMENT, *William*   Chichester
Add: West St.
Refs: PIG/LPCD/34.

WE(A)THERALD, *Walton*
              Sunderland
Add: Sussex St, Bishops Wearmouth.
Refs: DUR/DIR/27.
(See also Wetherald, below).

WEBB   Liverpool
E D: 20/40?
Refs: LAB/KNA: "Bound by/W./L." very wide range of date: Munby Coll: Label "B. by W, L." Vellum silk, 29.

WEBB, *Charles*   Cheltenham
  Add: 85 High St (20): 14 Portland
    Passage (22): 7 Winchcomb St
    (37).
  Refs: GLOU/DIR/20: PIG/LPCD/22:
    CHELT/ANN/37 to 40: ROB/NINE/
    DIR/39.

WEBB, *John*   Cheltenham
  Add: 23 Henrietta St.
  Refs: PIG/NCD/30.

WEBB, *William*   Cheltenham
  Add: St. Paul St.
  Refs: ROB/NINE/DIR/39.

WEBB & SIMMS   Manchester
  E D: 30?
  Refs: HOB/ABB. App. XI. p 194.

WEBBER, *Henry*   Bristol
  Add: St. Augustine's Back.
  Refs: PIG/LPCD/22.

WEBSTER, *John*   Birmingham
  Add: 104 Broomsgrove St.
  Refs: PIG/MND/42.

WEBSTER, *Samuel*   Whittlesea
  Add: Whitmore St.   (Cambs.)
  Refs: PIG/NCD/30.

WEBSTER, *William*   Leeds
  Add: 16 Newsam Yd, 135 Briggate.
  Refs: YORK/DIR/30: PIG/SEVEN/DIR/
    34: PIG/CDS/37.

WEIGHTMAN   Penrith
  E D: 00?   (Cumberland)
  Refs: HOB/ABB. App. XI. p. 194.

WEIGHTMAN, *Thomas*   York
  (Etc).
  Add: 44 Goodman Gate.
  Refs: PIG/SEVEN/DIR/34.

WENBAN & RANSOM
  (Printers &).   Hawkhurst (Kent)
  Refs: PIG/LPCD/32: 34.

WELLS, *John*   Newark (Notts.)
  Add: Barnby Gate.
  Refs: PIG/MID/DIR/35.

WESTON, *James P.*   Guernsey
         (St. Peter Port)
  Add: Le Marchant St.
  Refs: ROB/NINE/DIR/39: GUER/DIR/
    40.

WESTALL, *James*   Rochdale
  Add: Park Lane.
  Refs: PIG/SEVEN/DIR/34.

WETHERALD, *Walton*
         Sunderland
  Add: Coronation St (28): Sussex
    St (34).
  Refs: PIG/NCD/28: PIG/NAT/DIR/28/
    9: PIG/SEVEN/DIR/34.

WETTON, *George W.*   Maidenhead
  Add: High St.
  Refs: PIG/NCD/30.

WHEELER, *J. L.*   Oxford
Add: Magpie Lane.
Refs: PIG/LPCD/23.

WHEELER, *John*   Painswick
(Etc).   (Glos.)
Refs: ROB/NINE/DIR/39.

WHEELER, *William*   Northampton
Refs: See Hensman.

WHEREAT, *Wm.*   Bristol
Add: St. Michael's Hill.
Refs: ROB/NINE/DIR/39.

WHITAKER, *M. & A.* (21)
     Sheffield
WHITAKER, *Antony* (25)
Add: 18 Fargate (21): No. 13 (37).
Refs: SHEFF/DIR/21: 25: PIG/CDS/37.

WHITAKER, *Mark*   Sheffield
Add: 17 Allen St (25): Chapel
Walk (28).
Refs: SHEFF/DIR/25: 28.

WHITAKER, *M. & A.*   Sheffield
Add: 13 Fargate.
Refs: YORK/DIR/22.

WHITE, *William*   Bedford
Add: High St.
Refs: ROB/NINE/DIR/39: ROB/SIX/
DIR/39.

WHITE, *William*   Portsea
Add: 26 Unicorn St.
Refs: PIG/LPCD/23.

WHITEFIELD, *Joseph*
(& S T).   Newcastle-upon-Tyne
Add: North end Tyne Bridge.
Refs: NEW/DIR/82:87:95 (Stationer
only).

WHITEHEAD, *Charles*   Coventry
(& Copper Plate Printer).
Add: Hertford St.
Refs: PIG/NCD/28: PIG/NAT/DIR/28/
29: WARW/DIR/30: PIG/MID/DIR/
35.

WHITEHEAD, *J. Lawton*   Rochdale
E D: 35 to 40?
Add: Walk.
Refs: Label "J.L.W/BB/W,R"
seen on work dated 1826, but ½
calf binding probably about 10
years later.

WHITEHEAD & *Son*   Coventry

WHITEHEAD, *Richard* (28)
(& Copper Plate Printer).
Add: Cow Lane.
Refs: PIG/18/20: PIG/NCD/28:
PIG/NAT/DIR/28/29: WARW/DIR/
30.

WHITEHOUSE, *John*   Birmingham
Add: 18 Fleet St.
Refs: PIG/MND/42.

WHITESIDE, *Joseph*   Retford
(Bookseller, Stationer, Printer &).
Add: Grove St (32): New St (42).
Refs: NOTTSH/DIR/32: PIG/MID/DIR
/35: PIG/MND/42.

WHITLEY, *Nathan*   Halifax
(Apprentice to B. Frye).
Refs: Paid £3 6s. od. for masonic
binding for Probity Lodge, 1818.

WHITMAN, *Charles*   Reading
Add: 32 Castle St.
Refs: PIG/NCD/30.

WHITMAN, *Joseph*   Reading
Add: St. Mary's Butts.
Refs: PIG/LPCD/23: PIG/NCD/30.

WHITRIDGE   Carlisle
E D: 30?
Refs: (P) Label "Bound & sold by".

WHITTINGHAM, *James*
(S T &).   Nottingham
Add: Milton St (15): Clumber St
(18): · Parliament Row (22):
Lower Parliament St (40).
Refs: NOTT/DIR/14: 15: 18: 25: 34:
40: PIG/18/20: PIG/LPCD/22:
PIG/NCD/28: PIG/NAT/DIR/28/29:
NOTTSH/DIR/32: PIG/MID/DIR/35:
Label seen at Fletcher's, Nov., 50.

WHITTINGHAM, *Peter & Co.*
     Liverpool
Add: Slater Ct, Castle St (29):
14 Temple Lane (32) (No "&
Co.").
Refs: LIV/DIR/29: 32.

WHITTINGHAM, *William*
Add: High St.   King's Lynn
Refs: ROB/NINE/DIR/39: ROB/SIX/
DIR/39.

WHITTLE, *Peter*   Preston
Add: 5 Friargate.
Refs: PIG/LPCD/22.

WICKMAN   Cambridge
E D: 35?
Refs: Soth. Cat. 19.2.51. No. 309.

WICKHAM, *Thomas*   Maidstone
E D: 14?
Add: Week St.
Refs: PIG/LPCD/23: Munby Coll:
Label "T.W., BS & B, W.S.,
M, Magazines, etc". Mor. gilt
on 1810 book, dated 1814 at base
of spine.

WIGENS, *Charles*   Bath
Add: 14 King's-mead Sq. (30):
No. 2 (37): Res: 28 Kingsmead
Terrace (37): 8 Stanhope St (41).
Refs: PIG/NCD/30: BATH/DIR/33: 37:
41.

WILCOX, *Philip* Southampton
Add: Union Terrace.
Refs: PIG/NCD/30.

WILD, *Frederick* Hull
Add: 15 Bishop Lane.
Refs: WHI/WRY/37/8: HULL/DIR/38:
WHI/ENR/40.

WILD, *Henry* Nottingham
Add: Rutland St.
Refs: PIG/MID/DIR/35.

WILDE, *Frederick* Manchester

WILDE, *Henry M. P.* (38)
Add: 1 Cotton Court (32): 3 Star
Yard, Deansgate (38).
Refs: MAN/DIR/32: 38.

WILKINS, *Charles* Hull
(& S T).
Add: 13 Bishops Lane (22): 169
High St (28).
Refs: PIG/LPCD/22: YORK/DIR/22:
PIG/NCD/28: PIG/NAT/DIR/28/29:
HULL/DIR/22.

WILKINS, *George* Derby
(P R &).
Add: Queen St.
Refs: DERBY/DIR/23/4.

WILKINS, *Thomas* Norwich
Add: St. James.
Refs: PIG/LPCD/22.

WILKINS, *William* Swansea
Add: Mariner's Row.
Refs: PIG/LPCD/22: PIG/NCD/30:
SWAN/DIR/30.

WILKINSON, *C.* Hull
Add: 9 George Yard, Lowgate.
Refs: HULL/DIR/35: PIG/CDS/37:
PIG/MND/42.

WILKINSON, *Stephen*
Newcastle-upon-Tyne
Add: Opp. Castle-stairs, Close (78):
East end, Close (82).
Refs: NEW/DIR/78: 82: 87: 90: 95.

WILLANS, *Edward* Liverpool
(See Willans & Wood).
Add: 19 Rainford's Gdn. (05):
62 Bold St. (07 as Bookseller).
Refs: LIV/DIR/05: 07: 10.

WILLANS & WOOD Liverpool
(?Bookseller only).
E D: 25?
Add: Bold St.
Refs: O.C.: H. Kirke White,
Remains, f.c.g. Label gives him
as "Bookseller".

WILLIAMS, *Ben* Caerphilly
Refs: CARD/DIR/29.

WILLIAMS, *Charles* Dover
Add: 4 Townwall St.
Refs: PIG/HC/39: ROB/HOMCO/DIR/
39.

WILLIAMS, *David*   Llanelly
   Refs: PIG/MID/DIR/35.

WILLIAMS, *Edward*   Maidstone
   Add: King St.
   Refs: PIG/LPCD/23.

WILLIAMS, *John*
         Newcastle-under-Lyme
   Add: Ireland.
   Refs: NEW/LYME/DIR/22.

WILLIAMS, *John*   Plymouth
   (Etc).
   Add: 1 Old Town St (14): 31 (30).
   Refs: PIG/LPCD/23: PLYM/DIR/14:
    22: 30.

WILLIAMS, *Mary*   Birmingham
   Add: Fleet St.
   Refs: PIG/16/17.

WILLIAMS, *R.*   Devonport
   E D: 20?
   Add: 54 Fore St.
   Refs: LAB/KNA "RW/Bookbinder,
    etc/54 F.S/D" ca. 20.

WILLIAMS, *Thomas*   Norwich
   Add: St. Stephens.
   Refs: PIG/LPCD/22.

WILLIAMS, *William*   Liverpool
   Add: 2 Slater's Ct, Castle St.
   Refs: PIG/CDS/37.

WILLIAMS, *Thomas & Son*
   (B S, S T &).   Dover
   Add: Snargate St (23): 145 ditto
    (32) (No "& Son").
   Refs: PIG/LPCD/23: PIG/LPD/26/7:
    PIG/LPCD/32: 34: PIG/HC/39.

WILLIAMS, *Thomas & Son*
   Add: 175 Queen St.   Portsea
   Refs: PIG/NCD/30.

WILLIAMS & PULLINGER
   (& P R).   Chichester
   Add: East St.
   Refs: PIG/LPCD/34.

WILLIAMS & WILSON   Liverpool
   Add: 31 Castle St.
   Refs: LIV/DIR/34.

WILLIAMSON, *John*   Sheffield
   Add: 12 Sycamore St (22): 13
    Norfolk Row (25).
   Refs: YORK/DIR/22: SHEFF/DIR/25.

WILL(I)S, *Edward*   Plymouth
   (Etc).
   Add: Market St (22): 20 Briton
    Side (30).
   Refs: PLY/DIR/22: PIG/NCD/30.

WILSON, *Isaac*   Hull
   Add: 49 Lowgate.
   Refs: PIG/18/20: PIG/SEVEN/DIR/34.

WILSON, *J.* Wolverhampton
(Working Stationer).
Add: Snow Hill.
Refs: PIG/16/17.

WILSON, *John* Bath
Add: 22 Peter St.
Refs: BATH/DIR/29.

WILSON, *John* Berwick-on-Tweed
Add: Hide Hill.
Refs: PIG/SIN/20.

WILSON, *John* Hay
Refs: PIG/MID/DIR/35.

WILSON, *John Ralph* Deptford
Add: Newcross Road.
Refs: PIG/LPCD/32: 34.

WILSON, *Thomas* Whitehaven
Add: 45 King St. (Cumberland)
Refs: CUMWES/DIR/29.

WILSON, *William* Liverpool
Add: 4 Castle St (37): 1 Dale St
(40).
Refs: PIG/CDS/37: LIV/DIR/40.

WILSON & *Co.* Leeds
Add: 10 Trinity St.
Refs: PIG/MND/42.

WINGATE, *Jabez* Gloucester
Add: Northgate St (30): Worcester
St (39).
Refs: PIG/NCD/30: ROB/NINE/DIR/39.

WINSTANLEY, *John* Manchester
Add: 4 Taylor's Ct, Bootle St
(11.P): 13 Copperas St (13):
Old Exchange, King St (16):
St. Anne's Churchyard (18):
Cannon Ct, Cateaton St (21):
4 Old Church Yard (24): 25
Fountain St (28): No. 81 (32):
No. 81A (37): 25 Corporation
St (?).
Refs: MAN/DIR/11 P: 13: 21: 24:
28: 32: 38: PIG/16/17: 18/20:
PIG/NCD/24: LANC/DIR/25: PIG/
CDS/25/6: PIG/NCD/28: PIG/SEVEN
/DIR/34: PIG/CDS/37. O.C.
Heywood's Hierarchy: 1635,
Blind st. black mor. Label "Bd
by/JW/81 F.S/M". WSM/KC/
NEW mentions a ticket at 25
Fountain St, ca. 1850.

WINTER, *Thos.* Liverpool
Add: 20 Sir Thomas Bldgs.
Refs: LIV/DIR/40.

WISEMAN, *Henry Richard*
Add: Trinity St. Cambridge
Refs: PIG/NCD/30: PIG/HC/39:
ROB/NINE/DIR/39: ROB/SIX/DIR/
39: ?Still working in 1854: JA/
2379.

WITHER & HARTLEY
Manchester
Add: Wolstenholme Ct.
Refs: PIG/SEVEN/DIR/34.

PLATE XIII

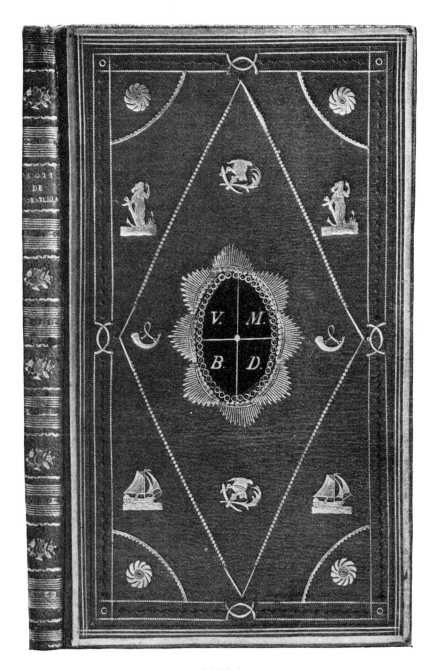

PLATE XIV

WOOD   Blackburn
  E D: 20?
  Refs: LAB/KNA: "Bound by/W/B"
  ca. 20.

WOOD   Worcester
  E D: 97?
    Refs: Wheeler, 167, on The
    Philanthrope, 1797.

WOOD, *A. P.*   Huntingdon
  Add: High St.
  Refs: ROB/NINE/DIR/39: ROB/SIX/
  DIR/39.

WOOD, *Charles*   Oxford
  Add: Tanner Yd, King St.
  Refs: PIG/NCD/30.

WOOD, *G.*   Liverpool
  (S T, P R &).
  E D: 29?
  Add: 11 Price's St, Old Dock.
  Refs: Label seen at Marks, Jan.
  1951.

WOOD, *George*   Bristol
  (P R, B B & S T).
  Add: 13 Castle St.
  Refs: ROB/NINE/DIR/39. Topo-
  graphical Dict. of Palestine by
  P. Graham, 1836. Patterned
  cloth bdg., with label "Geo.
  Wood/PR/BB & S/13 Castle St/
  Bristol".

WOOD, *James*   Leeds
  Add: 99 Kirkgate (17): 23 (22).
  Refs: PIG/16/17: 18/20: LEEDS/DIR
  /17: YORK/DIR/22: PIG/LPCD/22.

WOOD, *John*   Clapham
  (B S, S T &).
  Add: High St.
  Refs: PIG/LPCD/32.

WOOD, *John*   Birmingham
  Add: 14 Great Charles St (22):
  20 Holloway Head (28): 6 Court,
  Moor St (35).
  Refs: PIG/LPCD/22: PIG/NCD/28:
  PIG/NAT/DIR/28/29: WARW/DIR/
  30: PIG/MID/DIR/35: PIG/CDS/37:
  BIRM/DIR/25: 29: 33: 35: 39: PIG/
  MND/42.

WOOD, *John* (35)   Worcester

WOOD *& Son* (40)
  Add: 35 Foregate.
  Refs: PIG/DIR/WORC/35: WOR/DIR/
  40.

WOOD, *Primrose*   Liverpool
  Add: 62 Bold St.
  Refs: LIV/DIR/40.

WOOD   Rochdale
  (Etc, etc).
  Refs: F.m.g. binding, with ticket,
  on Ogilby Fables of Aesop, fol.,
  2 vol. in 1. Christie Sale, 1.4.53:
  306. Entwhistle of Foxholes Lib.,
  but doubtful if bound locally.

WOOD, *Thomas*   Birmingham
(P R, S T &, in 1808: etc, previously).

WOOD, *Joseph* (42)
  Add: High St (97): 17 New
    Meeting St (00).
  Refs: BIRM/DIR/97: 98: 08: 10: 12:
    15: 18: 21: 35: 39: PIG/16/17:
    18/20: PIG/LPCD/22: PIG/MID/DIR/
    35: PIG/CDS/37: PIG/MND/42.

WOOD, *Thomas*   Oxford
(decd. December, 1795, aged 72).
  Add: Catherine St.
  Refs: Jackson's Oxford Journal
    28.2.89 (advt. for servant) &
    2.1.96 (announcing his death).

WOOD, *William M.*   St. Helier
  Add: 70 King St.   (Jersey)
  Refs: ROB/NINE/DIR/39.

WOODHEAD, *Edmund George*
              Wath (?Cumberland)
(B S, S T &).
  Refs: PIG/MND/42.

WOODS, *G. & Co.*   Bristol
(& Bookseller).
  Add: 13 Castle St.
  Refs: ?

WOODWARD   Liverpool
(B S & S T).
  E D: ? 05.
  Add: 22 Lord St.

Refs: On a ticket seen on a contemporary Russia binding on a
1805 work, he states "Books
elegantly bound".

WOOLARD, *J.*   Brighton
  E D: 30?
  Add: 3 Prince's Place.
  Refs: LAB/KNA "Bound by/J.W/3
    P.P./B", ca. 30.

WOOLSTENCROFT   Warrington
  E D: 13?
  Add: King St.
  Refs: B.M., C 71, e 27 & O.C.
    (Hodgson, 23.1.53. No. 517).
    Green st. gr. mor. with ticket on
    Caulfield Ports. 3 vol. 1813.

WOON, *Thomas*   Witney
  Add: High St.
  Refs: ROB/SIX/DIR/39.

WOOTTON, *William*   Cambridge
  Add: Pembroke St.
  Refs: PIG/LPCD/23: PIG/NCD/30:
    O.C.: Vinci's Astronomy, 3 vol.
    40. 23, f. russia, g. (ticket).

WORRALL, *Philip*   Manchester
  Add: 2 Greengate, Salford.
  Refs: MAN/DIR/28.

WOSENCROFT, *Charles* Liverpool
(Printer, Medicine Vendor &).
  Add: 22 Cook St.
  Refs: LIV/DIR/90(W).

WRIGHT, *Christopher Norton*
(Etc.). Nottingham
Add: East Long Row.
Refs: PIG/MID/DIR/35: NOTT/DIR/40.

WRIGHT, *James* Manchester
Add: 6 King St.
Refs: PIG/NCD/28.

WRIGHT, *John* Macclesfield
(Etc.).
Add: Mill St.
Refs: MACC/DIR/25: PIG/NAT/DIR/28
/9.

WRIGHT, *John Butler* Liverpool
Add: Sweeting St.
Refs: PIG/SEVEN/DIR/34: PIG/CDS/37.

WRIGHT, *Joseph & Barnett*
Greenwich
WRIGHT, *Joseph* (39)
(B S, S T &).
Add: Church St (32): Croom's
Hill (39).
Refs: PIG/LPCD/32: PIG/HC/39:
Label seen on Chateaubriand's
Rancé, 2nd Ed., 1844, at
Grafton's, Jan. 1952.

WRIGHT, *Peter* Liverpool
(Grocer &).
Add: 34 Lord St.
Ref: LIV/DIR/90.

WRIGHT, *R.* Bristol
Add: 13 Old Market St.
Refs: BRIS/DIR/24.

WRIGHT, *Richard* Liverpool
Add: 14 Sweeting St (77): No. 9
(81) "and clerk of St. Catherine's
Church".
Refs: LIV/DIR/77: 81.

WRIGHT, *Richard* Liverpool
(& Victualler).
Add: 16 N. side Old Dock.
Refs: LIV/DIR/25.

WRIGHT, *Thomas* Leeds
Add: Rayson's Yard, Briggate.
Refs: LEEDS/DIR/00.

WRIGHT, *John Barber* Birmingham

WRIGHT, *Thomas Barber* (37)
Add: Union Passage, New St.
Refs: PIG/MID/DIR/35: PIG/CDS/37.

WRIGHT, *William* Hull
(S T &).
Add: 4 Lowgate.
Refs: HULL/DIR/22: PIG/NCD/28:
PIG/NAT/DIR/28/29.

WRIGHT, *William* Liverpool

WRIGHT, *William & Son* (18)
Add: 8 Elbow Lane, Sweeting St
(90): No. 7 (96): No. 5* (00):

No. 7 (07): No. 8 (13): 26
Sweeting St, Castle St (24):
No. 25 (29).
(* Dale St. between 00 & 18).
Refs: LIV/DIR/90 (G. & W.): 96:
00: 03: 05: 07: 10: 13: 16: 21:
25: 29: 32: BRI/DIR/91: PIG/16/
17: 18/20: YORK/DIR/22: PIG/
LPCD/22: LANC/DIR/24: PIG/NCD/
28.

WRIGHT & BAGNALL   Bristol
Add: 35 Bridge St.
Refs: BRIS/DIR/30.

WRIGHTSON, *Robert* Birmingham
(Etc, etc).
(See Thomson & Wrightson).

WRIGHTSON & WEBB (35).
Add: 7/8 New St.
Refs: WARW/DIR/30: BIRM/DIR/15:
18: 21: 25: 29: 33: 39: (See full
page advert. facing title page of
1818 Directory as to their binding
activities).

WROE, *James*   Manchester
(& Periodical Publisher).
Add: 218 Gt. Ancoats St.
Refs: PIG/NCD/24: MAN/DIR/24:
PIG/CDS/25/6.

YARINGTON, *Frederick*   Norwich
Add: Orford Hill (30): St. Stephens'
St (39).
Refs: PIG/NCD/30: PIG/HC/39.

YARROW   Birmingham
Add: Colmore St.
Refs: BIRM/DIR/98.

YELF, *William W.*   Newport
Add: Holyrood St.   (I. of W.)
Refs: PIG/NCD/30.

YEO, *Margery*   Exeter
E D: 90?
Add: Over against St. Martin's
Lane.
Refs: AE/HEAL/LAB.

YOUNG, *George*
          Newcastle-upon-Tyne
YOUNG, *James*
Add: Highbridge (78, George):
Queen St (01, James).
Refs: NEW/DIR/78: 01.

YOUNG, *James*   Hull
Add: 11 Bishop Lane.
Refs: PIG/SEVEN/DIR/34: PIG/CDS/
37: WHI/WRY/37/8: HULL/DIR/38:
WHI/ENR/40: PIG/MND/42.

YULE, *John*   York
Add: Stone Gate (87): Swine Gate
(18; no initial).
Refs: YORK/DIR/87: BRI/DIR/91:
PIG/18/20.

SCOTTISH ABBREVIATIONS

AE/GHB   Information communicated to A. Ehrman by G. H. Bushnell.

KAY   Kay's Portraits: 2 vol. 1837/8.

COSOC/BB/EDIN/75   Founders and signatories of Company & Society of Bookbinders in Edinburgh 1775. (Copy in Edinburgh City Library, IHS/1508/372).

SCOTTISH GENERAL DIRECTORIES

HOLD/11:   Holden's Annual Directory, 11, Vol. II (Norton 24).

PIG/SIN/20:   Pigot's Commercial Directory for Scotland, Ireland and the four northernmost counties of England, 20 (Norton 33).

PIG/CDS/25:   Pigot's New Commercial Directory of Scotland, 26/26 (Norton 40).

„   „ /26/7:   Ditto 26/27/(Norton 42).

„   „ /37:   „   Directory of Scotland & the Isle of Man, 37 (Norton 64).

DBP/1726/75:   Bibl. Soc. Dictionary of Booksellers, Printers, etc (1932) including Bushnell's List.

SCOTTISH LOCAL DIRECTORIES

ABER/DIR/24:	Aberdeen Directory 24/25.
,, ,, /28:	,, ,, 28/29.
*EDIN/DIR/73:	Edinburgh Directory 73/4.
,, ,, /80:	,, ,, 80.
,, ,, /04:	,, (& Leith) ,, 04/5.
,, ,, /09/11/16:	,, P.O. ,, 09/11/16.
,, ,, /20/23:	,, ,, ,, 20/23.
,, ,, /26/29:	,, ,, ,, 26/29.
,, ,, /33:	Gray's Annual Directory 33.
,, ,, /35/6:	,, ,, ,, 35/6.
,, ,, /36:	,, ,, ,, 36.
,, ,, /39:	Edin. P.O. ,, 39.
GLAS/DIR/83:	John Tait's Dir. for City of Glasgow, etc. May 83/4. (1871 reprint).
,, ,, /87:	Jones' Directory 1787 (1868 reprint).
,, ,, /89:	,, ,, 1789 (1866 ,,).
,, ,, /90/91:	,, ,, 1790/1.
,, ,, /01:	Glasgow Dir. 01.
,, ,, /13:	,, ,, 13.
,, ,, /17:	,, ,, 17.
,, ,, /18:	,, ,, 18.
,, ,, /23:	,, ,, 23.
,, ,, /26:	,, ,, 26.
,, ,, /28:	,, ,, 28.
,, ,, /40:	,, ,, 40.
DUND/DIR/24/5:	Colville's Dundee Register & Dir. 1824/5.
RENF/DIR/31/2:	Fowler's Renfrewshire Dir. 1831/2, dealing with Upper & Lower Wards, 2 vol.
,, ,, /36/7:	Ditto 1836/7, Lower Ward only.
PAIS/DIR/38/9:	Fowler's Paisley Dir., 1838/9.
PERT/DIR/23:	Morison's Perth Dir., 1823.
DUNF/DIR/35:	Miller's Dir. for Dunfermline, 1835.

* **NOTE.** Since the above list of Edinburgh directories was sent to the printers, the author has been able to go through another 20 such directories. References to them have, however, been included in the list of Scottish binders. As regards the year 1794, there are two Edinburgh directories distinguished as "94" & "94 W".

SCOTTISH BINDERS BY LOCALITY

ABERDEEN: Brown (2); Collie; Elmslie; Gordon; Inglis; Jackson; Johnson; Laurie; Low; Moffat; Mortimer; Philip; Philip & Moffat; Reid; Shirreffs; Strachan & Gellen; Wilson.

AIRDRIE: Ross; Turnbull.

ANNAN: Watt.

AYR: Goudie.

BATHGATE: McGriggow.

BEITH: Mitchell.

BIGGAR: Bothwick.

BRECHIN: Alexander; Scott; Willocks.

CARLUKE: Allan.

CASTLE DOUGLAS: Anderson.

CRIEFF: Maclaren.

CUPAR: Ness; Paul; Russell.

DALBEATTIE: McNish.

DALKEITH: Lyle; McIntosh; Robertson.

DUMBARTON: Miller.

DUMFRIES: Anderson (2); Dunbar; Dunlop; Henry; Robertson; Sinclair.

DUNBAR: Thompson.

DUNDEE: Forsyth; Mathers; Middleton; Robertson; Stevenson.

DUNFERMLINE: Campbell.

DUNKELD: Cant.

EDINBURGH: Affleck; Aitken; Alison; Allan (3); Anderson (2); Annan; Anton; Baillie; Banks (4); Bell; Bishop (2); Black; Borthwick; Bowack; Brown (2); Bruce (2); Burns; Butter; Cairns; Campbell (2); Carfrae (3); Caw (2); Christie (2); Claperton; Clark; Clarke; Cleghorn; Cleland; Cook; Cooper; Copland; Coupar; Crabbie; Crawford (2); Craw; Currie; Currie & Lamb; Darling; Dewar (2); Dickson; Donaldson; Duncan; Dundas; Dunlop; Elder; Elliott; Ellison; Fairbairn; Ferrier (2); Finlay; Fitch; Fitzpatrick; Fleming; Forbes (2); Forsyth; Frame; Fraser; Galloway (2); Gardiner; Gillies; Gillon; Gowan; Grant; Gray;

Gregory; Grieve (2); Guthrie; Halliday; Halliday & Ferrier; Hall & Muir; Hamilton (2); Hardie; Henderson; Henderson & Bisset; Heron; Herriot; Hill; Hogg; Howell; Hunter (3); Hutton; Inglis; Jamieson; Johnston; Jones; Keddie; Laing; Lauder; Laurie; Lawrence (2); Leckie; Leechman; Leighton; Logan; Low (2); Lumsden; McClelland; McDonald; McEwen; McIntosh; McLaggan; McLean; McLeish; McLellan; Manson; Marshall: Mathews; Meek; Millar; Miller (2); Mitchell; Moir; Moir & Watson; Monteith; Moodie; More (2); Muir (3); Muir & Mallock; Murray (2); Nicoll; Oliver & Boyd; Orrock; Orrock & Romanes; Paterson; Paton (3); Paul; Penson; Pettie; Porteous; Proctor; Rennie; Roch; Rogers; Ross; Sangster; Sawyer; Scott (2); Seton (2); Sinclair; Slater; Smith; Smiton; Souter; Steel; Steele; Steven; Stevens; Steward; Sutherland (3); Tait (3); Taylor (2); Taylor Seton; Thomson; Tod (3); Todd; Walker; Wallace; Watson (3); Watt; Weir; White (3); Whitelaw; Wilde; Wilson; Winckworth; Wood; Young.

ELGIN: Dunbar; Ettles & Young; McRae; Neilson.

FORFAR: Smith.

FRASERBURGH: Mitchell.

GIRVAN: McMorran.

GLASGOW: Aitken; Alexander; Blacklaws; Blair; Bogle; Bonnard; Brown (2); Bryce; Buchanan; Cairns; Cameron (2); Campbell; Carss; Chambers; Clacher; Clark; Colville (3); Crawford (2); Croiley; Cunningham; Donald; Duncan; Elliott; Farie; Ferguson; Findlay; Fisher; Fleckfield; Frye; Fulton; Gray; Hardie; Harrison; Henderson (2); Henderson & Hutheson; Heugh; Honeyman; Hutcheson; Hutchison; Jenkins; Johnston; Jones; Keddie (2); Keir; Kennedy; Laurie; Lishman; Love; Lyon; McFadyen; McGregor; McGregor & Cameron; McKendrick; McKenzie; McLaren; McLeod; McNair; McPherson; Marshall; Martin; Menzies (2); Millar; Moncrieff; Morrison (2); Muggoch; Muir (2); Neil (2); Neilson; Neilson & Moffatt; Niven; Peat; Rae; Rattray; Reid; Robinson; Scotland; Scott; Seller; Sheddon; Sinclair; Smith; Sommerville; Stewart; Swanston; Templeton; Thomson (2); Walker; Watson; Watt; Watt & McDonald; Watt & Prentice; Weir; Whelan; Wilson (2); Winning; Wood.

GREENOCK: Kerr; Laing; McGregor; McKelvie; Morrison; Watt; Young; Yuill.

HADDINGTON: Wood.

HAMILTON: Miller.

HAWICK: Ainslie; Elder.

INVERNESS: Douglas; Elltes; McCllough; McDonald; Sharp; Urquhart; Young.

KELSO: Grieve.

KIRKCALDY: Ford.

KIRKCUDBRIGHT: Gordon.

KIRRIEMUIR: Mills.

LESLIE: Brown.

LEVEN: Mitchell.

MAXWELLTOWN: Johnstone.

MAYBOLE: Campbell.

MONTROSE: Molison; Robertson; Scott: Shepherd.

MUSSELBURGH: Alison.

NEWTOWN STEWART: Kelly.

PAISLEY: Carswell; Condie; Dick; Low; Low & Knox; Mcfarlane; Moodie; Neilson; Stewart; Webster; White (2).

PERTH: Morison; Somner; Stobie; Tainsh; Wood.

PETERHEAD: Lawder.

ST. ANDREWS: Fletcher; McGregor.

STIRLING: Shearer.

STONEHAVEN: Duncan.

STRANRAER: McCredie.

STRICHEN: Campbell.

WIGTOWN: McBryde.

ALPHABETICAL LIST OF SCOTTISH BINDERS

AFFLECK, *Thomas*   Edinburgh
(& S T).
Add: 100 West Bow.
Refs: EDIN/DIR/19: 33: 35/6.

AINSLIE, *William*   Hawick
E D: 25?   (Roxburghshire)
Refs: JBO/AE.

AITKEN, *Andrew*   Glasgow
Add: 11 Bell St (16): Canon St
(26).
Refs: GLAS/DIR/16: 17: 18: 26.

AITKEN, *James*   Edinburgh
(& Machine Ruler, 26).
Add: 30 Old Fishmarket Close:
Res: 5 James St (16): 8 St. James'
Sq (35/6): No. 10 (39).
Refs: EDIN/DIR/16: 23: 26: 29:
35/6: 39: PIG/SIN/20: PIG/CDS/25:
26/7: 37.

ALEXANDER, *John*   Brechin
E D: ?
Add: Upper West Wynd.
Refs: WMS/KC/NEW.

ALEXANDER, *John*   Glasgow
Add: 29 Brunswick St (23): No.
77 (26).
Refs: GLAS/DIR/23 to 26: 28 to 31.

ALISON, *Robert*   Edinburgh
Add: Foot of Allan's Close (90):
President's Stairs (93): Parliament
Close (09): 10 Parliament Sq (20).
Refs: EDIN/DIR/90: 93: 94: 96: 01:
03: 07: 09: 11: 16: PIG/SIN/20.

ALLAN, *Charles*   Edinburgh
Add: Parliament Close (93): Old
P.O. Stairs (94): West Bow (01):
20 Carubber's Close (25).
Refs: EDIN/DIR/93: 94W: 96: 99: 01:
03: PIG/CDS/25: 26/7: DBP/1726/
75/p. 315 under "Grieve".

ALLAN, *George*   Edinburgh
E D: 94.
Refs: AE/GHB.

ALLAN, *James*   Carluke
Add: High St.   (Lanarkshire)
Refs: PIG/CDS/37.

ALLAN, *Thomas*   Edinburgh
(Married Samuel Campbell's
daughter in 1780).
E D: 80?
Refs: AE/GHB: DBP/1726/1775/p.289
(under Campbell).

ALLISON, *George*   Musselburgh
E D: 88.
Refs: AE/GHB.

ANDERSON, *Allan*   Dumfries
Add: 69 High St.
Refs: PIG/SIN/20.

ANDERSON, *James* Castle Douglas
(Kirkcudbrightshire)
Add: Cotton St (25): Market Hill
(37).
Refs: PIG/CDS/25/6: PIG/CDS/37.

ANDERSON, *John*   Dumfries
Add: 11 High St.
Refs: PIG/SIN/20.

ANDERSON, *John*   Edinburgh
E D: 98.
Refs: AE/GHB.

ANDERSON, *John*   Edinburgh
Add: Parliament Stairs (29): War-
riston Close, 323 High St (33).
Refs: EDIN/DIR/29: 33: 35/6: 39.

ANNAN, *John*   Edinburgh
Add: Luckenbooths (82): Castle
Hill (83).
Refs: EDIN/DIR/82: 83: 84: 86: 88:
90: AE/GHB.

ANTON, *John*   Edinburgh
E D: 96.
Refs: AE/GHB.

BAILLIE, *James*   Edinburgh

BAILLIE, *James & Robert* (03)
Add: Opp. Mealmarket (99):
Blackfriars Wynd (03): Back
Stairs, Parliament Close (04):
Burnet's Close (11).
Refs: EDIN/DIR/99: 00: 03: 04: 11.

BANKS, *Alexander* (09)   Edinburgh

BANKS, *Alexander & Son* (33)
Add: East Richmond St (09): 4
North St (11): No. 6 (16): 134
High St (20): 37 North Bridge
(25): Res: 8 Roxburgh St (26).
Refs: EDIN/DIR/09: 11: 16: 23: 29:
33: PIG/SIN/20: PIG/CDS/25: 26/7:
37.

BANKS, *Alexander Jun.*   Edinburgh
Add: 5 North Bridge.
Refs: EDIN/DIR/20: 26: 29: 33: 35:
PIG/CDS/37: O.C. Label from
plain $\frac{3}{4}$ calf binding. LAB/KNA.

BANKS, *James Haldane*   Edinburgh
(& Stationer).
Add: 51 S. Hanover St (33): No.
30 (37).
Refs: PIG/CDS/37: EDIN/DIR/33:
35/6: 39.

BANKS, *Peter*   Edinburgh
E D: 99.
Refs: AE/GHB.

BAXTER, *William*   Edinburgh
   Add: 39 South Bridge.
   Refs: EDIN/DIR/35/6.

BELL, *David*   Edinburgh
   (d. June, 1798).
   E D: 52.   L D: 1798.
   Add: North-West Kirk Parish (52):
   New North Kirk Parish (64):
   Potterrow Well (84).
   Refs: DBP/1726/75: (p. 282): EDIN/
   DIR/84: 86: 88: 90: COSOC/BB/
   EDIN/75.

BISHOP, *James*   Edinburgh
   Add: Chalmers' Close.
   Refs: EDIN/DIR/23.

BISHOP, *Thomas*   Edinburgh
   Add: Borthwick's Close, High St
   (20: Pig.): 201 High St (20 Ed/
   Dir.).
   Refs: PIG/SIN/20: EDIN/DIR/20.

BLACK, *John*   Edinburgh
   E D: 84.
   Refs: AE/GHB.

BLACKLAWS, *William*   Glasgow
   (Etc).
   Add: 218 Argyll St.
   Refs: GLAS/DIR/38 to 40: O.C. mor.
   gilt bdg. on Milton's works,
   London, 1839. Ticket "Bd by,
   etc".

BLAIR, *David & Co.*   Glasgow
   Add: 77 Brunswick St.
   Refs: PIG/CDS/37: GLAS/DIR/38 to 40.

BOGLE, *Robert*   Glasgow
   Add: Salt Market.
   Refs: GLAS/DIR/83.

BONNARD & DOUGLAS (11)
                      Glasgow
BONNARD, *John* (12)
   Add: Moodie's Court.
   Refs: GLAS/DIR/11 to 14.

BORTHWICK, *William* Edinburgh
   Add: 2 West Register St (04):
   Warriston's Close (07).
   Refs: AE/GHB/97: EDIN/DIR/04: 07:
   09.

BOTHWICK, *William*   Biggar
   Refs: PIG/CDS/25/6.   (Lanarkshire)

BOWACK, *Nicol*   Edinburgh
   Add: 46 Leith St (37): No. 60
   (33 & 39).
   Refs: PIG/CDS/37: EDIN/DIR/33: 39.

BROWN, *Alexander*   Aberdeen
   (b. 1766, d. 1848).

BROWN, *Alexander & Co.* (14)
   (B S &).
   Add: Upperkirkgate (85): Homer's
   Head, Broad St (93): & Co.
   (with his son William (14)): 38
   Broad St (24): Union St (31).

Refs: ABER/DIR/24: 28: Apollo Magazine, Jan., 1951, Art. by W. S. Mitchell: Sotheby Sale 24.7.50, No. 37.

BROWN, *George*   Glasgow
Add: Old Vennal.
Refs: GLAS/DIR/12: 13: 17.

BROWN, *Robert*   Edinburgh
Add: 15 Potter Row.
Refs: PIG/CDS/25: 26/27.

BROWN, *S.*   Glasgow
Add: 9 Prince's St.
Refs: GLAS/DIR/23: 24.

BROWN, *Thomas*   Leslie
Refs: PIG/CDS/37.   (Fifeshire)

BROWN, *William*   Aberdeen
Add: Nelson St.
Refs: PIG/CDS/37.

BROWN, *William*   Edinburgh
Add: New North Parish (68): Opp. the foot of Back Stairs (73): Rattery Close (82): Opp. Back Stairs (84): Ayer's Close, Cowgate (86): Rattery Close, Cowgate (93): Opp. Mealmarket (99): Entry between Forrester's & Liberton's Wynd (01).
Refs: EDIN/DIR/80: 82: 83: 84: 86: 88: 90: 93: 94W: 96: 99: 01: DBP/1726/75, p. 287.

BRUCE & MUNRO   Edinburgh

BRUCE, *George* (35)

BRUCE, *George Duncan* (37) (& S T).
Add: 6 Mound Place (33): No. 4 (35/6): Mound St (37).
Refs: EDIN/DIR/33: 35/6: PIG/CDS/37.

BRYCE, *D.*   Glasgow
E D: ca. 30.
Add: 84 Buchanan St.
Refs: AE/COLL/LAB.

BUCHANAN & BROWN
Add 77 Brunswick St.   Glasgow
Refs: GLAS/DIR/29.

BURNS   Edinburgh
Add: Bell's Wynd.
Refs: EDIN/DIR/04.

BUTTER, *John*   Edinburgh
Add: West Bow Head (80): North Side, Lawnmarket (94): Head of Lady Stair's Close (93 & 96).
Refs: EDIN/DIR/80: 82: 83: 84: 88: 90: 93: 94.W: 96: COSOC/BB/EDIN/75.

CAIRNS, *Peter*   Edinburgh
(& Auctioneer in 1823).
Add: 7 Richmond St (20): 263 Canongate (23).
Refs: PIG/SIN/20: EDIN/DIR/23.

CAIRNS, *Walter* Glasgow
  Add: 32 Argyll St (38): 35 Stock-
    well St (39).
  Refs: GLAS/DIR/38 to 40.

CAMERON, *Hugh* Glasgow
  Add: 27 Wilson St.
  Refs: GLAS/DIR/26: 28.

CAMERON, *James* Glasgow
  Add: 2 Prince's St (20): 27 Wilson
    St (26).
  Refs: PIG/SIN/20: GLAS/DIR/26.

CAMERON, *John* Glasgow
  Add: 38 High St (03): No. 98 (09).
  Refs: GLAS/DIR/03: 05-8: 09.

CAMPBELL, *D.* Edinburgh
  (& S T).
  Add: 36 Leith St.
  Refs: EDIN/DIR/29.

CAMPBELL, *Daniel* Strichen
  Refs: PIG/CDS/37. (Aberdeenshire)

CAMPBELL, *Duncan* Dunfermline
  Add: Chalmers St.
  Refs: DUNF/DIR/35: PIG/CDS/37.

CAMPBELL, *Samuel* Edinburgh
  Add: West Bow (73): New North
    Kirk Parish (80): Castle Barns (90).
  Refs: EDIN/DIR/73: 80: 82: 83: 84:
    86: 88: 90: DBP/1726/75, p. 289:
    COSOC/BB/EDIN/75.

CAMPBELL, *William* Glasgow
  Add: 187 Trongate (33): 179 Argyll
    St (37): Res: 50 Eglington St
    (40).
  Refs: PIG/CDS/37: GLAS/DIR/33/4:
    35/6: 37/8: 40.

CAMPBELL, *William* Maybole
  Add: Kirkwynd. (Ayrshire)
  Refs: PIG/CDS/37.

CANT, *James* Dunkeld
  (B S & Publisher).
  Refs: DBP/1726/75, p. 289. Said to
    have taken over R. Morison's
    Dunkeld branch in 1770 and to
    have worked till about 1812.
    The DBP states that he was no
    doubt also a BB, but gives no
    authority for the statement.

CARFRAE, *J. & A.* Edinburgh

CARFRAE, *John*
  E D: 11. L D: 20.
  Add: 101 Prince's St.
  Refs: Label as above, seen in
    Charing X Rd. on Burns' works,
    11. "A" seems to have left the
    firm by 20. O.C. A. Macdonald:
    Phingalers, 20. f. c. g. (J. only):
    AE/COLL/LAB: LAB/KNA ca. 20.

CARFRAE, *John Jun.* Edinburgh
  Add: 30 Old Fish Market Close.
  Res: 3 Jamaica St (20).
  Refs: PIG/SIN/20: EDIN/DIR/20.

191

CARSS & DRUMMOND (10)
Glasgow

CARSS & COLVILL (12)

CARSS, *John* (13)

CARSS, *J. & Co.* (23)
Add: 124 Trongate (10): No. 169
(11): Mudie's Court, Argyle St
(15): Res: Glenhead, Cadder
Parish (26).
Refs: GLAS/DIR/10: 11: 12: 13: 15:
17: 18: 23: 24: 26: 28/9: PIG/SIN/
20: PIG/CDS/25: PIG/CDS/37:
Dibden, N. E. & S. Tour 38,
p. 742/3 & 775/6: Sch. S. de R.
IV. 16 & 17: O.C. Cleland, Steam
Engine, 25, f.m.g. silk endpapers,
label, Lowther *ex-libris*. JA/1690.

CARSWELL, *Allan* Paisley
Add: 29 Old Snedden St & 77
High St (25): 5 New Snedden
St (37).
Refs: PIG/CDS/25/6: PIG/CDS/37:
PAIS/DIR/38/9.

CAW, *Alexander* Edinburgh
L D
Add: New North Kirk Parish (76):
Warriston's Close (84).
Refs: DBP/1726/75, p. 290: EDIN/
DIR/07: 09: 11: 16: 20: HOLD/11:
EDIN/DIR/84: 86: COSOC/BB/EDIN/
75.

CAW, *John* Edinburgh
(Bookseller &).
E D: 79.
Add: New North Kirk Parish.
Refs: DBP/1726/75, p. 291.

CHAMBERS, *W.* Glasgow
Add: 27 Shuttle St.
Refs: GLAS/DIR/35/6.

CHRISTIE, *Alexander* Edinburgh
E D: ca. 86.
Add: ? : Ryder St N.Y. 96/8.
Refs: DBP/1726/75, p. 292. BKBG.
p. 39.

CHRISTIE, *William* Edinburgh
E D: 73.
Add: Back Stairs (73): Head of
New Stairs (84): Back Stairs (86).
Refs: EDIN/DIR/73: 80: 82: 83: 84:
86: 93: 94: 96: 99: DBP/1726/75,
p. 292.

CLACHER, *David* Glasgow
Add: 8 East Clyde St (32): 43
Queen St (36).
Refs: GLAS/DIR/32/3: 35/6: 36/7.

CLAP(P)ERTON, *James* Edinburgh
Add: Luckenbooths.
Refs: EDIN/DIR/84: AE/GHB.

CLARK, *Alexander* Edinburgh
Add: Kincaid's Lane, Cowgate.
Refs: EDIN/DIR/93: 94.W.

PLATE XV

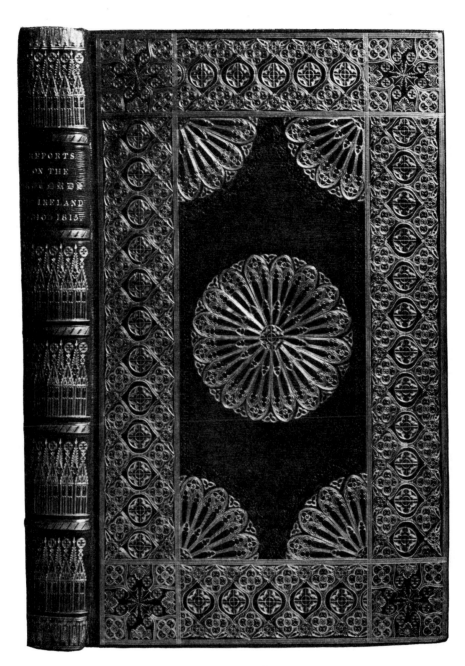

PLATE XVI

CLARK, *Alexander*   Glasgow
Add: 3 King St (23): No. 5 (26):
56 Bell St (39).
Refs: PIG/CDS/25/6: GLAS/DIR/23:
24: 26: 33/4: 35/6: 39/40: 40.

CLARK, *Robert*   Edinburgh
(b. 1738, d. 1810).
E D: 55?
Add: New North Kirk Parish (74):
Parliament House (82): Kincaid's
Lane, Cowgate (96).
Refs: EDIN/DIR/82: 83: 84: 96: 99:
DBP/1726/75, p. 293: Timperley
p. 837/8: Kay's Portraits, vol. 2,
p. 29: COSOC/BB/EDIN/75.

CLARKE, *K.*   Edinburgh
(See CLERK).
Add: 156 Cowgate.
Refs: EDIN/DIR/07: 09: 16: 20.

CLARKSON   Edinburgh
Add: Foot of Warriston Close,
Luckenbooths.
Refs: EDIN/DIR/04.

CLEGHORN, *William*   Edinburgh
E D: 55.
Add: N. W. Kirk Parish (55): Old
Church Parish (77): Old Post-
house Stairs (80).
Refs: EDIN/DIR/80: 82: 83: 84: 86:
88: 90: DBP/1726/75, p. 293.

CLELAND, *Charles*   Edinburgh
Add: Foot Allan's Close (84):
Craig's Close (86): Head of Fishmarket Close (88): Anchor Close
(90): Maiden Lane, N. Y. (92).
Refs: EDIN/DIR/84: 86: 88: 90:
BKBG/ pp. 39 & 78: Maggs Cat.
407/No. 303: Wheeler Cat. No.
145: AE/COLL/LAB.

CLERK, *K.*
(See CLARKE).

CLERK, *Robert*   Edinburgh
(See CLARK, *Robert*).

COLLIE, *William*   Aberdeen
(Bookseller &).
Add: 47 Upper Kirkgate: (Home)
71 North St.
Refs: PIG/CDS/25: 26/7: ABER/DIR/
24: 28: PIG/CDS/37.

COLVILL(E), *George*   Glasgow
Add: 8 Nelson St (13): 26 Bell St
(15): No. 36 (23): No. 55 (26):
Res: 10 College St (26): 67
Nelson St (29).
Refs: GLAS/DIR/13: 15: 17: 23: 24:
26: 28: 29/30: 36/7: PIG/SIN/20:
PIG/CDS/25/6.

COLVILL(E), *Robert* (I)   Glasgow

COLVILL(E), *Robert & John* (99)
 Add: 98 Trongate (83): Neilson's
  Land, Bell St (99): Old Wynd
  (01).
 Refs: GLAS/DIR/83: 87: 89: 99: 01:
  03: 05 to 14.

COLVILL(E), *Robert* (II)   Glasgow
 Add: 43 Queen St (37): Res. 48
  Garscube (40).
 Refs: PIG/CDS/37: GLAS/DIR/37/8:
  40.

CONDIE, *James*   Paisley
 Add: Moss St (11): 87 Moss St
  (20): (& Son): No. 42 (37): 6
  Christie Terrace: Res: 69 Moss
  St (38).
 Refs: HOLD/11: PIG/SIN/20: PIG/CDS
  /37: PAIS/DIR/38/9: JA/4956.

COOK, *William*   Edinburgh
 E D: 90.
 Refs: AE/GHB.

COOPER, *Thomas*   Edinburgh
 (See COUPAR?).
 Add: Mill's Close, Canongate.
 Refs: EDIN/DIR/09: 11.

COPLAND (or COUPLAND), *John*
     Edinburgh
 Add: Hyndford Close, 50 High St
  (29): South Gray's Close (37).

Refs: EDIN/DIR/29: 33: 35/6: PIG/
 CDS/37: (There was a *James*
 Copland, who was a journeyman
 bookbinder in Old Kirk Parish
 in 1773. See DBP/1726/75, p. 295).

COUPAR, *Thomas*   Edinburgh
 (See COOPER?).
 E D: 99.
 Refs: AE/GHB.

CRABBIE, *J.*   Edinburgh
 (& S T).
 Add: 49 Nicholson St.
 Refs: EDIN/DIR/33.

CRAW, *Alexander*   Edinburgh
 Add: Warriston Close (01): Bell
  Wynd (11).
 Refs: AE/GHB: EDIN/DIR/01: 09: 11:
  16: 20.

CRAWFORD, *A.*   Edinburgh
 (& S T).
 Add: 55 George St (27?): No. 69
  (33): 78 South Bridge (35/6).
 Refs: O.C. Vues d'Ecosse. Pichot:
  Brussels 27: f. r. g. sign. on inside
  edge on binding: EDIN/DIR/33:
  35/6.

CRAWFORD, *Andrew*   Edinburgh
 (& S T).
 Add: 55 George St (29): 4 Melville
  Place (33).
 Refs: EDIN/DIR/29: 33.

CRAWFORD, *Adam*   Glasgow
(Etc).
Add: 13 King St (25): No. 27 (33).
Refs: PIG/CDS/25/6: GLAS/DIR/33/4:
40.

CRAWFORD, *David*   Glasgow
(Bookbinders' Tool-cutters).
Add: 280 George St.
Refs: PIG/CDS/37.

CROILEY, *Peter & Co.*   Glasgow
Add: 106 George St.
Refs: PIG/SIN/20.

CUNNINGHAM, *James*   Glasgow
Add: 22 Trongate (24): No. 43 (28):
17 Brunswick Lane (37).
Refs: PIG/CDS/25/6: GLAS/DIR/24/5:
26: 28 to 31: PIG/CDS/37.

CURRIE, *William*   Edinburgh
Add: Opp. Mealmarket.
Refs: EDIN/DIR/93: 94W: 96: 99:
01: 03.

CURRIE & LAMB   Edinburgh
Add: 10 Hunter Square.
Refs: EDIN/DIR/36: PIG/CDS/37.

DARLING, *Robert*   Edinburgh
Add: Old Stamp Office Close (26):
221 High St (29): 1 Milne Sq
(33): 7 Old Fishmarket Close (37).
Refs: EDIN/DIR/26: 29: 33: 35/6:
39: PIG/CDS/37.

DEWAR, *John*   Edinburgh
(& S T).
Add: 59 Bristo St (25).
Refs: PIG/CDS/25: 26/27.

DEWAR, *John*   Edinburgh
Add: 12 N. Richmond St (11):
Parliament Stairs (20).
Refs: EDIN/DIR/11: 20: 23: PIG/CDS/
25: 26/7.

DICK, *David*   Paisley
Add: 3 High St, west end of Old
Bridge.
Refs: RENF/DIR/31/2.

DICKSON, *Joseph*   Edinburgh
E D: 87.
Refs: AE/GHB.

DONALD, *Andrew*   Glasgow
Add: 50 Adelphi St.
Refs: GLAS/DIR/33 to 36.

DONALDSON, *Alexander*
E D: 92.   Edinburgh
Refs: AE/GHB.

DOUGLAS, *K.*   Inverness
E D: 23.
Refs: Munby Coll: Label "K.D,
BS, S & BB, I" calf gilt, 27:
ABB/CBS.

DUNBAR, *John*   Dumfries
Add: 76 English St (20): 77 (25).
Refs: PIG/SIN/20: PIG/CDS/25/6.

DUNBAR, *John*   Elgin
  Add: Back St.
  Refs: PIG/CDS/37.

DUNCAN, *Charles*   Stonehaven
  Add: High St.   (Kincardineshire)
  Refs: PIG/CDS/37.

DUNCAN, *John*   Edinburgh
  E D: 73.
  Add: New Greyfriar's Parish.
  Refs: DBP/1726/75, p. 303.

DUNCAN, *Robert*   Glasgow
  Add: Salt Market.
  Refs: GLAS/DIR/83.

DUNDAS, *William*   Edinburgh
  E D: 48 (to 96?).
  Add: South South-West Kirk
  Parish.
  Refs: DBP/1726/75, p. 303.

DUNLOP, *Charles*   Dumfries
  Add: Maxwell-town.
  Refs: PIG/CDS/25/6.

DUNLOP, *Charles*   Edinburgh
  Add: 1 Milne Square.
  Refs: EDIN/DIR/33: 35/6: PIG/CDS/
  37.

ELDER, *John*   Edinburgh
  (B S &).
  Add: Posthouse Stair, Parliament
  Close, & foot New Bank Close.
  Refs: EDIN/DIR/03.

ELDER, *Walter*   Hawick
  Add: Howegate. (Roxburghshire)
  Refs: PIG/CDS/37.

ELLIOTT, *George*   Glasgow
  Add: 10 Bell St (20): No. 9 (24):
  23 Candlerigg St (25): No. 53
  (26): No. 20 (27): Tarbet St (29):
  239 George St (32).
  Refs: PIG/SIN/20: PIG/CDS/25/6:
  GLAS/DIR/23 to 33.

ELLIOT, *William*   Edinburgh
  E D: 70.
  Add: New North Kirk Parish.
  Refs: DBP/1726/75, p. 304.

ELLISON, *Robert*   Edinburgh
  Add: Foot of Allan Close.
  Refs: EDIN/DIR/88: 90.

ELLTES & *Co.*   Inverness
  E D: 21.
  Refs: AE/LAB.

ELMSLIE, *James*   Aberdeen
  (& Circulating Library).
  Add: 57 North St.
  Refs: ABER/DIR/28.

ETTLES & YOUNG   Elgin
  E D: 10?
  Refs: O.C. Doddridge, Rise &
  Progress, 1750, f.m.g. about 1810
  (?). Ticket.

FAIRBAIRN, *John*   Edinburgh
(Undoubtedly an important BB till 1780, after which date he always figures as ST).
E D: 61.
Add: Tolbooth Parish (61): Back of the Weighhouse (80).
Refs: DBP/1726/75, p. 305: EDIN/DIR /80: COSOC/BB/EDIN/75.

FARIE, *Robert*   Glasgow

FARIE, *Robert & Co.* (37).
Add: Old P.O. Court, 141 Trongate (20): 57 Argyll St. Res: 57 Osward St (26): 114 Trongate (28): Wilson Court, 57 Argyll St (29): "& Co." (37).
Refs: PIG/SIN/20: PIG/CDS/25/6: GLAS/DIR/23 to 30: PIG/CDS/37: Label seen in July, 1950, on a classic, dated 1818 on spine and bearing on the sides the arms of Glasgow City or University.

FERGUSON, *William*   Glasgow
Add: 159 Saltmarket (11): 1 Laigh Close (24).
Refs: GLAS/DIR/11: 17: 18: 24.

FERRIER, *Charles*   Edinburgh
Add: 306 Lawnmarket (23): West Bow (26): 306 High St (33).
Refs: PIG/SIN/20: PIG/CDS/25: 26/ 27: EDIN/DIR/20: 23: 26 (& 64 West Bow) 33.

FERRIER, *William*   Edinburgh
Add: Strichen's Close (16): 13 Old Fishmarket: Res.: 13 Salisbury (20): Old Assembly Close (26): 1 Milne Sq (33): No. 6 (37): No. 7 (39).
Refs: EDIN/DIR/16: 20: 23: 26: 29: 33: 35/6: 39: PIG/CDS/25: 26/27.

FINLAY, *Alex.*   Glasgow
Add: 10 Old Wynd.
Refs: GLAS/DIR/23.

FIN(D)LAY, *William*   Edinburgh
(Inventor of a new ruling machine in 93).
E D: ca. 75.
Add: Castle Hill (84): Kennedy's Close, Castle Hill (93): opp. Weighhouse (96).
Refs: EDIN/DIR/84: 93: 96: COSOC/ BB/EDIN/75.

FISHER, *John*   Glasgow
(& S T).
Add: 29 Virginia St (05 & 08): 76 Hutcheson St (06): 69 Glassford St (07): 62 Trongate (09).
Refs: GLAS/DIR/05 to 09: 13: 17: 18: 23: PIG/SIN/20.

FITCH, *Alexander*   Edinburgh
(Journeyman BB in 1771).
Add: Old Greyfriars' Parish (71/3): opp. the Cornmarket (80): Horse Wynd (84): Potter row port (90).

197

Refs: DBP/1726/75, p. 305: EDIN/
DIR/80: 84: 86: 88: 90: 93: 96:
99: 01: 03: 04.

FITZPATRICK, *D.*   Edinburgh
Add: Old Assembly Close.
Refs: EDIN/DIR/23.

FLECKFIELD, *Robert*   Glasgow
(& S T).
Add: 119 Candleriggs.
Refs: PIG/CDS/39.

FLEMING, *David*   Edinburgh
(Burgess of Edinburgh).
E D: ca. 75.
Add: Portsburgh.
Refs: EDIN/DIR/80: COSOC/BB/EDIN
/75.

FLETCHER   St. Andrews
E D: ca. 30.   (Fifeshire)
Add: Opp. the University Library.
Refs: Pupil of C. Lewis. See Dibden
N. E. & S. Tour, p. 921.

FORBES, *Alexander*   Edinburgh
Add: 5 Milne's Court.
Refs: PIG/CDS/37: EDIN/DIR/33:
35/6: 39.

FORBES, *John*   Edinburgh
Add: Dickson's Close (96): 115
Cowgate (16): No. 127 (20):
6 Horse Wynd, Cowgate (23):
16 Rose St (35/6).

Refs: EDIN/DIR/96: 16: 20: 23: 26:
35/6: PIG/SIN/20: PIG/CDS/25: 26/
7: 37.

FORD, *John*   Kirkcaldy
(B S, S T &).   (Fife)
Refs: HOLD/11.

FORSYTH, *James*   Edinburgh
E D: ca. 1747.
Add: Mealmarket Stairs.
Refs: DBP/1726/75, p. 307: EDIN/
DIR/73/4: 80: 82: 83: 84: 86: 88:
90: 93: 94.

FORSYTH, *John*   Dundee
Add: Barrack St.
Refs: PIG/CDS/37.

FRAME, *Lockhart*   Edinburgh
Add: 10 Parliament Sq (20): 322
High St: Res. 54 Bristo St (26):
322 Lawnmarket (29): 2 James
Ct & Mound Place (37): 6 James
Ct (39).
Refs: EDIN/DIR/20: 23: 26: 29: 33:
35/6: 39: PIG/CDS/25: 26/7: 37.

FRASER, *John*   Edinburgh
Add: Warriston's Close.
Refs: EDIN/DIR/16.

FRYE, *John & Co.*   Glasgow
Add: 285 Argyll St.
Refs: GLAS/DIR/30/1.

FULTON, *Thomas*   Glasgow
    Add: 125 Trongate (27): No. 131
    (29).
    Refs: PIG/CDS/37: GLAS/DIR/27 to
    36: S. Fulton may have been
    associated with Thomas about
    1835.

GALLOWAY, *Robert*   Edinburgh

GALLOWAY, *A.*
    Add: 25 Thistle St (35/6): 17 West
    Register St (37): 29 W. Register
    St (39).
    Refs: PIG/CDS/37: EDIN/DIR/35/6:
    39.

GARDNER, *Alexander*   Edinburgh
    E D: 94.
    Refs: AE/GHB.

GILLIES, *William*   Edinburgh
    Add: 5 Salisbury St.
    Refs: PIG/CDS/37.

GILLON, *John*   Edinburgh
    Add: 27 Jamaica St.
    Refs: EDIN/DIR/35/6.

GORDON, *Alexander*
    (P R &).   Kirkcudbright
    Add: High St.
    Refs: PIG/SIN/20.

GORDON, *William*   Aberdeen
    (B S, etc).
    Add: 20 Upper Kirkgate: (Home)
    No. 19 Upper Kirkgate,
    Bountie's Court.
    Refs: PIG/CDS/25: 26/27.

GOUDIE, *Daniel*   Ayr
    Add: 11 New Market St.
    Refs: PIG/NCDS/25: PIG/CDS/37.

GOWAN, *N.*   Edinburgh
    Add: Forrester's Wynd.
    Refs: EDIN/DIR/07.

GRANT, *Robert*   Edinburgh
    Add: 23 Lothian St.
    Refs: PIG/SIN/20.

GRAY, *George*   Glasgow
    (Bookbinders' Toolcutters).
    Add: 24 Trongate.
    Refs: PIG/CDS/37.

GRAY, *John*   Edinburgh
    Add: 57 Pleasance (16): Nether-
    bow: Res: 13 Salisbury St (20):
    7 Mound (35/6).
    Refs: EDIN/DIR/16: 20: 23: 26: 35/6:
    39: PIG/CDS/37: LAB/KNA.

GREGORY, *John Preston*
                  Edinburgh (?)
    Add: 7 Temple Court.
    Refs: PIG/CDS/37.

GRIEVE, *Alexander*   Edinburgh
   E D: ca. 71.
   Add: College Kirk Parish (71):
     Bell's Wynd (73): Allan's Close
     (80): President's Stair (84): Par-
     liament Close (90): Old Kirk
     Parish (94).
   Refs: EDIN/DIR/84: 86: 88: 90: 94:
     96: COSOC/BB/EDIN/75.

GRIEVE, *Robert*   Edinburgh
   Add: Allan's Close (82).
   Refs: EDIN/DIR/82: 83. WSM/KC/
     NEW mentions a binding with
     stamp, and quotes him as ap-
     pearing in the EDIN/DIR/24/5 at
     32 College Wynd.

GRIEVE, *W.*   Kelso
   E D: ca. 26.
   Refs: Ticket "Bd. by/W.G./BS/
     ST & BB/Kelso" ½ calf on Scott's
     Woodstock, 1826, in Edin. City
     Library.

GUTHRIE, *John*   Edinburgh
   (& B S). b. 1748, d. 1823.
   Add: Linen Hall, Cowgate (68?):
     Netherbow (?): opp. Fountain-
     well (86): Nicolson St (14).
   Refs: EDIN/DIR/86. For his book-
     selling and other activities, see
     DBP/1726/75, p. 315. TIMP/p. 890:
     Kay.

HALIDAY, *John*   Edinburgh
   Add: 42 Old Fishmarket Close.
   Refs: EDIN/DIR/16.

HALIDAY & FERRIER   Edinburgh
   Add: 42 Old Fishmarket Close.
   Refs: HOLD/11: EDIN/DIR/11.

HALL & MUIR   Edinburgh
   Add: High St.
   Refs: HOLD/11.

HAMILTON, *Alexander*   Edinburgh
   Add: 9 High School Yard.
   Refs: PIG/SIN/20.

HAMILTON, *Robert*   Edinburgh
   Add: Old Assembly Close (09):
     Back Stairs (16): Parliament Stairs
     (20).
   Refs: EDIN/DIR/09: 11: 16: 20: 23:
     PIG/SIN/20.

HARDIE, *James*   Edinburgh
   Add: Gosford's Close.
   Refs: EDIN/DIR/93: 96.

HARDIE, *James*   Glasgow
   Add: 277 High St.
   Refs: GLAS/DIR/01: 03: 08.

HARRISON, *Robert*   Glasgow
   Add: 22 Saracen Lane.
   Refs: GLAS/DIR/24.

HENDERSON, *James*   Edinburgh
(See Henderson & Bisset).
Add: 25 St. James' Square.
Refs: PIG/CDS/25: 26/27: Note
book dated 1816 extant. See Edn.
Journal of Royal Scottish Society
of Arts, Vol. XVI, Part I, Oct.,
1941.

HENDERSON, *Peter & Co.*
Add: 18 or 46 Nelson St. Glasgow
Refs: GLAS/DIR/26.

HENDERSON & BISSET
                           Edinburgh
(Founded in 1823: B B to Her
Majesty (39)).
Add: 25 St. James' Sq (23): West
Register St & Craig's Close (25):
W. Market St & Mound Place
(26): Mound Place (29): 21
George St (31): 19 Hill St (36).
Refs: There is a long reference to
these binders, who worked for
Thomas Maitland, in Dibden's
S.E. & N. Tour, 38. Henderson is
stated to have been a pupil of
C. Lewis.
PIG/CDS/37: EDIN/DIR/29: 33: 35/
6: 39. See long article by Camp-
bell White in Edn. Journal of
Royal Scott. Socy. of Arts, Vol.
XVI, Part I, Oct., 1941. The
firm is still in existence (1952).
I am indebted to Mr. Campbell
White for much information
supplied to me.

HENDERSON & HUT(C)HESON
(or Hutchison).   Glasgow
Add: 72 Trongate (23): 62 (24).
Refs: GLAS/DIR/23: 24/5: PIG/CDS/
25/6.

HENRY, *James*   Dumfries
Add: 28 Buccleuch St (26): 35
Irish St (37).
Refs: PIG/CDS/25/6: PIG/CDS/37.

HERON, *Lauchlan*   Edinburgh
Add: Forrester's Wynd (93): Borthwick's Close (09): 469 High St
(11): Covenant Close (16).
Refs: EDIN/DIR/93: 94W: 96: 99: 03:
07: 09: 11: 16.

HERRIOT, *Mrs.*   Edinburgh
(Widow of William?).

HERRIOT, *Charles*
(Still alive in 1775, when he signed
Soc. of B B articles).
E D: 1773 & 1768 respectively.
Add: Old Fishmarket Close (Mrs.)
(73): Parliament House (73).
Refs: DBP/1726/75, p. 319.

HEUGH, *Walter*   Glasgow
Add: Salt Market.
Refs: GLAS/DIR/83.

HILL, *Alexander*   Edinburgh
Add: 10 St. James' Sq.
Refs: EDIN/DIR/29.

HOGG, *William*   Edinburgh
   E D: ca. 75.
   Add: Old Bank Close.
   Refs: COSOC/BB/EDIN/75: EDIN/
     DIR/84.

HONEYMAN, *M.*   Glasgow
   Add: 53 Kirk St, Calton.
   Refs: PIG/CDS/25/6.

HOWELL, *John*   Edinburgh

HOWELL, *William* (26)
   Add: 30 Thistle St.
   Refs: PIG/SIN/20: EDIN/DIR/20: 23:
     26: PIG/CDS/25: 26/7.

HUNTER, *Charles*   Edinburgh
   Add: Tolbooth Parish (57): Ham-
     mermen's Close, Cowgate (73/4):
     Parliament House (80): Par-
     liament Sq. Res: foot of West
     Bow (82): opp. Cornmarket (84).
   Refs: DBP/1726/75, p. 319: EDIN/DIR
     /80: 82: 83: 84: COSOC/BB/EDIN/
     75.

HUNTER, *David*   Edinburgh

HUNTER, *Mrs.* (35/6)
   Add: 52 Cowgate.
   Refs: EDIN/DIR/20: 23: 26: 29:
     35/6: PIG/CDS/25: 26/27.

HUNTER, *John*   Edinburgh
   Add: Hastie's Close, Cowgate (80):
     opp. Magdalen Chapel (90):
     Cowgate Head (94).
   Refs: EDIN/DIR/80: 84: 90: 94W.

HUNTER, *Mrs.*   Edinburgh
   Add: Opp. Magdalen Chapel,
     Cowgate.
   Refs: EDIN/DIR/07: 09: 11.

HUTCHESON, *Alexander* Glasgow
   (or HUTCHISON).

HUTCHESON, *James* (13)

HUTCHESON, *David* (26)
   (See Henderson &).
   Add: Salt Market (83 "A")*: 159
     Salt Market (13): 43 Trongate
     (17): Gibson's Ct, Salt Market
     (20): 53 Spoutmouth (23): 158
     Trongate (24/5, as J. Hutchison,
     Wholesale): No. 80 (26): No.
     125 (David) (26): 27 King St (28):
     12 Prince's St (29): 46 Salt
     Market (38).
   Refs: GLAS/DIR/13: 17: 18: 23: 24/5:
     26 (David): 27 to 39: PIG/SIN/20:
     PIG/CDS/25: 37.
   * May be the continuation of the
     business of Alexander (I). (See
     DBP/1726/75, p. 320).

HUTCHISON, *Robert*   Glasgow

HUTCHISON, *James* (26)
     Add: 159 Salt Market.
     Refs: PIG/SIN/20: GLAS/DIR/26.

HUTTON, *John*   Edinburgh
     (Was undoubtedly a B B of impor-
     tance in 1775, but from 1782 is
     styled as S T in the directories).
     E D: ca. 75.
     Add: Parliament Square.
     Refs: EDIN/DIR/82: 83: 84: 86:
     COSOC/BB/EDIN/75.

INGLIS, *Alexander*   Aberdeen
     (& S T).
     Add: Causewayend.
     Refs: ABER/DIR/28.

INGLIS, *Archibald*   Edinburgh

INGLIS, *James* (37)
     Add: 11 Bristo Port (11): Carubber's
     Close, High St (25): 127 Nicol-
     son St (33): 16 Roxburgh Place
     (35).
     Refs: EDIN/DIR/11: 16: 20: 23: 26:
     33: 35/6: PIG/CDS/25: 26/7: 37
     (James).

JACKSON, *William Ltd.*   Aberdeen
     Refs: Apollo Magazine, Jan., 1951,
     Art. by W. S. Mitchell.

JAM(I)SON, *Robert*   Edinburgh
     (B B & later Bookseller).
     Add: Tolbooth Parish (71): Par-
     liament Sq. (73).
     Refs: DBP/1726/75, p. 322.

JENKINS, *Wm.*   Glasgow
     (B S, S T &).
     Add: Salt Market (20): 125 Tron-
     gate (26).
     Refs: PIG/SIN/20: GLAS/DIR/26.

JOHNSTON, *J. & Co.*   Glasgow
     Add: 2 Hutcheson St.
     Refs: O.C. Holy Bible, Edin. 4d.
     22, superbly blind stamped &
     gilt on purple mor., with 2in.
     inside doublures similarly treated,
     & pink silk endpapers. Green
     oblong ticket "Mfd. by/J.J. &
     Co./2 H. St./Glasgow". Binding
     between 1822/30.

JOHNSTON, *Robert*   Aberdeen
     (& S T).
     Add: 19 Gallowgate: Res: 3 Black-
     friar St.
     Refs: ABER/DIR/28.

JOHNSTON, *William*   Edinburgh
     Add: 183 Cowgate.
     Refs: EDIN/DIR/16.

JOHNSTONE, *William Francis*
         Maxwelltown (Dumfries)
     Add: 50 Glasgow St.
     Refs: PIG/CDS/37.

JONES, *John*   Edinburgh

JONES, *John & Son* (26)
   Add: 2 Drummond St (25): 59
   South Bridge St (26): 4 In-
   firmary St (29): 59 S. B. St. &
   Salisbury St (35/6).
   Refs: EDIN/DIR/26: 29: 33: 35/6:
   PIG/CDS/25: 26/7: 37.

JONES, *John*   Glasgow
   Add: McNair's Land, Trongate
   (99): 43 Trongate (05): No. 141
   (09): P.O. Court, Trongate (17):
   11 Nelson St (20).
   Refs: GLAS/DIR/99: 01: 05 to 15:
   17: PIG/SIN/20.

KEDDIE, *Archibald*   Glasgow

KEDDIE, *Archibald & Thomas* (10)

KEDDIE, *Thomas* (09)
   Add: 2 Prince's St (03): No. 3 (05):
   Moodie's Ct (09): 6 Bell St (11).
   Refs: GLAS/DIR/03: 05 to 09: 09
   (T.): 10 (A. & T.): 11 (A.): 11 (T.).

KEDDIE, *Archibald*   Edinburgh
   Add: Covenant Close (16): Old
   Bank Close (20).
   Refs: EDIN/DIR/16: PIG/SIN/20.

KEIR & MILLER   Glasgow
   Add: 18 Hutcheson St.
   Refs: GLAS/DIR/38/9.

KELLY, *Bruce*   Newton-Stewart
   Refs: PIG/CDS/37.   (Wigtonshire)

KENNEDY, *D.*   Glasgow
   (Etc, etc).
   Add: 16/17 Gt. Clyde St.
   Refs: GLAS/DIR/39/40.

KENNEDY, *James*   Glasgow
   (& S T).
   Add: 115 Ingram St.
   Refs: PIG/CDS/37.

KERR, *James Jun.*   Greenock
   (B S &).
   Add: 10 Hamilton St.
   Refs: RENF/DIR/31/2: 36/7 (no
   "Jun.").

LAING, *Andrew*   Greenock
   (Etc, in 1836).
   Add: 14 William St (31): 1 Hamil-
   ton St (36).
   Refs: RENF/DIR/31/2: 36/7.

LAING, *John*   Edinburgh
   Add: Libberton's Wynd (09):
   Byres' Close (16).
   Refs: EDIN/DIR/09: 16.

LAUDER, *John*   Edinburgh
   Add: 155 Cowgate (20): No. 165
   (26).
   Refs: PIG/SIN/20: EDIN/DIR/26: 29.

LAURIE, *Alexander*   Edinburgh
  Add: 126 Cowgate.
  Refs: PIG/CDS/25: 26/27.

LAURIE, *Robert*   Glasgow
  (& Librarian).
  Add: 27 Commerce St (28): 8
  King St, Tradeston (32): No. 3
  (39).
  Refs: PIG/CDS/37: GLAS/DIR/28 to 40.

LAURIE, *William*   Aberdeen
  (& Circulating Library).
  Add: 38 Gallow Gate (20): 11 St.
  Nicholas St. Res: Cruickshank's
  Court, 46 Shiprow (28).
  Refs: PIG/SIN/20: PIG/NCDS/25: 26/
  7: ABER/DIR/24: 28: PIG/CDS/37.

LAWDER, *Andrew*   Peterhead
  Add: Long-gate.   (Aberdeen)
  Refs: PIG/NCDS/26.

LAWRENCE, *Abraham*   Edinburgh

LAWRENCE, *Alexander* (23)
  Add: 126 Cowgate.
  Refs: EDIN/DIR/23: PIG/CDS/25: 26/
  27.

LECKIE, *David*   Edinburgh

LECKIE, *David & Co.* (29)
  Add: 30 W. Register St (20): 3
  Forth St (29).
  Refs: PIG/SIN/20: EDIN/DIR/29: 33.

*LEECHMAN, *James*   Edinburgh

LEECHMAN & *Son* (07)
  E D: ca. 66: (but there may be two
  James).
  Add: New Kirk Parish (66): Gos-
  ford Close (86): St. Andrew's St
  (88): Byer's Close (90): Bow
  Head (93): Fountain Close,
  Netherlaw (99): Cowgate (09).
  Refs: EDIN/DIR/86: 88: 90: 93:
  94W: 96: 99: 07: 09: HOLD/11:
  COSOC/BB/EDIN/75.
  * Is on occasion spelt as Leishman,
  which may suggest German origin,
  but see DBP/1726/75, p. 324.

L(E)IGHTON, *John*   Edinburgh
  Add: Head of Horse Wynd.
  Refs: EDIN/DIR/96.

LEICHMAN, *James*   Edinburgh
  (See Leechman).

LISHMAN, *J.*   Glasgow
  Add: 109 Dale St, Tradeston.
  Refs: GLAS/DIR/24.

LOGAN, *Robert*   Edinburgh
  E D: 1765.
  Add: Old Kirk Parish (65): Foot of
  West Bow (73/4).
  Refs: DBP/1726/75, p. 325: COSOC/
  BB/EDIN/75.

LOVE, *George*   Glasgow

LOVE, *George & Co.* (29)
(& P R).
   Add: 169 Trongate (24): 1 Wallace
   Court (25): 3 (26): 17 Bazar (30):
   28 Salt Market (29/30 "& Co.").
   Refs: PIG/CDS/25/6: GLAS/DIR/24 to
   33.

LOW, *Carnegie*   Edinburgh
   Add: Bow Head (93): Baxter's
   Close, Lawnmarket (99): Middle
   of Mealmarket Stairs (04): 388
   Castle Hill (25).
   Refs: EDIN/DIR/93: 94W: 96: 99:
   01: 04: 07: 11: 16: 20: 23: 26:
   29: PIG/CDS/25: 26/7.

LOW, *Ernest*   Aberdeen
   Add: 6 Blackfriars St (24): No. 7
   (25): 22 Wollmanhill: Res: 22
   Black's Bldgs. (28).
   Refs: PIG/CDS/25: 26: 27: ABER/DIR/
   24: 28.

LOW, *William*   Paisley

LOW & KNOX (31)
   Add: 26 High St (20): 10 Gauze St
   (25): 2 New St (31).
   Refs: PIG/SIN/20: PIG/CDS/25/6:
   RENF/DIR/31/2 (L. & K.): PAIS/
   DIR/38/9 (W. L. again).

LUMSDAINE (or LUMSDEN),
   William   Edinburgh
   Add: 60 North Bridge (26): 10
   South St. David St (29).
   Refs: EDIN/DIR/26: 29.

LYLE, *Peter*   Dalkeith
(Doubtfully a binder by 1826).
   Add: High St.
   Refs: PIG/SIN/20: PIG/CDS/26.

LYON, *John*   Glasgow
   Add: 15 Gallowgate.
   Refs: GLAS/DIR/03: 05 to 08.

McBRYDE, *James*   Wigtown
   Add: Main St.
   Refs: PIG/SIN/20.

McCLELLAND, *John*   Edinburgh
   Add: 29 Thistle St (16): 29 Register
   St (20).
   Refs: EDIN/DIR/16: 20: PIG/SIN/20.

McCREDIE, *William*   Stranraer
   Add: Fisher St.   (Wigtownshire)
   Refs: PIG/CDS/37.

McCULLOUGH, *Daniel*   Inverness
   Add: East St.
   Refs: PIG/CDS/25/6.

McDONALD, *Archibald*   Inverness
   Add: 7 High St.
   Refs: PIG/CDS/37.

McFADYEN, *Alexander*   Glasgow
Add: 9 Argyll St (25): No. 21 (26):
17 Stockwall (27): 13 Argyll St
(33).
Refs: GLAS/DIR/25 to 34.

McFARLANE, *William*   Paisley
(& Bookseller (37): & Hairdresser
(38)).
Add: 4 New St.
Refs: PIG/CDS/37: PAIS/DIR/38/9.

McGREGGOR, *John*   St. Andrews
Add: Market St.
Refs: PIG/CDS/25/6.

McGREGOR, *D.*   Greenock
Add: 1 Bank St.
Refs: RENF/DIR/31/2.

McGREGOR, *William*   Glasgow
Add: Old Wynd.
Refs: GLAS/DIR/26.

McGREGOR & CAMERON
    Glasgow
(Or McGrigor & Cameron).
Add: 12 Wilson St (24): 12 Bell St
(25).
Refs: GLAS/DIR/24/5: PIG/CDS/25/6.

McGRIGGOR, *Willaim*   Bathgate
(& S T).   (Linlithgowshire)
Add: Jarvey St.
Refs: PIG/CDS/25/6.

McINTOSH, *Allan*   Edinburgh
Add: 11 Heriot's Buildings, Leith
Walk (29): 70 Nicolson St (39).
Refs: EDIN/DIR/29: 33: 35/6: 39:
PIG/CDS/37.

McINTOSH, *G. L.*   Dalkeith
Refs: EDIN/DIR/35/6.

McINTOSH, *John*   Dalkeith

McINTOSH, *J. & W.* (35/6)
Refs: PIG/CDS/25: 26/7: EDIN/DIR/
35/6.

McKELVIE   Greenock
E D: 32.
Refs: Stamped address seen at
Fletcher's on Bibliophobia (?
Dibden) by Mercurius Rusticus,
1832, tree calf gilt.

McKENDRICK, *John*   Glasgow
Add: 75 Argyll St.
Refs: GLAS/DIR/39/40.

McKENZIE, *Peter*   Glasgow
Add: 31 Argyll St.
Refs: PIG/CDS/37.

McLAG(G)AN, *James*   Edinburgh
(Late Bookbinder in 1826).
Add: Covenant Close, High St
(11): 17 Shakespeare Sq (23):
Res: 24 Gardner's Crescent (26).
Refs: EDIN/DIR/11: 16: 20: 23: 26:
29: PIG/SIN/20: PIG/CDS/25: 26/7.

McLAREN, *John*   Edinburgh
Add: Halkerston's Wynd.
Refs: EDIN/DIR/20.

McLAREN, *John*   Glasgow
(From the 1826 Glasgow Directory
    he would appear to have worked
    with J. Carss & Co., but was
    allowed to sign certain works on
    his own; later he appears to have
    worked on his own).
Add: Moodie Ct. (26): 157 Tron-
    gate (28): 64 Queen St (33): 23
    Glassford St (34).
Refs: GLAS/DIR/26 to 40: LAB/KNA:
    ca. 25: Munby Coll: Label "Sold
    & Bd. by J. M., G" Green m.g.,
    ca. 1830.

McLAREN, *William*   Crieff
Add: Old Square.   (Perthshire)
Refs: PIG/CDS/25.

McLELLAN, *C.*   Edinburgh

McLELLAN, *Mrs. Cathleen* (26)
Add: 63 North Bridge (25): No. 60
    (35/6).
Refs: PIG/CDS/25: 26/27: 37: EDIN/
    DIR/26: 29: 33: 35/6.

McLEOD, *James*   Glasgow
Add: 15 Melville Place.
Refs: GLAS/DIR/27.

McMORRAN, *William*   Girvan
Add: Bank St.   (Ayrshire)
Refs: PIG/CDS/37.

McNAIR, *Robert*   Glasgow
Add: Salt Market (83): Head of
    Back-Wynd (99).
Refs: GLAS/DIR/83: 99: 01: 03: 05
    to 09: AE/COLL/LAB.

McNISH   Dalbeattie
E D: 06?   (Kirkcudbrightshire)
Refs: O.C. Thomson. Seasons.
    Perth. 93. 4°. dark green back,
    tree calf sides. M.S. note inside:
    "Bound by McNish/Dalbeattie,
    1806" (in 2 different scripts).

McPHERSON, *Evan*   Glasgow
Add: Salt Market.
Refs: GLAS/DIR/83.

McRAE, *John*   Elgin
Add: High St.
Refs: PIG/CDS/37.

MALLOCK, *Patrick*   Edinburgh
Add: 51 North Bridge.
Refs: EDIN/DIR/26.

MANSON, *John*   Edinburgh

MANSON & *Son* (33: B S)

MANSON & *Co.* (37)
Add: 3 Carnegie St (09): Riddell's
    Close (16): Advocate's Close, 357
    High St (26): W. Register St &
    357 High St: Res: Advocate's
    Close (29): 41 St. Andrew Sq &
    46 W. Register St (33): 21

George St (35/6): 21 George St (& Co., 37).
Refs: EDIN/DIR/09: 11: 16: 20: 23: 26: 29: 33: 35: PIG/CDS/25: 26/7: 37: AE/LAB (& Son: ca. 30).

MARSHALL, *John*   Glasgow
Add: High St.
Refs: GLAS/DIR/83.

MARSHALL, *H.*   Edinburgh
Add: 71 Prince's St.
Refs: EDIN/DIR/39.

MARSHALL, *Thomas*   Edinburgh
Add: Allan's Close, High St.
Refs: EDIN/DIR/20: 23: 26: PIG/SIN/ 20: PIG/CDS/25: 26/27.

MARTIN, *Thomas*   Glasgow
(& Pocket-book Maker).
Add: 74 Argyll St.
Refs: GLAS/DIR/38 to 40.

MATHERS, *David*   Dundee
Add: Hawk Hill.
Refs: PIG/CDS/37.

MATHEWS, *J. A.*   Edinburgh
Add: 16 Parliament Sq.
Refs: EDIN/DIR/16.

MEEK, *William*   Edinburgh
Add: 265 High St (35): Craig's Close (37).
Refs: EDIN/DIR/35/6: PIG/CDS/37.

MENZIES, *R. & A.* (20)   Glasgow

MENZIES, *William* (26)
Add: 127 Trongate (20): 11 Salt Market (26): No. 39 (26).
Refs: PIG/SIN/20: GLAS/DIR/23: 26.

MENZIES, *John*   Glasgow
(A rather mysterious person or persons, no doubt from the co-incidence of addresses related to the above).
Add: 11 Salt Market (12): No. 30 (25): No. 39 (26): 27 Wilson St (29): 77 Brunswick St (31).
Refs: GLAS/DIR/12: 25 to 32.

MENZIES, *William*   Glasgow
Add: 11 Salt Market.
Refs: GLAS/DIR/13: PIG/SIN/20.

MIDDLETON, *William*   Dundee
(& Account Book Manufacturer).
Add: 45 Union St.
Refs: PIG/CDS/37.

MILLAR, *Ebenezer*   Glasgow
Add: Salt Market.
Refs: GLAS/DIR/83.

MILLAR, *George*   Edinburgh
E D: 91.
Refs: AE/GHB.

MILLER, *Andrew*   Hamilton
(P R &).
Add: Castle-Wynd.
Refs: PIG/SIN/20.

MILLER, *John*   Dumbarton
    Add: High St.
    Refs: PIG/NCDS/25.

MILLER, *Robert*   Edinburgh
    Add: Forrester's Wynd (04): Royal
    Bank Close (09): Carubber's
    Close (11): 149 Richmond Lane
    (16).
    Refs: EDIN/DIR/04: 07: 09: 11: 16.

MILLER, *William*   Edinburgh
    Add: Sciennes: Res. Duncan St,
    Newington (23): 1 Duncan St,
    Newington (25): 3 Gilmour St,
    Simon Sq. (33).
    Refs: PIG/CDS/25: 26/27: EDIN/DIR/
    23: 33.

MILLS, *W. B.*   Kirriemuir
    E D: ca. 40.   (Forfarshire)
    Refs: P. Labels.

MITCHELL, *Adam*   Edinburgh
    Add: 46 Abbeyhill.
    Refs: EDIN/DIR/35/6.

MITCHELL, *James*   Edinburgh
    Add: Crosscauseway (07): East 1
    Richmond St (11).
    Refs: EDIN/DIR/07: 09: 11: 16.

MITCHELL, *John*   Fraserburgh
    (B S &).   (Aberdeen)
    Refs: PIG/NCDS/26.

MITCHELL, *William*   Beith
    Add: New St.   (Ayrshire)
    Refs: PIG/CDS/37.

MITCHELL, *William*   Leven
    Add: Shore St.   (Fifeshire)
    Refs: PIG/CDS/25/6.

MOFFAT, *Francis*   Aberdeen
    (See Philip & Moffat).
    Add: 50 Queen St.
    Refs: ABER/DIR/24.

MOFFAT, *P.*   Aberdeen
    E D: ca. 93.
    Refs: JA/2334.

MOIR, *James*   Edinburgh

MOIR, *Mrs.* (86)
    Add: Brown's Close.
    Refs: EDIN/DIR/82: 83: 84: 86: 88.

MOIR & WATSON   Edinburgh
    Add: Old Assembly Close.
    Refs: EDIN/DIR/23.

MOLISON, *Thomas*   Montrose
    Add: Bridge St.
    Refs: PIG/CDS/37.

MONCRIEFF, *Alexander*   Glasgow
    Add: Head of the New Wynd (99):
    McNair's Land, Trongate (01).
    Refs: GLAS/DIR/99: 01.

MONTEITH, *Edward*   Edinburgh
    Add: 7 Lothian St.
    Refs: PIG/SIN/20.

MOODIE, *George*   Edinburgh
    (May have succeeded Patrick Boyd,
      whose daughter he married).
    Add: Head of the Horse Wynd (80):
      Old Assembly Close (84).
    Refs: EDIN/DIR/80: 84: DBP/1726/
      75, p. 335.

MOODIE, *Matthew*   Paisley
    E D: 86.
    Refs: AE/GHB.

MORE, *James*   Edinburgh
    Add: Allan's Close, High St.
    Refs: EDIN/DIR/93:94W:96:99:01:
      03:07:09:11:16:20:23:33:35/6:
      PIG/SIN/20: PIG/CDS/25: 26/7.

MORE, *John*   Edinburgh
    E D: 55?
    Add: Brown's Close.
    Refs: EDIN/DIR/73:80: DBP/1726/75,
      p. 335.

MORISON, *David H. & Co.*   Perth
    (Publisher, S T, etc).
    Add: 2 Watergate: Res: No. 8.
    Refs: PERT/DIR/23: Munby Coll:
      engraved label "M & Co., ST &
      BB P" on 1819 work.
    The N.L.S. copies of the Perth
      Dir. for 1823 & 1824 are bound

in neat red morocco by the firm
who published these Directories.
They have each different labels.

MORISON, *Robert Sen.*
              Perth & Dunkeld
MORISON *& Co.* (ca. 1815) (S T &)
    Refs: DBP/1725, p. 336.

MORRISON, *David*   Glasgow
    Add: 460 Argyll St.
    Refs: GLAS/DIR/38/9.

MORRISON, *John*
      Greenock & Glasgow (32)
    Add: 14 Hamilton St (20): No. 46
      (31) (& Ruler): 30 King St,
      Tradeston (32): 45 Oxford St
      (33): No. 51 (34): 21 New Bridge
      St (40): ("& Librarian").
    Refs: PIG/SIN/20: PIG/CDS/25/6:
      RENF/DIR/31/2: 36/7: GLAS/DIR/32
      to 40.

MORTIMER, *William*   Aberdeen
    E D: ?
    Add: 58 Guestrow.
    Refs: ABER/DIR/28.
    Styles himself "late bookbinder".
    May be a relation of the person of
    the same names, who was a boot
    and shoe maker at the same epoch
    at 62 Guestrow.

MUGGOCH, *James*   Glasgow

MUGGOCH, *J. J.* (28)
(& Printer's Joiner).
Add: 23 King St (25): No. 47 (26).
Refs: GLAS/DIR/25: 26: 28 to 33.

MUIR, *David*   Edinburgh
Add: 159 High St.
Refs: EDIN/DIR/11.

MUIR, *James & Geo.*   Glasgow

MUIR, *G.* (38)
Add: 18 Hutcheson St (33): No. 15
(34): No. 34 (38): 51 Brunswick
St: Res: 4 Dunlop St (39).
Refs: PIG/CDS/37: GLAS/DIR/33 to 40.

MUIR, *Thomas*   Edinburgh
Add: 134 High St (35/6): Steven-
law's Close (37).
Refs: EDIN/DIR/35/6: 39: PIG/CDS/37.

MUIR, *William*   Edinburgh
Add: Bailie Fyfe's Close (26): 56
High St (33).
Refs: EDIN/DIR/26: 29: 33: 35/6.

MUIR & MALLOCH   Edinburgh
Add: 51 North Bridge.
Refs: PIG/CDS/25: 26/27.

MURRAY, *James*   Edinburgh
Add: Middle College Wynd (07):
23 College Wynd (20).
Refs: EDIN/DIR/07: 09: 11: 16: 20:
PIG/SIN/20.

MURRAY, *William*   Edinburgh
Add: Allan's Close (33): 11 George
St (37): 12 Rose St (39).
Refs: EDIN/DIR/33: 35/6: 39: PIG/
CDS/37.

NEIL, *James*   Glasgow
Add: 29 Brunswick St.
Refs: PIG/SIN/20.

NEIL, *Thomas*   Glasgow
Add: Smith's Ct, 53 Candleriggs
(28): 175 Buchanan St (34): Res.
94 W. Nile St (40).
Refs: PIG/CDS/37: GLAS/DIR/28: 34/
5: 40.

NEILSON, *Charles*   Elgin
(Etc).
Add: Batchen Lane (25).
Refs: PIG/CDS/25/6.

NEILSON, *John & Co.* (24)
     Glasgow
NEILSON, *J. & A.* (27)

NEILSON, *John* (32)
Add: 32 Nelson St, 6 Candleriggs
(27): 21 Argyll St (32): No. 31
(35): No. 57 (38): 45 Candleriggs: Res: 27 Union St (39).
Refs: GLAS/DIR/24: 27 to 40.

NEILSON, *John*   Paisley
(Etc).
Add: 18 St. Mirren's St: Res. 21
St. James' St.
Refs: PAIS/DIR/38/9.

NEILSON & MOFFAT (25)
Glasgow
Add: 32 Nelson St (25): No. 67 (26).
Refs: PIG/CDS/25/6: GLAS/DIR/25:26.

NESS, *Thomas*   Cupar (Fife)
Add: Crossgate.
Refs: PIG/CDS/37.

NICOL(L), *Mungo*   Edinburgh
E D: 98?
Add: Brown's Close, Luckenbooths.
Refs: EDIN/DIR/04: 07: 09: HOLD/11: AE/GHB (98).

NIVEN, *William*   Glasgow
Add: 43 Argyll St (27): No. 87 (36): 8 Turner's Ct (37) (?same address): 55 Glassford St (39).
Refs: GLAS/DIR/27 to 40: PIG/CDS/37.

OLIVER & BOYD   Edinburgh
(Etc, etc).
Add: Baron Grant's Close, High St.
Refs: PIG/SIN/20. Billhead in Munby Coll: dated 16.2.19.

ORROCK (ORRECK), *George*
Edinburgh
Add: 35 West College St (16): 20 Clerk St (20).
Refs: EDIN/DIR/16: 20: PIG/SIN/20: Crushed mor. binding, ca. 1840, on BM. C. 38 C. 25. Bruce's Sermons, 1589.

ORROCK & ROMANES
Edinburgh
E D: ca. 30.
Add: 94 South Bridge St (33): No. 35 (39).
Refs: PIG/CDS/37: EDIN/DIR/33: 35/6: 39.

PATERSON, *Maurice*   Edinburgh
E D: 25?
Add: 15 Broughton St (?): 1 St. James' St (33): 21 Catherine St (39).
Refs: LAB/KNA: ca. 25: EDIN/DIR/33: 35/6: 39.

PATERSON, *Philip*   Edinburgh
E D: 96.
Refs: AE/GHB.

PATON, *George*   Edinburgh

PATON, *John*
(B S &).
(Doubtful if they bound in the period).
Refs: DBP/1726/75, p. 344.

PATON, *Philip*   Edinburgh
E D: 96.
Refs: AE/GHB.

PAUL, *John*   Cupar (Fife)
Add: Bonnygate.
Refs: PIG/CDS/37.

PEAT, *Thomas*   Glasgow
    (B S &).
    Add: 35 Thistle St (24): 35 Shuttle
    St (25).
    Refs: GLAS/DIR/24 to 26.

PEATTIE, *George*   Edinburgh
    E D: ca. 75.
    Add: Allan's Close (H. 11): 306
    High St (11 F.D.).
    Refs: HOLD/11: EDIN/DIR/11: COSOC
    /BB/EDIN/75.

PENSON, *Richard*   Edinburgh
    Add: 8 St. David St.
    Refs: EDIN/DIR/33.

PETTIE, *George*   Edinburgh
    Add: 391 High St.
    Refs: EDIN/DIR/33.

PHILIP, *John*   Aberdeen
    Add: 50 Queen St (24): No. 46 (28).
    Refs: PIG/CDS/37: ABER/DIR/24: 28:
    WSM/KC/NEW.
    Apollo, Jan., 1951, Art. by W. S.
    Mitchell.

PHILIP & MOFFAT   Aberdeen
    Add: 50 Queen St.
    Refs: PIG/SIN/20: PIG/CDS/25: 26/7:
    ABER/DIR/24.
      Seem to have sometimes adver-
    tised as a firm and sometimes
    separately.

PORTEOUS, *James*   Edinburgh
    E D: 62.
    Add: New Grayfriars' Parish (62):
    Nicolson's St (80): Chapel St
    (82): No. 72 (90).
    Refs: EDIN/DIR/80: 82: 83: 84: 90:
    DBP/1726/75, p. 345: COSOC/BB/
    EDIN/75.

PROCTOR, *Joseph*   Edinburgh
    Add: 5 Brown St.
    Refs: EDIN/DIR/33.

PROCTOR & CHISHOLM
    (& S T).   Edinburgh
    Add: 29 Frederick St.
    Refs: EDIN/DIR/26.

RAE, *John*   Glasgow

RAE, *T. & A.* (39)
    Add: 5 South Hanover St (36): 42
    Argyll St (37): 14 Garthland St
    (39).
    Refs: PIG/CDS/37: GLAS/DIR/36 to 40.

RATTRAY, *Charles*   Glasgow
    (Etc).
    Add: 480 Argyll St.
    Refs: GLAS/DIR/40.

REID, *Henry*   Glasgow
    Add: 159 Salt Market.
    Refs: GLAS/DIR/05 to 08.

REID, *John* Glasgow
    Add: 36 Queen St.
    Refs: PIG/CDS/37.

REID, *Peter* Aberdeen
    Add: 5 Long Acre: (Res: W. Henderson's Court, 161 Gallowgate).
    Refs: ABER/DIR/28.

RENNIE, *E.* Edinburgh
    E D: 11?
    Refs: AE/LAB.

ROACH, *Peter* Edinburgh
    Add: Boyd's Close, Canongate (09): Don's Close (20): Weir's Close, 208 Canongate (23).
    Refs: EDIN/DIR/09: 11: 20: 23: 26: 33: 35/6: 39: PIG/SIN/20: PIG/CDS /25: 26/7.

ROBERTSON, *James* Dalkeith
    Add: High St West.
    Refs: PIG/CDS/37.

ROBERTSON, *James* Dumfries
    Add: 27 Buccleuch St.
    Refs: PIG/SIN/20.

ROBERTSON, *John* Dundee
    Add: Nethergate (24): Matthewson's Close (25).
    Refs: DUND/DIR/24: PIG/CDS/25/6.

ROBERTSON, *John* Montrose
    Add: Shore Wynd (20): High St. (25).
    Refs: PIG/SIN/20: PIG/CDS/25/6.

ROBINSON, *H. & Co.* Glasgow
    Add: 7 Brunswick Place.
    Refs: GLAS/DIR/39/40.

ROCH, *Patrick* Edinburgh
    E D: 91.
    Refs: AE/GHB.

ROGERS, *William* Edinburgh
    (& S T).
    Add: 12 Melville Place.
    Refs: EDIN/DIR/35/6: PIG/CDS/37.

ROSS, *John* Airdrie
    Add: Stirling St. (Lanarkshire)
    Refs: PIG/CDS/37.

ROSS, *Thomas* Edinburgh
    (P R &).
    E D: 63 (?to 98).
    Add: New Grayfriars' Parish (63): Old Church Parish (98).
    Refs: DBP/1726/75, p. 349: COSOC/ BB/EDIN/75.

RUSSELL, *John* Cupar (Fife)
    Add: Lady-Wynd.
    Refs: PIG/CDS/37.

SANGSTER, *Peter* Edinburgh
    Add: Tron Parish (65): Peebles Wynd (73/4): Sandiland's Close (82): Wardrop's Court (01).
    Refs: EDIN/DIR/73: 82: 83: 84: 86: 88: 90: 93: 94: 96: 99: 01: DBP/1726/75, p. 351.

SAWERS, *James*   Edinburgh

SAWERS, *William* (11)
   Add: 59 South Bridge (09): Stamp
   Office Close (20).
   Refs: EDIN/DIR/09: 11 (WM.): PIG/
   SIN/20.

SCOTLAND, *G. D.*   Glasgow
   Add: 51 Stockwell St.
   Refs: GLAS/DIR/40.

SCOTT, *Daniel*   Glasgow
   Add: P.O. Court.
   Refs: GLAS/DIR/03.

SCOTT, *David*   Montrose
   E D: (pre) 99.
   Refs: AE/GHB.

SCOTT, *James*   Edinburgh
   Add: Gabriel Road (73/4): For-
   rester's Wynd (80).
   Refs: EDIN/DIR/73: 80: 82: 83: 84:
   86: 88: 90.
   O.C. F. Hopkins. Tentamen
   Medicale 77: c.g. Baskett's Bible
   & Psalms: 1741 & 72 m.f.g.:
   Bible, 1653.
   HOB/ABB/Nos. 95/7: pp. 132/4:
   DBP/1726/75, p. 351: I feel that
   both of these require revision in
   view of my note on Scott:
   William (?): SCH/S. de R. IV.
   8: JA: 937.

SCOTT, *Robert*   Brechin
   Add: High St.   (Forfarshire)
   Refs: PIG/CDS/37.

SCOTT, *William* (?)   Edinburgh
   Refs: The only evidence for his
   existence as a binder is the note
   on a book in the Edin. Univ. Lib.
   (press-mark, Df.2.43) "Bound by
   Willm. Scott, Edinburgh". He
   is certainly not the "Scott, Edinburgh", who was without a
   doubt "James". A careful search
   of Edinburgh directories between
   1773 & 1790 shows no trace of a
   William Scott having existed as a
   binder. The inscriber of the Edin.
   Univ. Library volume has, I
   believe, started a "false" hare,
   which had no existence.

SELLER, *William*   Glasgow
   (Paper Ruler & S T).
   Add: 114 Trongate (35 & 40): No.
   91 (37).
   Refs: PIG/CDS/37: GLAS/DIR/35 to 40.

SETON, *Robert*   Edinburgh
   (S T &: to the King, 35).
   (See J. *Taylor* Seton).
   Add: Old Assembly Close (09):
   Brown's Close (11): 423 Lawn-
   market (29): The Mound (30):
   3 Mound Place (37): The Mound
   (40).

Refs: EDIN/DIR/09: 11: 16: 29: 33: 35/6: 39: PIG/CDS/37.
O.C. Label "R/S/ST/&/BB/to the King/The Mound/E" on full calf binding on "Present State of Banking" 1840: P. Labels.

SHARP, *William*   Inverness
(B S, S T &). Decd. 1797.
E D: 62?
Refs: DBP/1726/75, p. 352.

SHEARER, *John*   Stirling
Add: Bakers-Wynd.
Refs: PIG/SIN/20.

SHEDDEN, *J.*   Glasgow
Add: 88 John St.
Refs: GLAS/DIR/35/6.

SHEPHERD, *James*   Montrose
Add: 19 High St.
Refs: PIG/CDS/25/6: PIG/CDS/37.

SHIRREFFS, *Andrew*   Aberdeen
E D: 62 (to 00?).
Refs: AE/GHB.

SINCLAIR, *Alexander & Donald*
                    Edinburgh
SINCLAIR & Co. (30?)
E D: 20.   L D.
Add: 23 Warriston's Close, High St (20): 54 North Bridge (26): 16 Rose St (29).

Refs: PIG/SIN/20: EDIN/DIR/23: 26: 29: PIG/CDS/25: 26/7.
Munby Coll: Label "Bd. by S. & Co., 16 RS, E", calf gilt, ca. 1830.

SINCLAIR, *Hugh*   Glasgow
Add: 11 Bell St.
Refs: GLAS/DIR/08.

SINCLAIR, *James*   Dumfries
Add: 90 High St.
Refs: PIG/SIN/20.

SLATER, *A.*   Edinburgh
Add: 1 Holyrood St.
Refs: EDIN/DIR/35/6.

SMITH, *David*   Glasgow
Add: 11 Canon St.
Refs: GLAS/DIR/30/1.

SMITH, *George*   Forfar
Add: Castle St.
Refs: PIG/CDS/25.

SMITH, *Wm.*   Edinburgh
(& S T).
Add: 16 West Bow (20): 10 Parliament Sq (23): Allan's Close (26): 306 Lawnmarket (37): 269 High St (?).
Refs: EDIN/DIR/23: 26: 29: 33: 35/6: 39: PIG/SIN/20: PIG/CDS/25: 26/7: 37. WSM/KC/NEW mentions a stamp by him. O.C. Ticket "Bd. by/W.S./269/HS/E".

SMITON, *Alexander* (54?)
                                  Edinburgh
(Also Smeaton (84) & Smeiton).

SMETON, *Mrs.* (86)

SMEITON & MILLER (94)
  Add: Brown's Close, Luckenbooths
    (73): Forrester's Wynd (93).
  Refs: DBP/1726/75, p. 355: EDIN/
    DIR/73: 80: 82: 83: 84: 86: 88:
    90: 93: 94W: 96: COSOC/BB/75.

SOM(M)ERVILLE & AITKEN (15)
                                  Glasgow
SOM(M)ERVILLE, *George* (16)
  Add: 169 Trongate (15): 4 Salt
    Market (20).
  Refs: GLAS/DIR/15 to 18: PIG/SIN/20.

SOMNER, *George*   Perth
  Add: Barrosa St.
  Refs: PIG/CDS/25/6.

SOUTER   Edinburgh
  (B S & Musical Binder).
  Add: 15 Parliament Sq.
  Refs: HOLD/11: EDIN/DIR/11.

STEEL, *Maitland*   Edinburgh
  Add: Riddell's Close, Lawnmarket
    (25): 7 James Ct (33): 4 Mound
    Place (37 PIG).
  Refs: PIG/CDS/25: 26/27: 37: EDIN/
    DIR/33: 35/6: 39.

STEELE, *Mathew*   Edinburgh
  Add: 322 Lawnmarket.
  Refs: EDIN/DIR/23: 26.

STEVEN, *John*   Edinburgh
  E D: 79.
  Refs: AE/GHB.

STEVENS, *Alex.*   Edinburgh
  (& S T).
  Add: 34 North Bridge Street.
  Refs: EDIN/DIR/29: 33: 35/6: PIG/
    CDS/37.

STEVENSON, *William*   Dundee
  Add: Castle Lane.
  Refs: PIG/CDS/37.

STEWART, *Andrew*   Edinburgh
  Add: College Wynd.
  Refs: EDIN/DIR/83.

STEWART, *D.*   Glasgow
  Add: 190 Argyll St.
  Refs: GLAS/DIR/34/5.

STEWART, *Daniel*   Edinburgh
  Add: Niddry's Wynd.
  Refs: EDIN/DIR/81: 82: 83.

STEWART, *John*   Edinburgh
  E D: ca. 75.
  Refs: AE/GHB.
    In the 1786 Edinburgh Directory
    he figures as a BS, but was a
    signatory of COSOC/BB/EDIN in
    1775.

STEWART, *Robert*   Paisley
  Add: 1 Lillia's Wynd (37): No. 3:
    Res: 69 High St (38).
  Refs: PIG/CDS/37: PAIS/DIR/38/9.

STOBIE, *John*   Perth
  Add: 102 High St.
  Refs: PIG/CDS/25.

STRACHAN & GELLEN
                   Aberdeen
  Add: 8 & 10 Long Acre.
  Refs: ABER/DIR/24: PIG/CDS/25:
    26/7.

SUTHERLAND, *Alexander*
                  Edinburgh
  Add: Advocate's Close, Lucken-
    booth (07): Old P.O. Close (16):
    Old Bank Close (20): Craig's
    Close (25).
  Refs: EDIN/DIR/07: 09: 11: 16: 20:
    PIG/SIN/20: PIG/25: 26/7.

SUTHERLAND, *John*   Edinburgh
  Add: 12 Calton St.
  Refs: PIG/CDS/37.

SUTHERLAND, *Robert*   Edinburgh
  Add: Anchor Close.
  Refs: EDIN/DIR/29.

SWANSTON, *William*   Glasgow
  Add: 26 Nelson St (24): No. 53
    (26): 55 Bell St (27).
  Refs: GLAS/DIR/24 to 27.

TAINSH, *James*   Perth
  Add: 48 St. John St.
  Refs: PIG/CDS/37.

TAIT, *Alexander*   Edinburgh
  (Son of James?).
  Add: Parliament Stairs (09): 126
    Cowgate (11): 5 Bristo St (16):
    3 Parliament Sq (23): 134 High
    St (26): No. 265 (33).
  Refs: EDIN/DIR/09: 11: 16: 23: 26:
    33: 35/6: PIG/CDS/25: 26/7.

TAIT, *George*   Edinburgh
  Add: 20 Warriston's Close, High
    St (16): Craig's Close (23): Milne
    Sq (26): 317 High St (33):
    Writer's Court (37).
  Refs: EDIN/DIR/16: 20: 23: 26: 33:
    35/6: PIG/SIN/20: PIG/CDS/25: 26/
    7: 37.

TAIT, *James*   Edinburgh
  (Still alive in 1788, when he married
    his second wife).
  Add: Old Kirk Parish (68): College
    Wynd (73).
  Refs: EDIN/DIR/73/4: 80: 82: 83:
    84: 86: DBP/1726/75, p. 358.

TAYLOR, *James*   Edinburgh
  (See J. *Taylor* Seton).
  Add: Back of Exchange (84): Par-
    liament Close (88): Gosford's
    Close (93): Kintore's Court,
    Luckenbooth (04): 4 Mound
    Place (16).

Refs: EDIN/DIR/84: 86: 88: 90: 93: 96: 99: 00: 01: 03: 04: 07: 09: 11: 16: 20: 23: PIG/SIN/20.

TAYLOR, *William* Edinburgh
Add: 4 Mound Place.
Refs: PIG/CDS/25: 26/7.

TAYLOR, SETON, *J.* Edinburgh
(See Taylor, J. & Seton, R.).
Add: 3 Mound Place (26): 6 St. Andrew Square (33).
Refs: EDIN/DIR/26: 29: 33: 35/6: LAB/KNA.

TEMPLETON, *Thomas* Glasgow
Add: 5 Salt Market (17): Hutcheson St (20): 77 Brunswick St (31).
Refs: GLAS/DIR/17: 31/3: PIG/SIN/20.

THOMPSON, *Andrew* Dunbar
     (Haddingtonshire)
Add: Westport St.
Refs: PIG/CDS/37.

THOMSON, *Abram* Edinburgh
(Etc).
Add: 6 Old Fishmarket Close (07): Res: 11 Broughton Place (26).
Refs: EDIN/DIR/07: 16: 23: 29: 33: 35/6: PIG/SIN/20: PIG/CDS/25: 26/7: 37: AE/LAB.

THOMSON, *James* Glasgow
Add: 15 New Wynd (25): No. 15 (26): 153 Trongate (29): 5 Hutcheson St (31).
Refs: GLAS/DIR/25 to 32: PIG/CDS/37.

THOMSON, *James* Glasgow
Add: 47 Montrose St (37): 5 Hutcheson St (40).
Refs: PIG/CDS/37: GLAS/DIR/40.

TOD, *George* Edinburgh
Add: 12 Clyde St.
Refs: PIG/CDS/37: EDIN/DIR/39.

TOD, *John* Edinburgh
Add: 19 Clyde St: Res: Old P.O. Close (26): No. 12 (33): 1 Forth St (39).
Refs: EDIN/DIR/26: 29: 33: 35/6: 39.

TODD, *William & Co.* (33). Edinburgh

TODD, *William* (37)
(Plain & ornamental).
Add: 1 Forth St.
Refs: EDIN/DIR/33: 35/6: PIG/CDS/37.

TURNBULL, *Robert* Airdrie
     (Lanarkshire)
Add: 43 South Bridge St.
Refs: PIG/CDS/25.

URQUHART, *Donald* Inverness
Add: 45 High St.
Refs: PIG/CDS/37.

WALKER, *John* Edinburgh
Add: Foot of Roxbrough Close (96): 22 Libberton's Wynd, Cowgate (16).
Refs: EDIN/DIR/96: 99: 01: 03: 16: 20: PIG/CDS/25: 26/7.

WALKER, *William*   Glasgow
   Add: 37 Trongate (27): No. 114
   (29): Res: Bloomfield Cottage,
   Carngadhill (40).
   Refs: GLAS/DIR/27 to 40: PIG/CDS/
   37.

WALLACE, *William*   Edinburgh
   Add: Cowgate Head.
   Refs: EDIN/DIR/90.

WATSON, *Daniel*   Edinburgh
   Add: 36 Niddry St (33): 23 South
   Bridge St (37): No. 23 (39).
   Refs: EDIN/DIR/33: 35/6: 39: PIG/
   CDS/37.

WATSON, *James*   Edinburgh
   Add: Grant's Close, West Bow (96):
   6 Milne's Square (26): No. 7 (39).
   Refs: EDIN/DIR/96: 26: 33: 35/6:
   39: PIG/CDS/37.

WATSON, *John*   Edinburgh
   Add: Foot of Stevenlaw Close (23):
   Covenant Close (25).
   Refs: EDIN/DIR/23: PIG/CDS/25:
   26/27.

WATSON, *John*   Glasgow
   (& Paper Ruler).
   Add: 96 George St (26): 9.
   Gallowgate (35).
   Refs: GLAS/DIR/26: 35/6.

WATT, *David*   Annan
   Add: Murray St. (Dumfriesshire)
   Refs: PIG/CDS/37.

WATT, *James*   Edinburgh
   Add: Foot of Allan's Close (93):
   Parliament Square (07).
   Refs: EDIN/DIR/93: 96: 03: 07: 09.

WATT, *John*   Glasgow

WATT & MACDONALD
   Add: 5 Hutcheson St.
   Refs: GLAS/DIR/28 to 31.

WATT, *John*   Greenock
   (Etc).
   Add: 6 William St.
   Refs: RENF/DIR/36/7.

WATT & PRENTICE   Glasgow
   Add: Wellington Ct, 22 Argyll St.
   Refs: PIG/CDS/25/6.

WEBSTER, *David*   Paisley
   Add: 210 High St.
   Refs: PIG/CDS/25.

WEIR, *David*   Edinburgh
   E D: 78.
   Refs: AE/GHB.

WEIR, *Robert*   Glasgow
    Add: 6 Argyll St (09): No. 9 (12).
    Refs: GLAS/DIR/09 to 14.

WHEL(L)AN (or WHALLAN),
    Abraham   Glasgow
    Add: 394 Gallowgate (33): No. 138
    (36): 94 Stockwell (35).
    Refs: GLAS/DIR/33 to 38.

WHITE (or WHYTE), *Andrew*
                            Paisley
WHITE, *Miss Margaret* (38)
    Add: 3 St. Mirren St (25): Coffee
    Room Buildings, 4 Lillias Wynd
    (31).
    Refs: PIG/CDS/25/6: RENF/DIR/31:
    PAIS/DIR/38/9.

WHITE, *James*   Edinburgh
    Add: West Port.
    Refs: EDIN/DIR/93: 94W: 96.

WHITE, *Patrick*   Edinburgh
    (Two generations?).
    (See Peter).
    Add: Bow Head (86): Dunbar's
    Close, Lawnmarket (93): Fish-
    market Close (94): East Camp-
    bell's Close, Cowgate (99): 145
    Cowgate (25): 106 West Bow
    (29): No. 100 (33): James' Court
    (35).
    Refs: EDIN/DIR/93: 94W: 96: 99: 01:
    03: 04: 29: 33: 35/6: PIG/CDS/25:
    26/7.

WHITE, *Peter*   Edinburgh
    (See Patrick).
    Add: Advocate's Close (80): West
    Bow Head (82): below Milne's
    Court (84): Campbell's Close
    (07): 145 Cowgate (11).
    Refs: EDIN/DIR/80: 82: 84: 88: 07:
    09: 11: 16: 20: 26.

WHITELAW, *Thomas*   Edinburgh
    Add: 11 Drummond St.
    Refs: PIG/SIN/20.

WILDE, *F. C.*   Edinburgh
    (& S T).
    Add: 16 Parliament St.
    Refs: PIG/CDS/37.

WILLOCKS, *Day*   Brechin
    Add: High St.
    Refs: PIG/CDS/25.

WILSON, *A.*   Edinburgh
    (Pocket-book Maker, BB, etc).
    Add: 233 High St.
    Refs: EDIN/DIR/20.

WILSON, *Andrew*   Aberdeen
    (& Dealer in books).
    Add: 155 Gallowgate.
    Refs: ABER/DIR/28.

WILSON, *Archibald*   Edinburgh
    Add: 55 Potter Row (16): 3
    Drummond St (29).
    Refs: EDIN/DIR/16: 20: 23: 29:
    PIG/CDS/25: 26/7.

WILSON, *John*   Glasgow
    Add: 2 Blair St, Calton (25):
      Barrowfield Toll (37).
    Refs: PIG/CDS/25: GLAS/DIR/37/8/9.

WILSON, *William*   Glasgow
    Add: 159 Salt Market (11): 30
      Trongate (13).
    Refs: GLAS/DIR/11 to 17.

WINCKWORTH, *James* Edinburgh
    (& S T).
    Add: Parliament Stair (25): Back-
      stairs: Res: 2 Argyll Sq (26).
    Refs: PIG/CDS/25: 26: 27: EDIN/DIR
      /26.

WINNING, *Archibald*   Glasgow
    Add: High St (20): 43 Trongate
      (24): No. 85 (26 & 30): 25 Bell St
      (27).
    Refs: PIG/SIN/20:   PIG/CDS/25:
      GLAS/DIR/24 to 35.

WOOD, *David*   Perth
    (& S T, etc).
    Add: 157 High St.
    Refs: PIG/CDS/37.

WOOD, *John*   Edinburgh
    (B S &).
    Add: South West Kirk Parish (45):
      Luckenbooths (73/4).
    Refs: DBP/1726/75, p. 369.

WOOD, *John*   Glasgow
    (Publisher &).
    Add: 10 New Wynd (13): 6 York
      St (16).
    Refs: GLAS/DIR/13 to 18.

WOOD, *John*   Haddington
    Add: North-East Port.
    Refs: PIG/CDS/25/6.

YOUNG, *J.*   Inverness
    Refs: LAB/JONES.

YOUNG, *John*   Edinburgh
    Add: Castlehill (96): Parliament Sq
      (16): Covenant Close (23): 6
      Meuse Lane (37).
    Refs: EDIN/DIR/96: 03: 07: 09: 11:
      16: 20: 23: 26: 35/6: PIG/SIN/20:
      PIG/CDS/25: 26/7: 37.

YOUNG, *Thomas*   Greenock
    Add: Watson's Lane.
    Refs: PIG/CDS/25.

YUILL, *Robert*   Greenock
    E D: 74?
    Refs: DBP/1726/75, p. 371.

IRISH DIRECTORIES AND OTHER REFERENCES

HOLD/09:	Holden's Triennal Directory 09.
PIG/SIN/20:	Pigot's Directory Scotland, Ireland and Northern Counties 20.
„ „ /21:	Ditto 21.
PCD/DUB/24:	Pigot's Dublin Directory 24.
PIG/DHD/26:	„ „ & Hibernian Directory 26.
TIA/46:	Thom's Irish Almanach & Directory 46.

ARM/DIR/40:	Lennox's Directory of Armagh, etc 40.
BELF/DIR/19:	Bradshaw's Belfast Directory 19.
SMY/BELF/DIR/19:	Smyth's „ „ 19.
BELF/DIR/20:	Belfast Almanach & Directory 20.
„ „ /31:	Donaldson's Belfast Directory 31/2.
„ „ /35:	Matier's „ „ 35/6.
„ „ /39:	Martin's „ „ 39.
„ „ /40:	„ „ „ 40/1.
„ „ /42:	„ „ „ 42/3.
„ „ /43:	„ „ „ 43/4.
„ „ /46:	„ „ „ 46.
CORK/DIR/20:	Connor's Cork Directory 20.
„ „ /27:	„ „ „ 27.
DUB/DIR/—/—:	Wilson's Dublin Directory, *anno citato*.
DUB/PO/DIR/33:	Dublin Post Office Directory 33.
„ „ „ /34:	„ „ „ „ 34.
„ „ „ /35:	„ „ „ „ 35.
„ „ „ /40:	„ „ „ „ 40.
DUB/ALM/38:	Pettigrew & Oulton's Dublin Almanach 38.
NEWRY/DIR/20:	Bradshaw's Directory of Newry, etc 20.
„ „ /40:	„ „ „ 40.

NAT/LIB:	National Library, Dublin.
R I A:	Royal Irish Academy, Dublin.
T C D:	Trinity College, Dublin.
EVANS:	Edward Evans: Hist. & Bibl. Account of (Irish) Almanachs, Directories, etc. Office of the Irish Builder, 1897. (Somewhat incomplete).
M C:	Maurice Craig, student & collector of Irish bindings, especially of the XVIIIth century.

IRISH BINDERS BY LOCALITY

ARMAGH: McWatters; Scott; White; Young.

BALLIBAY: McClatchey.

BALLYMONEY: Griffith.

BANDON: Coombs.

BELFAST: Archbold; Archer & Son; Barnes; Boyd (2); Brady; Brown; Campbell (2); Cinnamond; Conn; Connan; Gold; Greer (2); Gurney; Harrison; Henderson; Hodgson (2); Ireland; Kelly; Lamont; Linn; McBurney; McCann; McDonald; McGeary; McLaughlin; McWilliams; Magee; Manning; Mitchell; Moore (2); Rusk; Searson; Simms & McIntyre; Stephenson; Tate; Ward (2); Watt; Weir; Winnington; Young.

CASHEL: Connolly.

CLONMELL: Hackett; Higgins (2).

COLERAINE: Gaw; Hart.

COOKSTOWN: Richardson.

CORK: Burke; Carr; Carver; Cottrell; Drew; King; Lee; Massey; Redmond; Thompson; Whitney (2).

DROGHEDA: O'Donegan.

DROMORE: Gibson.

DUBLIN: Adams (2); Barker; Battersby; Bell; Bellew; Bigger; Boland; Booth (4); Boylan; Bradley; Brown (2); Bradley; Byrne; Callan; Carroll (3); Chandler; Challoner; Collins; Colombine; Connelly; Connolly (2); Costigan; Courtney; Cumming; Curran; Cuthbert; Cutler; Darcy; Day; Devoy; Dickinson; Donaldson; Donnellan; Dornin; Dowell; Dowling; Doyle; Dunbairn (2); Duncan; Dunn; Eden; Eustace; Evans; Field; Fitzgibbon (2); Fox (3); Frazer; Galway (2); Gibney; Gibson; Grant; Greene (2); Gritten; Hall (2); Hammond & Coyne; Hanlon; Harford (3); Hogan, Linden & Co.; Hutchinson; Iver; Jones; Cavanagh; Keane; Keating; Keightley; Keogh; Kiddie; Leatham; Leech (3); Linden; Litton; Lynch; McCafferty; McDermott; McDonough; McDoole; McKenzie; McNeill; Maher: Maillie & Farrell; Maloney; Manley; Moore; Mowatt; Mullen (3); Murray; Nelson; Nowlan; O'Donoghue; Oliver; Pettigrew & Oulton; Phelan; Plunkett; Purcell; Rainsford (2);

Reid; Reillie; Roche; Rogers; Ryan; Saloon; Searson; Servant; Shaw; Sinclair; Stevenson; Stewart; Sweeney; Taaffe; Thacker; Tucker; Tyrrell; Walsh; Watters; White; Wilkinson (2); Wilson; Wright.

DUNDALK: Curry; Reilly.

DUNGANNON: Kelly; Richardson; Tipping.

ENNIS: Considine.

FERMOY: Lindsay.

KILKENNY: Pemberton; Pembroke (2).

LIMERICK: Donnellan; Grogan; Hahir; O'Mealy; O'Shea.

LISBURN: McCully.

LONDONDERRY: Boyd; Hays; Ireland.

LURGAN; Humphries; Iver; Reilley.

MALLOW: Lindsey.

MONAGHAN: Cass; Greacen; Robinson.

MULLINGAR: Hammond.

NEWRY: Blackham (2); Burgess; Corry; Greer.

OMAGH: Nelis.

SLIGO: Drennan: Somerville.

WATERFORD: Harvey; Leech; Morrison; Thomson.

WEXFORD: Wheelock.

YOUGHAL: Cox.

ADAMS, *James*   Dublin
Add: 17 Chatham St (24): 56
Exchange St (29): Wicklow Place
(38): 11 Wicklow St (38): No. 56
(39): 36 Cuffe St (46).
Refs: PCD/DUB/24: PIG/DHD/26:
DUB/DIR/27 to 40: DUB/PO/DIR/
34/40: DUB/ALM/38: TIA/46.

ADAMS, *John*   Dublin
Add: 15 Golden Lane.
Refs: DUB/DIR/13/14.

ARCHBOLD, *Samuel*   Belfast
Add: 82 High St.
Refs: PIG/SIN/20: 21.

BARKER, *Thomas*   Dublin
Add: Clarke's Court (83): Hoey's
Court (84).
Refs: DUB/DIR/83 to 88.

BARNES, *Jackson*   Belfast
Add: 2½ North St.
Refs: BELF/DIR/31.

BATTERSBY, *William Joseph*
(B S &).   Dublin
Add: 5 Essex Bridge.
Refs: DUB/DIR/29.

BELL, *Robert*   Dublin
Add: 18 Trinity Place.
Refs: DUB/DIR/08 to 10.

BELLEW, *Gerald*   Dublin
(& S T).
Add: 21 S. King St (36): 79 Grafton
St (46).
Refs: DUB/DIR/36/40: DUB/ALM/38:
DUB/PO/DIR/40: TIA/46: LAB/
PEARSON.
O.C. Eustace: Classical Tour. 8th
Ed. 1841. 3 vol. red m.g. Binder's
name stamped on inside edge of
binding.

BIGGER, *James*   Dublin
Add: 51 New St (38): No. 61 (46).
Refs: DUB/DIR/38: 40: DUB/PO/DIR/
40: TIA/46.

BLACKHAM, *Richard*   Newry
Add: Boat St.
Refs: NEWRY/DIR/20.

BLACKHAM, *William*   Newry
Add: 43 Hill St.
Refs: PIG/SIN/20: 21: NEWRY/DIR/
20: DIR/ARM/40.

BOOTH, *John*   Dublin
Add: 37 Bow St.
Refs: DUB/DIR/15/16.

BOOTH, *William*   Dublin
Add: 20 Back Lane.
Refs: DUB/DIR/02.

BOOTH, *William*   Dublin
(& Blank-card Maker 1802).

BOOTH, *Jane* (16)
  Add: 67 Exchequer St (91 to 09):
    No. 82 (10 to 40).
  Refs: DUB/DIR/09 to 40.
  (The directories do not mention
  any bookbinding activities after
  1834).

BOYD, *Henry*   Belfast
  Add: 14 Crown Entry (31): 12 (35).
  Refs: BELF/DIR/31: 35.

BOYD, *John*   Belfast
  Add: 136 North St.
  Refs: BELF/DIR/39.

BOYD, *John*   Londonderry
(B S etc).
  Add: Castle St.
  Refs: PIG/SIN/20: 21. PCD/24 (ex-
    pressly includes bookbinding).

BOYLAN, *Thomas*   Dublin
  Add: 7 Smock Lane.
  Refs: DUB/DIR/93 to 02.

BRADLEY, *Abraham*   Dublin
E D: 03 (?).
  Refs: AE/COLL.

BRADY, *Samuel*   Belfast
  Add: 8 Cole Alley.
  Refs: BELF/DIR/35.

BROWN, *George*   Dublin
  Add: 3 Bedford Row.
  Refs: DUB/DIR/03 to 09.

BROWN, *James*   Belfast
  Add: 1 Pottingers Entry.
  Refs: BELF/DIR/19: PIG/SIN/20.

BROWN(E), *William*   Dublin
(S T &, in 1809).
  Add: 16 Boot Lane (96): 38 Capel
    St (09): 39 (10).
  Refs: DUB/DIR/96 to 10.

BURGESS, *J.*   Newry
  Add: Corry Place.
  Refs: PIG/SIN/20: 21.

BURKE, *John*   Cork
  Add: Collectors Lane, Grand
    Parade.
  Refs: CORK/DIR/20.

BYRNE, *Laurence S.*   Dublin
(B S &).
  Add: 25 Anglesea St.
  Refs: DUB/DIR/35 to 37.

CALDWELL, *Matthew*   Dublin
  Add: 33 Eustace St (40): 31 Fred-
    erick St (46).
  Refs: DUB/DIR/40: TIA/46: Munby
    Coll: label "C, BB, No. 9 F.S.,
    D".

CALLAN, *Patrick*   Dublin
Add: 5 Johnston Ct (24): No. 8 (33).
Refs: PCD/24: PIG/DHD/26: DUB/DIR/26 to 35: DUB/PO/DIR/34.

CAMPBELL, *Cosin*   Belfast
Add: 8 Michael St.
Refs: BELF/DIR/35.

CAMPBELL & McBURNEY (39)
                  Belfast

CAMPBELL, *Robert* (40)
Add: 70 High St.
Refs: BELF/DIR/39: 40: 42: 43: 46.

CANDLER, *Paul*   Dublin
Add: 63 Gt. George St.
Refs: PIG/SIN/20: PCD/24: PIG/DHD/26.

CAREY, *Patrick*   Dublin
Add: 11 Crow St (15): No. 2 (16).
Refs: DUB/DIR/15: 16.

CARR, *Henry*   Cork
Add: Christchurch Lane.
Refs: CORK/DIR/20.

CARROLL, *D. W.*   Dublin
Add: 44 Lower Sackville St.
Refs: DUB/PO/DIR/40.

CARROLL, *Laurence*   Dublin
Add: 3 East Hanover St.
Refs: DUB/PO/DIR/40.

CARROLL, *William*   Dublin
(Morocco Leather Seller).
Add: 19 New Row.
Refs: DUB/DIR/29.

CARVER, *William*   Cork
Add: 1 Brown St.
Refs: PCD/24: PIG/DHD/26: CORK/DIR/27.

CAVANAGH, *Francis*   Dublin
Add: 26 Wicklow St.
Refs: TIA/46: LAB/KNA.

CHALLONER (or Challener),
William   Dublin
(B S &).

CHALLONER, *John* (40)
Add: 1 Little Britain St (17): 60 Henry St (28): 138 Dorset St (46).
Refs: DUB/DIR/17 to 35: PIG/SIN/20: PCD/DUB/24: PIG/DHD/26: DUB/PO/DIR/34: 40: TIA/46.

CHAMBERS, *John*   Dublin
E D: 1790?
Add: 4 Abbey St (40).
Refs: DUB/DIR/40: TIA/46.
M.C. reports that he did a lot of account book and ledger binding back to 1790 and that there are samples in the Guinness Brewery. He may also have worked for Government Depts.

CINNAMOND, *William*   Belfast
Add: 41 John St (19): 17 Pottinger's
Entry (35).
Refs: BELF/DIR/19: 35: PIG/SIN/20:
PCD/DUB/24: PIG/DHD/26.

COLDWELL, *Thomas*   Dublin
(Supplied, *inter alia*, Bookbinders'
tools).
Add: 50 Capel St.
Refs: DUB/DIR/31 to 40.

COLLINS, J.   Dublin
Add: 34 Temple Bar (40).
Refs: DUB/PO/DIR/40: TIA/46: AE/
COLL/LAB.

COLOMBINE, *Joseph*   Dublin
Add: 19½ Anglesea St (24): 5 S.
Cope St (33 as Columbine, J.):
10 Bedford Row (32).
Refs: PCD/DUB/24: DUB/DIR/24: 32:
35: PIG/DHD/26: DUB/PO/DIR/33.
Variously spelt, and appears only
sporadically in the directories.

CONN, *John*   Belfast
Add: 4 Hammond's Court (27):
19 Castle St (35): 16 Crown
Entry (39).
Refs: BELF/DIR/31: 35: 39.
The *Northern Whig* of 21.6.27
contains an advertisement as to
new binding materials recently
received.

CONNAN, *Michael*   Belfast
Add: 57 Smithfield Court.
Refs: BELF/DIR/35.

CONNELLY, *George*   Dublin
Add: Fishamble St.
Refs: DUB/DIR/96.

CONNOLLY, *Caleb*   Dublin
(S T).
Add: 36 Camden St (23): 2 Cut-
purse Row (40).
Refs: PCD/DUB/24: PIG/DHD/26:
DUB/DIR/25 to 40: DUB/PO/DIR/
34: 40.
Seems to have concentrated on
lower end of his stationery
business about 1836, and to have
ceased his BB activities.

CONNOLLY, *John*   Cashel
Add: Main St.   (Tipperary)
Refs: PCD/DUB/24: PIG/DHD/26.

CONOLLY, *T. & C.*   Dublin
(& P R).
Add: 115 New St.
Refs: DUB/DIR/38.

CONSIDINE, *Martin*   Ennis
Add: Church St.   (Co. Clare)
Refs: PCD/DUB/24.

COOMBS, *Thomas*   Bandon (Cork)
Add: Watergate.
Refs: PIG/SIN/20.

CORRY, *John*   Dundalk
  (Etc).
  Add: Middleward.
  Refs: PIG/SIN/20.

CORRY, *Samuel*   Newry
  (& B S).
  Add: Market St.
  Refs: PIG/SIN/20: 21: NEWRY/DIR/20
  which also notes him as umbrella
  maker.

COSTIGAN, *Christopher*   Dublin
  Add: 37 S. St. George's St.
  Refs: DUB/DIR/13: 14.

COTTRELL, *Francis*   Cork
  Add: Hanover St.
  Refs: PIG/SIN/20: CORK/DIR/20: 27.

COURTNEY, *William*   Dublin
  Add: 3 St. George's Place, Hard-
  wicke St (37): 98 Dorset St (46).
  Refs: DUB/ALM/38: DUB/DIR/37 to
  40: DUB/PO/DIR/40: TIA/46.
  M.C. has a binding with his
  ticket on a book dated 1835.

COX, *John*   Youghal (Cork)
  Add: Mall.
  Refs: PIG/SIN/20.

CUMMING, *William*   Dublin
  (B S &).
  Add: 27 Gt. Britain St (16): 52
  Moore St (21).
  Refs: DUB/DIR/16 to 40: PCD/DUB/
  24: PIG/DHD/26: DUB/PO/DIR/34:
  DUB/ALM/38.

CUNNINGHAM, *W.*   Dublin
  (& S T).
  Add: 1 Chatham Row, William St.
  Refs: DUB/DIR/03 to 05.

CURREN, *Patrick*   Dublin
  Add: 9 Derby Square.
  Refs: DUB/DIR/86 to 87.

CUTHBERT, *Daniel* (34)   Dublin

CUTHBERT, *Henry* (35)
  Add: 3 Bishop St.
  Refs: DUB/PO/DIR/34: 40: DUB/DIR/
  36 to 40: DIR/ALM/38.

CUTLER, *George*   Dublin
  (& S T).
  (Etc in 39).
  Add: 56 Upper Stephen St.
  Refs: PIG/SIN/20: PCD/DUB/24: PIG/
  DHD/26: DUB/PO/DIR/34: DUB/
  DIR/35 to 40.

DARCY, *John*   Dublin
  (B S &).
  Add: 32 Mary St.
  Refs: DUB/DIR/38: 39

DAY, *Joseph*   Dublin
(B S &).
Add: 24 N. Summer St.
Refs: DUB/ALM/38: DUB/DIR/38: 40:
     DUB/PO/DIR/40.

DEVOY, *Joshua*   Dublin
(Binder to the University in 1836).
Add: 6 Pitt St (21): 27 Exchequer
     St (34 & 39): 30 Wicklow St
     (38).
Refs: DUB/DIR/21 to 40: PCD/DUB/
     24: PIG/DHD/26: DUB/PO/DIR/34:
     40: DUB/ALM/38.

DICKINSON, *George*   Dublin
Add: 15 Sycamore Alley.
Refs: DUB/DIR/87 to 94.

DONALDSON, *John*   Dublin
Add: 24 Anglesea St (15): 6 Bed-
     ford Row (21): 21 Anglesea St
     (24): No. 24 (31): No. 20 (32).
Refs: DUB/DIR/15 to 35: PCD/DUB/
     24: PIG/DHD/26: DUB/PO/DIR/34.

DONNELLAN, *W.*   Dublin
E D: 18 (?).
Add: Jervis St.
Refs: St. gr. red mor. gilt binding
     in M.C. Coll. with ticket.

DONNELLAN, *William*   Limerick
Add: Mary St.
Refs: PCD/DUB/24: PIG/DHD/26.

DORNIN, *Thomas & Co.*   Dublin
(& S T).
Add: 33 St. Anne's St.
Refs: PIG/SIN/20: DUB/DIR/27: 31 to
     35.

DOYLE, *P. J.*   Dublin
(B S &).
Add: 18 Anglesea St.
Refs: O.C. ½ mor. on selections
     from Madame de Genlis. n.d.

DOWELL, *George*   Dublin

DOWELL, *John* (33)
(& Account Book Manufacturer).

DOWELL, *M.* (38)
Add: 10 Charlemont St.
Refs: DUB/DIR/28 to 40: DUB/PO/
     DIR/34.

DOWLING, *Michael Jun.*   Dublin
Add: 11 Wood Quay.
Refs: DUB/DIR/37: DUB/ALM/38:
     DUB/PO/DIR/40.

DRAPER, *William*   Dublin
Add: 3 Bedford Row.
Refs: DUB/DIR/08.

DRENNAN, *Alexander*   Sligo
Add: Bridge St.
Refs: PIG/SIN/20.

DREW, *Barry*   ?
E D: 00?
Refs: AE/COLL/LAB.

DUNBAVIN, *Peter*   Dublin

DUNBAVIN, *Thomas* (16)
Add: Gt. Strand St.
Refs: DUB/DIR/13 to 22: PIG/SIN/20:
PCD/DUB/24: PIG/DHD/26.

DUNCAN, *Thomas*   Dublin
Add: 15 Crow St (20): 32 Ex-
chequer St (24).
Refs: PIG/SIN/20: DUB/DIR/21 to 26:
PCD/DUB/24: PIG/DHD/26.

DUNN, *Frederick*   Dublin
Add: 17 Aungier St (13): 12
Skinner Row (24).
Refs: DUB/DIR/13: 14: PCD/DUB/24:
PIG/DHD/26.

EDEN, *Richard*   Dublin
(& S T).
Add: 33 S. Gt. George St (35):
18 Fade St (46).
Refs: DUB/ALM/38: DUB/DIR/35 to
40: DUB/PO/DIR/40: TIA/46.

EDMONDS, *William*   Dublin
Add: 72 Camden St.
Refs: DUB/DIR/25: 26.

EUSTACE, *Christopher*   Dublin
Add: 13 Charles St.
Refs: DUB/DIR/35.

EVANS, *H.*   Dublin
(Etc).
Add: 35 Lower Sackville St.
Refs: DUB/PO/DIR/33.

FALCONER, *J.*   Dublin
(Still in existence as printers. M.C.).
E D: 20?
Add: Sackville St.
Refs: LAB/KNA.

FIELD, *Isaac*   Dublin
(P R &).
Add: 4 Stafford St.
Refs: DUB/DIR/31 to 33.

FITZGIBBON, *Richard*   Dublin

FITZGIBBON, *Elisa*
Add: 18 S. King St.
Refs: DUB/DIR/11 to 25: 26 (Elisa).

FOX, *George*   Dublin
Add: 55 Fishamble St.
Refs: DUB/DIR/94: 5.

FOX, *John*   Dublin
Add: 24 Anglesea St.
Refs: DUB/PO/DIR/33: DUB/DIR/33.

FOX, *Patrick*   Dublin
Add: 4 York St.
Refs: DUB/DIR/36: 37.

FRAZER   Dublin
  E D: 00?
  Add: 37 Annan Quay.
  Refs: AE/COLL/LAB.

GALWAY, *Edward*   Dublin
  Add: Smock Alley (20): 24 Fish-
    amble St (23).
  Refs: PIG/SIN/20: DUB/DIR/23 to 26
    to 35: DUB/PO/DIR/34.

GALWAY, *Robert*   Dublin
  Add: 65 Gt. Strand St (36): No. 59
    (40): 9 Abbey St (33).
  Refs: DUB/DIR/33 to 40: DUB/ALM/
    38: DUB/PO/DIR/40.

GALWEY *& Co.*   Dublin
  E D: (Possibly after 40).
  Add: 22 Eustace St.
  Refs: LAB/KNA/3: O.C. Inlaid
    vellum binding with ticket, ca.
    1860 (as fascinating as the Albert
    Memorial).

GASS, *Charles*   Monaghan
  (& P R).
  Add: Dublin St.
  Refs: PCD/DUB/24.

GAW, *Thomas*   Coleraine
  E D: 26 (?).
  Refs: Poor ½ calf bindings on 3
    vols. of Lander's Conversations
    1824/6, in M.C. Coll., with
    ticket.

GIBNEY, *Thomas*   Dublin
  Add: 159 Gt. Britain St.
  Refs: DUB/PO/DIR/34: DUB/DIR/32
    to 35.

GIBSON, *Henry*   Dromore
  (& Grocer).   (Co. Down)
  Refs: PCD/DUB/24.

GIBSON, *James*   Dublin
  (Plain and fancy).
  Add: 32 Upper Ormond Quay.
  Refs: PIG/SIN/20.

GOLD, *John*   Belfast
  Add: 9 Mustard St (09): No. 49 (11).
  Refs: HOLD/09: 11.

GRANT, *William*   Dublin
  Add: 30 George St South.
  Refs: DUB/DIR/33: 37: DUB/ALM/38:
    DUB/PO/DIR/40: TIA/46.

GREACEN, *Nathaniel*   Monaghan
  Add: Diamond.
  Refs: PCD/DUB/24.

GREENE, *Michael William* Dublin
  (B S &).
  Add: 23 Anglesea St.
  Refs: DUB/DIR/17 to 19.

GREEN(E), *Robert*   Dublin
(& P R 1840).
    Add: 50 Lower Stephen St (23):
    7 Bedford Row (40).
    Refs: DUB/DIR/23: 24: PCD/DUB/24:
    PIG/DHD/26: DUB/PO/DIR/40.

GREER, *Henry*   Belfast
    Add: 2 King St.
    Refs: BELF/DIR/31: 35: 39.

GREER, *R.*   Belfast
    Add: 11 Long Lane.
    Refs: BELF/DIR/35.

GREER, *Robert*   Newry
(Etc, etc).
    Add: 4 Margaret Sq.
    Refs: ARM/DIR/40.

GRIFFITH, *Benjamin*   Ballymoney
(Etc).   (Co. Antrim)
    Add: Main St.
    Refs: PCD/DUB/24.

GRITTON, *Percival R.*   Dublin
    Add: 14 Moira Place (38): 9 Gt.
    Strand St & 53 Capel St (40).
    Refs: DUB/ALM/38: DUB/PO/DIR/40:
    DUB/DIR/38: 39.

GROGAN, *Michael*   Limerick
(& Copper Plate Printer).
    Add: 1 Brunswick St.
    Refs: PCD/DUB/24: PIG/DHD/26.

GURNEY, *John*   Belfast
    Add: Hammonds Ct.
    Refs: BELF/DIR/19: PIG/SIN/20.

HACKETT, *John*   Clonmell
(& B S).
    Add: Main St.
    Refs: PCD/DUB/24.

HAHIR, *William*   Limerick
    Add: Mary St.
    Refs: PCD/DUB/24: PIG/DHD/26.

HALL, *William*   Dublin
(& B S in 1831).
    Add: 55 St. George St (12): No. 8
    (16): 17 Fade St (24): 26 Temple
    Bar (28): 12 Cope St (31): 44
    French St (34).
    Refs: DUB/DIR/12 to 37: PIG/DHD/
    26: DUB/PO/DIR/34.

HALLHEAD, *William*   Dublin

HALLHEAD, *Sara*
(See Mackenzie, W.).
    E D: 72/6 (W): 83 (S).
    Add: 63 Dame St.
    Refs: Though W. and S. both style
    themselves as booksellers, M.
    Craig thinks that they both may
    have done binding. W. H. bought
    out the business of Anne Leathley,
    widow of Joseph Leathley, some
    time between 1772/6. (M.C.).

HAMMOND, *J.*   Mullingar
  E D: 12?
  Refs: Ticket as "Binder" reported
    by Mr. Stevens Cox, of Ilchester,
    on an 1812 book by Sir Humphry
    Davy.

HAMMOND, *John*   Dublin
  Add: 4 George Quay.
  Refs: DUB/PO/DIR/40.

HAMMOND & COYNE   Dublin
  Add: 15 Gt. Brunswick St (33):
    No. 20 (34).
  Refs: DUB/DIR/33 to 35.

HANLON, *James*   Dublin
  (& Ruler, Printer, etc).
  Add: 105 Thomas St (38): 1 Temple
    Lane (39): 9 Bedford Row (46).
  Refs: DUB/ALM/38: DUB/DIR/38 to
    40: DUB/PO/DIR/40: TIA/46.
    M.C. queries if he is the well-
    known engraver.

HANLON & WILSON   Dublin
  (Rulers &).
  Add: 14 Temple Lane.
  Refs: DUB/DIR/36.

HARFORD, *P.* (13)

HARFORD, *J. P.* (17, 28 & 35)

HARFORD, *Susannah* (24)
  Add: 20 Anglesea St (13): 4
    Trinity Place (16): No. 5 (28):
    Trinity Place (35).
  Refs: DUB/DIR/13 to 23: PIG/SIN/20:
    PCD/DUB/24: 28 (JP): PIG/DHD/26:
    DUB/DIR/35 (JP).
    J.P. makes sporadic appearances
    in 1817, 28 & 35.

HARRISON, *George*   Belfast

HARRISON, *George & Co* .(40)
  Add: 5 Pottinger (19): No. 2 (39):
    51 High St (see below?).
  Refs: BELF/DIR/19: 39: 40: 42: 43:
    46: PIG/SIN/20.
    O.C. Gell's Rome, 3 vol. 34.
    stamped calf or paper carries
    label "H/BD/BS & ST/51 High
    St. B". It is of excellent quality
    and probably contemporary.

HARVEY, *T. N.*   Waterford
  E D: 20?
  Refs: LAB/KNA: ca. 20.

HAYS, *Henry*   Londonderry
  (& Copper Plate Printer).
  Add: 7 Richmond St.
  Refs: PCD/DUB/24: Munby Coll:
    Label "H, BB, 7 RS, D": Sheep
    gilt.

237

HIGGINS, *Cornelius*   Clonmell
(& B S).
   Add: Dublin St.
   Refs: PCD/DUB/24.

HIGGINS, *George*   Clonmell
   Add: Duncan St.
   Refs: PIG/SIN/20.

HODGSON, *John*   Belfast
   Add: 9 High St.
   Refs: PCD/DUB/24: PIG/DHD/26.

HODGSON, *R. & J.*   Belfast
(& S T).
   Add: High St.
   Refs: HOLD/09.

HOGAN, *William* (22)   Dublin

HOGAN LINDEN *& Co.* (29)*
   *See Linden.

HOGAN, *W. & Jas.* (32)

HOGAN, *W.* (35).
   (& S T, Ruler & A/c book Mfr.
   passim).
   Add: 7 Anderson Ct (22): 1 Aston
   Quay (32).
   Refs: DUB/DIR/26 to 36: DUB/PO/
   DIR/40.

HUMPHRIES, *John*   Lurgan
(Etc).
   Add: Main St.
   Refs: DIR/ARM/40.

HUTCHINSON, *John*   Dublin
   Add: 33 William St.
   Refs: DUB/DIR/21 to 40: PCD/DUB/
   24: PIG/DHD/26: DUB/PO/DIR/34:
   40: DUB/ALM/38: TIA/46.

IRELAND, *Henry*   Londonderry
(Etc).
   Add: Ferry-Quay St.
   Refs: PCD/DUB/24.

IRELAND, *Thomas*   Belfast
   Add: 134 High St.
   Refs: BELF/DIR/35.

IVER, *George* Lurgan (Co. Armagh)
   Refs: PCD/DUB/24: PIG/DHD/26.

JONES, *John*   Dublin
   Add: 26 New Row S.
   Refs: DUB/PO/DIR/33.

KEATING, *George*   Dublin
   Add: 56 Fleet St.
   Refs: DUB/DIR/91.

KEENE, *Martin*   Dublin
(Book, Stationery and Patent
   Medicine Warehouse).
(This combination is quite usual).

KEENE, *Martin & Son*
Add: 6 College Green.
Refs: DUB/DIR/04 to 37.
O.C. Bensley's Bible, 2 vol. L.P.
1795, f.m.g. Bookplates of W.
Cairns & Ld. Cairns. Elaborate
yellow ticket in each vol. "Sold
by/Martin Keene/at his/Book/
Stationery / and / Patent Medicine
/ Warehouse / 6 / College Green
/Dublin" and in oval around
(right to left) "Engraving and
Printing neatly executed, Law &
Mercantile Stamps, Account
Books ruled and bound to any
pattern".

KEIGHTLEY, *Benjamin*   Dublin
Add: 4 Coghill's Ct.
Refs: DUB/DIR/91 to 94.

KELLY, *Matthew*   Dungannon
Add: Milltown.   (Co. Tyrone)
Refs: DIR/NEWRY/20.

KELLY, *N. D.*   Dublin
(Printers'& Bookbinders' Materials).
Add: 6 Gt. George St.
Refs: DUB/DIR/29.

KEOGH, *James*   Dublin
Add: 8 Anglesea St (40): 19
Anglesea St (46).
Refs: DUB/DIR/40: DUB/PO/DIR/40:
TIA/46.

KIDDIE (or KEDDIE), *Thomas*
Add: 7 Swift's Row.   Dublin
Refs: PIG/SIN/20 (Kiddie): DUB/DIR/
21 (Keddie).

KING, *Abraham Bradley*   Dublin
Refs: Joined his grandfather as
Parliamentary binder in 1780 and
later worked alone from 1784
until the Union. Was Lord Mayor
of Dublin about 1812. He had a
bindery, rather than was a binder,
but one binding is known, signed
at the base of the spine "A. B.
King, Binder" on Castlereagh's
copy of the Report of the Select
Committee of the House of
Commons, 1798, with red mor.
spine, and calf sides with Etruscan
decorations and allegorical
painting. (See M. Craig's Irish
Bindings, 1600-1800).

KING, *Jonas*   Cork
Add: Ann St (20): Half Moon St
(24).
Refs: CORK/DIR/20: PCD/DUB/24:
PIG/DHD/26.

LAMONT *Brothers*   Belfast
Add: Donegall Place Bldgs.
Refs: BELF/DIR/26.

LEATHAM, *J. C.*   Dublin
Add: 5 Digges St.
Refs: DUB/DIR/33 to 40: DUB/PO/
DIR/33 to 35-40.

LEE, *James*   Cork
Add: 11 Paul St.
Refs: PCD/DUB/24: PIG/DHD/26.

LEECH, *Arthur*   Dublin
Add: 1 York Row, Aungier St
(35): 12 Mercer St (40).
Refs: DUB/DIR/36 to 40: DUB/ALM/
38: DUB/PO/DIR/40: TIA/46.

LEECH, *George*   Dublin
Add: 3 York Row.
Refs: DUB/PO/DIR/34.

LEECH, *John*   Dublin
Add: 30 Gt. Strand St.
Refs: DUB/DIR/18 to 21: PIG/SIN/20.

LEECH, *John*   Waterford
Add: Quay.
Refs: PIG/SIN/20.

LINDEN, *Arthur*   Dublin
(& S T).
Add: 19 Anglesea St.
Refs: DUB/DIR/32.
(See Hogan).

LINDSAY, *John Wesley*   Fermoy
(& B S).   (Munster)
Add: King St.
Refs: PCD/DUB/24.

LINDSEY   Mallow
(P R etc).   (Co. Cork)
Refs: LAB/JONES.

LINN, *Henry*   Belfast
E D: pre-1786.
Refs: Walker's Hibernian Magazine
for Nov., 1786, contains the
following obituary notice: "In
the poorhouse of Belfast, aged
90, Mr. Henry Linn, the oldest
bookbinder probably in Ireland".

LITTON, *Richard*   Dublin

LITTON, *Anne*
Add: 1 Dawson Ct (14): 23 Lower
Stephen St (23).
Refs: DUB/DIR/14 to 24: PIG/SIN/20:
PCD/DUB/24: PIG/DHD/26.

LYNCH, *John*   Dublin
Add: 30 Gt. Strand St.
Refs: DUB/DIR/17.

MACANULTY, *Brian*   Ireland
E D: Left Ireland about 1785.
Add: Philadelphia (U.S.) (85/94):
Salem (94).
Refs. BKBG/AMER/p. 73.

McBURNEY, *Robert*   Belfast
Add: 35 Hill St.
Refs: BELF/DIR/35.

McCAFFERTY, *George*   Dublin
(& S T).
Add: 157 Gt. Brunswick St.
Refs: DUB/DIR/37.

McCANN, *Thomas*   Belfast
    Add: 19 Wilson Ct (31): Joy's Ct
    (35).
    Refs: BELF/DIR/31: 35.

MACCLATCHEY, *William* Ballibay
    (& B S).   (Co. Monaghan)
    Refs: PCD/DUB/24.

McCULLY, *Hugh*   Lisburn
    Add: Jackson's Lane. (Co. Antrim)
    Refs: BELF/DIR/19: PIG/SIN/20.

McDERMOTT, *Laurence*   Dublin
    Add: 18 Gt. Britain St.
    Refs: DUB/DIR/19: 20.

McDONOUGH, *Michael*   Dublin
    Add: 1 Temple Lane.
    Refs: DUB/DIR/32: 33.

McDOOLE, *Hugh*   Dublin
    Add: 14 Gt. Strand St.
    Refs: DUB/DIR/91 to 95.

McGEARY, *James*   Belfast
    Add: 30 Little Donegall St.
    Refs: BELF/DIR/19.

McKENZIE, *John*   Dublin
    Add: 12 Gt. Ship St.
    Refs: DUB/DIR/13 to 18.

McKENZIE, *William*   Dublin
    Add: 63 Dame St (84 to 92): 33
    College Green (92 to 11): 7
    Merriam Row (11).
    Refs: HOB/ABB p. 116: DUB/DIR/84
    to 17.
    O.C. Warton's English Poetry,
    3 vol. 1774, Trinity College arms
    and prize ticket (ticket): Boyle's
    works, seen at Story's, 6 vol 1772:
    1784. T.C. prize ticket. On some
    T.C.D. prize tickets McK.'s name
    is engraved as bookseller and
    printer to the University.

McKENZIE, *William*   Dublin
    The following information has, in
the main, been kindly supplied to me
by M. Craig, who has made a special
study of early Irish bindings.
    Apparently not related to any of
the London McKenzies. But may be
related to a Benjamin McKenzie who
was a shoemaker in Tighe Street,
Dublin, 1781 onwards.
    Up to 1782 inclusive, William Hall-
head, bookseller, appears at 63 Dame
Street in the Dublin Directories. 1783
Sara Hallhead, bookseller, at same
address. 1783, May 20th, William
McKenzie married Sara Hallhead,
widow of William Hallhead (q.v.) in
St. Andrew's Church, Dublin (Dub.
Par. Reg. Soc.).
    1784, William McKenzie, bookseller,
    63 Dame Street, and so till 1810

inclusive. At no time is he described as a binder in the Directories. He was bookseller to the University. He printed the 1791 edition of the College Statutes (copy in T.C.D., dark green morocco, prob. bd. by McK., but not ticketed).

1811, William McK., bookseller & stationer, 7 Merrion Row, and so till 1817 inclusive, after which he disappears.

A good many ticketed bindings by McKenzie are known, on imprints of date 1772, 1774, 1777, 1779, 1780, 1784, etc. All tickets seen by M.C. read "Bound by McKenzie, 63 Dame Street". Ticketed bindings in *Nat. Lib.*, *Nat. Mus.*, *R.I.A.*, T.C.D., Abbey coll., Henry Davis coll., Ramsden coll., and doubtless elsewhere.

There is reason to suppose that not all McKenzie's best bindings were ticketed. Perhaps he only used the ticket for a few years, from about 1784. He worked mainly in green morocco and tree calf. The sides of his bindings are rarely decorated with more than a roll and perhaps a tool in the corners. There is also reason to suppose that he was, if not the originator, at least one of the chief exponents of the Dublin style of lettering bindings at the head of the back, usually with the place of publication, the date being at the foot.

These were usually on strips of red leather or some other contrasting colour. His backs were sometimes in three colours, formed by successive overlays. Some of his ticketed bindings were by no means fine. His edges were rarely, perhaps never, gilt, but were stained green or marbled. His endpapers are of the splash-marbled variety.

Finally there is reason to suppose that when he married Mrs. Hallhead in 1783 he took over an existing bindery which had already some fine bindings to its credit.

M.C. has never seen any signed bindings by John McKenzie (q.v.). He seems to have been too young to be McKenzie's son by Sara Hallhead.

McLAUGHLIN, *William*   Belfast
Add: Hammond Ct (19): Rosemary St (24).
Refs: BELF/DIR/19: PIG/SIN/20: PCD/DUB/24: PIG/DHD/26.

McNEILL, *Joseph*   Dublin
Add: 2 Drury Lane: No. 9 (19 & 20).
Refs: DUB/DIR/16 to 32.

McWATTERS, *John*   Armagh
(& S T, P R).
Add: Upper English St.
Refs: BELF/DIR/43: DIR/ARM/40.
M.C. reports that the firm still exists.

McWILLIAMS, *Thomas*   Belfast
    Add: 11 Pottinger's Entry.
    Refs: BELF/DIR/39.

MAGEE, *Adam*   Belfast
    Add: 16 Thomas St.
    Refs: BELF/DIR/35.

MAHER, *George*   Dublin

MAHER, *C. W.* (27)

MAHER, *Christopher* (32)
    Add: Coghill Ct, Dame St (20):
      2 Temple Lane, Dame St (ca. 27):
      76 Fleet St (32).
    Refs: PIG/SIN/20: DUB/DIR/32.
    O.C. Fine binding in mor., with
      broad inside borders and silk end-
      papers on Milton Paradise Lost,
      1827.
    Ticket "CWM/BB/2 TL/DS/D".

MAILIE & FARRELL   Dublin
    Add: Wolf's Alley.
    Refs: PIG/SIN/20.

MALONEY, *Charles*   Dublin
    Add: 28 Little Strand St.
    Refs: DUB/DIR/37.

MANLEY, *George*   Dublin
    Add: 2 Tinkler's Court.
    Refs: DUB/DIR/40.

MANNING, *William*   Belfast
    Add: 30 Chapel Lane.
    Refs: BELF/DIR/19.

MASSEY, *Henry*   Cork
    Add: 8 Meeting House Lane.
    Refs: PCD/DUB/24: PIG/DHD/26:
      CORK/DIR/27.

MITCHELL, *Robert*   Belfast
    Add: 20 Chapel Lane.
    Refs: BELF/DIR/35.

MOORE, *Cunningham*   Dublin

MOORE, *E.* (46)
    Add: 57 Jervis St: No. 61 (46).
    Refs: DUB/DIR/36: DUB/PO/DIR/40:
      TIA/46.

MOORE, *William*   Belfast
    Add: 33 Donegall St.
    Refs: BELF/DIR/19.

MORRISON, *Samuel*   Waterford
    Add: Parliament St (20): Quay (24).
    Refs: PIG/SIN/20: PCD/DUB/24:
      PIG/DHD/26.

MOWAT(T), *John*   Dublin
    (& B S etc).
    Add: 60 Marlborough St (36): 64
      William St (38): 30 Upper
      Sackville St (40): 45 Jervis St (46).
    Refs: DUB/DIR/36 to 40: DUB/PO/
      DIR/40: TIA/46.

MULLEN, *George* Dublin
Add: 27 Temple Bar (03): 38
Nassau St (23): 61 William St
(28): 62 King William St (46).
Refs: DUB/DIR/03 to 40: PIG/SIN/20:
PIG/DHD/26: DUB/ALM/38: DUB/
PO/DIR/34: 40.
O.C. Charles Fox: Life of James
II, 1808, f.m.g., pink silk e.p.:
pink label at first address: WM 08.
I have recently added to my O.C.
about six Mullen bindings, ca.
1815, bound for the Lord Lieu-
tenant, Ld. Whitworth.
HOB/ABB. 112: Sch. S. de R. IV,
41, 42, 43.

MULLEN, *John* Dublin
(& Account Book Manufacturer).
Add: 81 Upper Abbey St.
Refs: DUB/DIR/38: 40.

MULLEN, *T.* Dublin
Add: 27 Anglesea St: No. 20 (27):
No. 21 (29).
Refs: DUB/DIR/16 to 29.
O.C. Pinelli Costumi, 17 f.m.g.
Cupid & harp on sides (ticket):
Fenelon, Livre de Prières, 26.
Lamb and Flag on sides (ticket).
M.C. reports plain ½ binding on
Fulton's Inland Navigations, 1796,
in his O.C., which he thinks is
roughly contemporary.

MURRAY, *David* Dublin
(Ruler &).
Add: 6 Hawkins St.
Refs: DUB/DIR/35 to 39.

NELIS, *John* Omagh
(Etc, etc).
Add: Main St.
Refs: ARM/DIR/40.

NOLAN, *Peter* Dublin
(& Machine Ruler).
Add: 7 Anderson St.
Refs: DUB/DIR/19 to 21.

NOWLAN *& Co.* (32) Dublin

NOWLAN, *Matthew* (34)

NOWLAN, *Matthew & Son* (35)

NOWLAN, *Samuel* (46)
Add: 11 St. Mary's Abbey (32):
No. 12 (46).
Refs: DUB/DIR/32 to 40: DUB/PO/
DIR/34: 40: TIA/46.

O'DONEGAN Drogheda

O'DONNAGAN, *John* Drogheda
Add: James St.
Refs: PIG/SIN/20: PCD/DUB/24:
PIG/DHD/26.

244

O'DONOGHUE, *F.*   Dublin
    E D: 30?
    Add: Elephant Lane.
    Refs: Green mor. $\frac{1}{2}$ binding on Sir
    W. Petty's tracts, 1769, in M.C.
    Coll. M.C. dates it about 1830.

OLIVER, *George*   Dublin
    Add: 48 Abbey St.
    Refs: DUB/DIR/27: 28.

O'MEALY, *James*   Limerick
    Add: Shannon St.
    Refs: PCD/DUB/24: PIG/DHD/26.

O'SHEA, *Maurice*   Limerick
    Add: 1 Bedford Row (20): Cath-
    erine St (24).
    Refs: PIG/SIN/20: PCD/DUB/24:
    PIG/DHD/26.

PANORMO, *Alexander*   Dublin
    (& Copper Plate Printer).
    Add: 5 Pitt St.
    Refs: DUB/DIR/25 to 28.

PEMBROKE, *Thos.*   Kilkenny
    Add: Chapel Lane.
    Refs: PIG/SIN/20: PCD/DUB/24:
    PIG/DHD/26: PIG/NAT/28/9.

PEMBROKE, *Laurence*   Kilkenny
    Add: Rose & Inn St.
    Refs: PCD/DUB/24: PIG/NAT/28/9.

PLUNKET(T), *Peter*   Dublin
    Add: 5 Chancery Place (36): No. 4
    (40).
    Refs: DUB/DIR/35: DUB/PO/DIR/40.

PURCELL, *David*   Dublin
    Add: 50 Temple Bar.
    Refs: DUB/DIR/96.

RAINSFORD, *Margaret* (96)
                            Dublin
RAINSFORD, *James* (01)
    Add: 22 Andrew St.
    Refs: DUB/DIR/96 to 10.

REDMOND, *James*   Cork
    Add: South Main St.
    Refs: CORK/DIR/20.

REID, *William*   Dublin
    (B S &).
    Add: 26 Anglesea St (32): No. 7
    (33): No. 8 (36).
    Refs: DUB/DIR/32 to 39: DUB/ALM/
    38: DUB/PO/DIR/33: 34.

REILLEY, *Thomas*   Lurgan
    (Etc).
    Add: Main St.
    Refs: ARM/DIR/40.

REILLIE, *Michael*   Dublin
    Add: Cook St.
    Refs: PIG/SIN/20.

245

REILLY, *William*   Dundalk
  Add: Wellington Place.
  Refs: DIR/ARM/40.

RICHARDSON, *Leander*
            Cookstown (Co. Tyrone)
  Refs: PCD/DUB/24.

RICHARDSON, *Lewis*
            Dungannon (Co. Tyrone)
  Add: Perry St.
  Refs: PCD/DUB/24.

ROBINSON, *Joseph*   Monaghan
  (& P R).
  Add: Diamond.
  Refs: PCD/DUB/24.

ROCHE, *F. J.*   Dublin
  (Die Sinker, Letter Cutter & Book-
    binding Ornament Manufacturer).
  Add: Garter Court, Castle St.
  Refs: DUB/DIR/31 to 33.

ROGERS, *Robert*   Dublin
  (Ornamental & plain).
  Add: 12 Skinner Row.
  Refs: DUB/DIR/00 to 08: PIG/SIN/20.

RUSK, *John*   Belfast
  (Publican &).
  Add: 4 Crown Entry.
  Refs: BELF/DIR/35: 41: 42.

RYAN, *Francis*   Dublin
  (& S T).
  Add: 4 Dame Court (24): 13
    Trinity St (29).
  Refs: PCD/DUB/24: PIG/DHD/26:
    DUB/DIR/29 to 31.

SALMON, *John*   Dublin
  Add: 12 S. Gt. George St (96):
    6 Barrack St (05): 9 S. Cope St
    (09).
  Refs: DUB/DIR/96 to 09

SAUNDERS, *R.* (35)   Dublin

SAUNDERS, *Mrs. E.* (36)
  Add: 16 Chatham St.
  Refs: DUB/DIR/35: 36.

SCOTT, *Samuel*   Armagh
  Add: Rokeby Green (24): Thomas
    St (40).
  Refs: PCD/DUB/24: PIG/DHD/26:
    ARM/DIR/40: BELF/DIR/43.

SEARSON, *Henry*   Belfast
  Add: 1 Elliott's Ct (19): & Hamil-
    ton Place (20): 10 John St (24):
    6 Crown Entry (31).
  Refs: BELF/DIR/19: 20: 31: PCD/DUB
    /24: PIG/DHD/26.

SERVANT, *David*   Dublin
  (& S T).
  Add: 2 Crow St.
  Refs: DUB/DIR/01 to 08.

SHAW, *Thomas*   Dublin
     Add: 3 Bedford Row.
     Refs: PCD/DUB/24: PIG/DHD/26.

SIMMS & McINTYRE   Belfast
     (Etc, etc).
     Add: 18 Donegall St.
     Refs: SMY/BELF/DIR/19: 20: BELF/
     DIR/46.

SINCLAIR, *James*   Dublin

SINCLAIR, D. (25)
     Add: 36 Stafford St.
     Refs: PCD/DUB/24: DUB/DIR/25/6
     ("D"): PIG/DHD/26.

SOMERVILLE, *Benjamin*   Sligo
     Add: Castle St.
     Refs: PIG/SIN/20.

STEVENSON, *Alexander*   Dublin

STEPHENSON, *John* (01)
     Add: 3 Metcalf Court.
     Refs: DUB/DIR/85 to 12.

STEPHENSON, *William*   Belfast
     (Or Stevenson)
     Add: 16 Henry St.
     Refs: BELF/DIR/31: 35.

STEWART, *James*   Dublin
     Add: 29 Usher's Quay.
     Refs: PCD/DUB/24: PIG/DHD/26.

SWEENEY, *George*   Dublin
     Add: 30 Low Strand St (20): 3
     Abbey St (29).
     Refs: PIG/SIN/20: DUB/DIR/20 to 31.

TAAFFE, *William*   Dublin
     Add: 14 Stephen St.
     Refs: DUB/DIR/14: 15.

TATE, *John*   Belfast

TATE, *John & Co.* (42)
     Add: 5 Crown Entry (31): 13 High
     St (35): 3 Crown Alley (42).
     Refs: BELF/DIR/31: 35: 39: 40: 42:
     43: 46.
     The *Northern Whig* of 27.6.27
     contains a long advertisement to
     the effect that he is adding paper-
     ruling and stationery to his
     previous bookbinding activities.
     O.C. Anastasius, 3 vol. ½ calf, g.
     1820.

THACKER, *James*   Dublin
     Add: 7 Mark St (33): Shaw St (36).
     Refs: DUB/PO/DIR/33 to 35: DUB/
     DIR/36.

THOMPSON, *S. M.*   Cork
     E D: ca. 35.
     Refs: Noted in Sotheby's Sale,
     31.7.50, No. 110. Sub-Lewis style
     in poor condition

THOMSON, *George*   Waterford

THOMSON, *Edward* (24)
(& Copper Plate Printer).
Add: Peter St (11): Printer St.
Refs: HOLD/11: PCD/DUB/24: PIG/
DHD/26.

TIPPING, *Henry*   Dungannon
Add: Perry St.   (Co. Tyrone)
Refs: PCD/DUB/24.

TUCKER, *Thomas*   Dublin

TUCKER & BEERE
(Between about 1824 & 30).
Add: 14 Gt. Strand St (20): No. 25
(24): No. 45 (31): 62 Jervis St
(40).
Refs: PIG/SIN/20: PCD/DUB/24: DUB/
DIR/21 to 40: PIG/DHD/26: DUB/
PO/DIR/34.

TYRRELL, *Silvester*   Dublin
B S (& B B in 33).
Add: 1 Essex Quay.
Refs: DUB/DIR/32 to 35.

WALSH, *Nicholas*   Dublin
(P R, S T &).
Add: 24 Lower Sackville St.
Refs: DUB/DIR/35: 37.

WARD, *James*   Belfast
Add: 2 Wilson Court.
Refs: HOLD/11.

WARD, *Marcus*   Belfast
(An account of the firm's very wide
range of activities is contained in
the advertisement in Martin's
1840/1 Belfast Directory).
E D: 39.
Add: 14 Pottinger's Entry (39):
6 Cornmarket (42).
Refs: BELF/DIR/39: 40: 42: 43.
O.C. Borrow, G. Bible in Spain.
43. ¾ m.g. (ticket): Wordsworth's
Works, Paris, 1828 (binding may
be 10 years later).

WATT, *J. & R.*   Belfast
Add: 1 Joy's Court (27): 3 Skipper
St (31).
Refs: BELF/DIR/31.
The *Northern Whig* of 21.6.27
contains a long advertisement,
dated 11.6.27, describing the
firm's capabilities both as bookbinders and as manufacturers of
all kinds of leather fancy work.

WATTERS, *John*   Dublin
(& Blank Card Maker).
Add: 14 Gt. Strand St (20): 9 Crow
St (21): No. 8 (40): No. 6 (46).
Refs: PIG/SIN/20: DUB/DIR/21 to 40:
PCD/DUB/24: PIG/DHD/26: DUB/
PO/DIR/34: 40: DUB/ALM/38: TIA/
46.

WEIR, *Richard*   Belfast
(Or Wier).
   Add: 34 High St (19): 3 Church
   Lane (24).
   Refs: SMY/BELF/DIR/19: PIG/SIN/20:
   PCD/DUB/24: PIG/DHD/26.
   Quite possibly the son of the
   famous Richard Wier, partner of
   Roger Payne. (See Howe's
   London BB, 1648-1815, p. 99).

WHEELOCK, *Samuel*   Wexford
(Bookseller, etc. Expressly stated to
   be a bookbinder).
   Add: (Intelligence Office, Saturday)
   & Main St.
   Refs: PIG/SIN/20: PCD/DUB/24.

WHITE, *Hamilton*
   Add: 1 Stafford St.
   Refs: DUB/PO/DIR/32: 33.

WHITE, *John*   Dublin

WHITE, *John Jun.* (40)
(& Circulating Library).
   Add: 21 N. Brunswick St.
   Refs: DUB/DIR/35 to 40: DUB/PO/DIR
   /40.

WHITE, *Samuel*   Armagh
(& Stationer).
   Add: Scotch St (40): 5 English St
   (42): Upper English St (43).

Refs: DIR/ARM/40: BELF/DIR/42: 43.
M.C. reports a ticketed ½ binding
in his collection which he dates
about 1830.
O.C. Nice ½ calf binding on
Rush's Residence at Court of
London, 1833. Also several bind-
ings in coll. of E. H. Leslie of
Ballybea, sold Nov., 1952.

WHITNEY, *Thos.*   Cork
   Add: Paul St (11): 49 George St
   (20).
   Refs: HOLD/11: PIG/SIN/20: PCD/
   DUB/24: PIG/DHD/26: CORK/DIR/
   27.

WHITNEY, *William*   Cork
   Add: Wandesfords Bridge St.
   Refs: CORK/DIR/27.

WILKINSON, *Thomas*   Dublin
   Add: 155 Francis St.
   Refs: DUB/DIR/89 to 94.

WILKINSON, *William*   Dublin
   Add: 1 Crown Alley.
   Refs: DUB/ALM/38: DUB/PO/DIR/40.

WILSON, *W. J.*   Dublin
(Ruler &).
   Add: 70 Gt. George St S.
   Refs: DUB/DIR/38.

WINNINGTON, *James* Belfast
    Add: 28 Chapel Lane.
    Refs: BELF/DIR/19: PCD/DUB/24:
    PIG/SIN/20: PIG/DHD/26.

WRIGHT, *William* Dublin
    Add: 25 Stafford St (32): No. 35
    (34).
    Refs: DUB/DIR/32 to 40: DUB/PO/
    DIR/33 to 35.

YOUNG, *James* Belfast
    (& Copper Plate Printer).
    Add: High St.
    Refs: HOLD/09.

YOUNG, *John* Armagh
    (& P R, S T).
    Add: Market St.
    Refs: PIG/SIN/20: 21: NEWRY/DIR/20.